Employee Assistance Law Answer Book

Sandra G. Nye

THE PANEL ANSWER BOOK SERIES

ISBN 1-878375-12-1

Printed in the United States of America

How to Use the *Employee Assistance Law Answer Book*

The *Employee Assistance Law Answer Book* is divided into 13 chapters, which are intended to offer to the reader the fundamentals of law and clinical practice issues common to employee assistance programs (EAPs). An understanding of the relationship of legal and clinical concepts is necessary to an understanding of the EAP client and the practice of EAP providers.

The questions are numbered in consecutive sequence in each chapter. Of necessity, the reader will sometimes be directed from one chapter to another when cross-referencing will add to an understanding of the issue being explored.

Subheadings before groups of related questions should be helpful in locating material. In addition, the question numbers beginning each left page and ending each right page appear in the upper left and right corner of each page, respectively, for easy reference.

Listing of Questions: The list of questions in the beginning of the book will help the reader locate areas of immediate interest. The questions are identified by number and the pages on which they appear. A short description of the chapter content heads each section of the book, followed by a list of subheadings in each chapter.

Appendices: Appendix materials are samples and models. They are intended as suggestions and starting points for the reader. For the most part, they should be freely adapted to the needs of the individual. With respect to consent forms, however, any adaptation must be scrutinized for compliance with local and federal regulations. Note that appendix materials, although not strictly keyed to chapter, appear in the order in which they are first mentioned in the question-and-answer portion of the book.

Index: At the back of the book is a traditional topical index as a further aid to locating specific information.

Preface

EAPs are the front line of defense for many employers against loss and liability arising as a result of employee dysfunction. EAPs operate at the interface of employment law, law related to certain common disease entities (for example, substance abuse or mental illness), and malpractice law. These relevant areas of law are so diverse that, until now, there was little reason for one lawyer, human resources professional, or clinician to be familiar with all of them. This book is a response to many requests for an integrated representation useful to all of the disciplines involved with EAPs. It is intended to provide an introduction and overview of the law as it applies to clinical service delivery in the workplace.

The *Employee Assistance Law Answer Book* is intended for interdisciplinary use, and not as a legal treatise. As a general rule, only one example is offered as illustrative authority for each concept. It is hoped that this method will help to avoid distractions to the nonlawyer reader, while offering the lawyer a key case from which to start any serious legal research that is required. This book does not give legal advice, and reference to it cannot and should not substitute for consultation with knowledgeable legal counsel. However, human resources professionals and their lawyers and EAP sponsors and providers will find that they have in hand a comprehensive reference on EAP law as it currently exists.

Sandra G. Nye
June 1, 1990

About the Author

SANDRA G. NYE is principal of Sandra G. Nye and Associates, a firm providing consultation, representation, continuing education, and in-service training to mental health and social service providers and to business. She is also an assistant professor of jurisprudence in psychiatry at the University of Illinois Abraham Lincoln School of Medicine in Chicago, and an adjunct faculty member at the Center for Family Studies, Institute of Psychiatry, Northwestern University Medical School. Ms. Nye is the author of a number of publications and a videotape series entitled *The Clinician in the Courtroom*. She received a JD from DePaul University College of Law, an MSW from Loyola University Graduate School of Social Work, and a BA from the University of Chicago.

Table of Contents

Listing of Questions

Chapter 2 Policy and Procedure Issues for EAPs

Chapter 3 The Clinical Care Contract

Chapter 4 Confidentiality Requirements

Chapter 5 Professional Liability

Chapter 6 Malpractice Liability Stemming From Common Clinical Problems

Chapter 7 Ethics and Professional Liability

Chapter 8 Legal Issues in EAP Operations

Chapter 9 Substance Abuse Laws

Chapter 10 EAPs and Employment and Labor Laws

Chapter 11 Mental Health Law

Chapter 12 Legal Problems of EAP Clients

Chapter 13 Preparing for Trial: The Courts, Evidence, and Expert Testimony

Chapter 1

The Development of Workplace Employee Assistance and EAP Law

EAPs are the natural successors of early occupational alcoholism programs. They are effective vehicles for addressing the substance abuse crisis in industry and government. New EAPs are being established daily in the public and private sectors and are being required of federal contractors and grantees. Programs exist in various forms, each of which has innumerable possible permutations. The legal implications of various program forms are briefly introduced.

EAPs are mental health and social service clinical care or information-and-referral programs serving employees and their dependents. They are operated for the mutual benefit of employers and employees in the workplace context. The EAP concept evolved from an earlier idea, the occupational alcoholism program, which developed along with Alcoholics Anonymous (AA) in the early 1940s. As the AA program gained recognition as a vehicle for controlling alcoholism, its enthusiastic members brought it into their workplaces. It did not take long for forward-thinking employers to begin participating in the identification of employees with alcohol problems and encouraging them to get help before poor job performance resulted in their termination.

Limitations of Occupational Alcoholism Programs

Early occupational alcoholism programs had limited success for several reasons. First, the workplace did not recognize early-stage alcoholism, so employees were not identified as needing services until their disease was so far advanced as to make effective intervention problematic. Chronic alcoholism was generally thought to be untreatable, and many workplace decision makers did not consider it worthwhile to expend resources for employees who were thought to be "lost causes."

The programs that did develop usually relied exclusively or largely on supervisors as casefinders trained to recognize the symptoms of alcoholism. As a result, it was almost always nonsupervisory, lower-level workers, rarely executives, who were identified and referred for services. Understandably, rank-and-file workers singled out in this manner claimed discrimination, which effectively stonewalled action, often until it was too late to save lives and jobs. Perhaps more significantly, alcohol abusers became more anxious to conceal their problems at work, so that it was only after years of drinking that they exhibited the late stage symptoms that finally called attention to their problem.

James T. Wrich states:

> The third major problem encountered by traditional alcohol identification programs was that alcoholic people are extremely skillful at diverting attention from their real problem. Alcoholics can easily convince lay people that the "cause" of the drinking and therefore the "real problem," is a nagging or spendthrift spouse, an unmanageable child, a physical ailment, money problems, or plain bad luck. When a supervisor with one or two hours training in alcoholism symptomatology was matched against a practicing alcoholic who had stored up scores of excuses and alibis over the years, it was no contest—the supervisor nearly always lost.

The Employee Assistance Program—Updated for the 1980s (Center City, Minn.: Hazelden, 1980).

The Rise of EAPs

Over time, the focus began to shift from alcoholism symptoms per se to poor job performance as the condition triggering program intervention. This strategy may have helped avoid the problem of denial regularly encountered in confronting an alcoholic, but the referring supervisors were still, in fact, looking for alcoholism symptoms and often did not consider referral of employees who did not exhibit the symptom pattern they could recognize. Further, the only resource available for referral of the problem worker was an alcoholism counselor, so the problems of stigma and narrow focus remained.

For those employees who were identified and referred, the success rates were high. For the many other employees—early stage alcoholics or employees whose work performance was impaired by other kinds of problems—there was no help, and many were lost. By the 1970s, it became evident that a broader approach was necessary, both to reduce the antagonism and denial of employees with alcohol-related problems, and to help employees with other difficulties. Additionally, drug abuse had become a recognized problem in industry, so that people began to talk about "substance abuse" or "chemical dependency" rather than just alcoholism.

Today, EAPs are concerned with identifying and assisting not only chronic-stage substance abusers, but the vast majority of employees with chemical dependency problems—those who are unidentified as needing help because they do not meet the common stereotypes—as well as employees with mental health and other problems. EAPs emphasize employee well-being, which makes these programs more attractive both to unions and to management. The reality is that employees with job-performance problems, whether or not related to chemical dependency, also have a wide variety of other problems: psychological or medical, psychosocial, financial, interpersonal, familial, and legal. These problems interfere with work, and it is work-related problems that EAPs are really designed to address.

Further, because impaired job performance may be one of the last firm symptoms to appear, early intervention is the key to a genuinely effective EAP. The National Institute on Alcohol Abuse and Alcoholism suggests that delay in intervention with an alcohol abuser may cut the probability of recovery from 80% to 15% or lower. The workforce—that is, human resources—is a major asset of any company, and the cost of impairment is astronomical. An estimated 10% of American workers have their productivity impaired by substance abuse, and 10%–15% of all highway fatalities involve drug use. Compared to nonusers, drug users are three times as likely to be involved in on-the-job accidents, are absent from work twice as often, and have three times the average level of sickness. Substance abuse costs industry around $100 billion each year.

Growth of Employee Assistance

Since chemical addiction is a handicapping condition protected by federal (and some state) law, employers must deal with impaired workers whether they want to or not, and the EAP appears to be the single most effective approach to dealing with substance abuse. The success of the EAP approach is measurable in the phenomenal growth of the field; there are thousands of EAPs worldwide, and their number is growing.

The employee assistance field has been given a tremendous boost with the enactment of the Drug-Free Workplace Act of 1988 (as part of the Anti-Drug Abuse Act of 1988, Pub. L. No. 100-690, 41 U.S.C. §701 et seq.), which requires federal contractors and grantees to certify that they will provide drug-free workplaces. On June 7, 1989, the Nuclear Regulatory Commission promulgated 10 C.F.R. Part 26, a regulation requiring any licensee authorized to operate a nuclear power reactor, its vendors, and its contractors to institute fitness-for-duty programs. (10 C.F.R. §26.25 (1989) issued under 42 U.S.C. §§2201(b) and 2201(i) (1989)) As part of the fitness-for-duty program, any such licensee must maintain an EAP that offers assessment, short-term counseling, referral services, and treatment monitoring to employees with problems that could adversely affect their job performance. The EAP must be designed to achieve early intervention and provide for confidential assistance, but must also notify a licensee if an employee constitutes a hazard. Other government agencies already, or soon will, require their contractors to provide EAPs, and the implications for private industry are clear.

EAPs deliver clinical services within the context of work. Substance abuse is a fairly new field of clinical concentration and the subject of a rapidly growing collection of clinical law. In addition, employment law relating to substance abuse is generated almost daily. Therefore, EAP law can be defined as the area where these bodies of law come together and overlap. EAPs come in various forms, and to a large extent, the shape of the EAP will determine which laws it is governed by.

Types of EAP Programs

Internal Programs

An *internal* or *in-house* program is formed by the sponsor as a separate department or service within the sponsor's organization. The EAP staff members are employees of the sponsor and thus subject to its control, as are any other employees. In-house EAPs may be sponsored by employers, unions, or jointly by management and labor.

- *Employer-sponsored* EAPs serve only one company's employees and their dependents. They may be located on the employer's premises—sometimes in conjunction with the medical or personnel department—or at a remote location leased or owned by the company.
- *Union-sponsored* in-house programs, organized by unions for their members and members' dependents, may be based at the union headquarters, a remote location, or—by agreement—on an employer's premises.
- *Joint programs* are organized under an agreement between a union and a single employer or association of employers.

There is an essential tension between employers and organized labor around issues of control of working conditions and employee discipline which often causes the individual employee to lose out. Approximately 20% of the American workforce is organized. When the union is in the position of having to defend the substance-abusing employee against the employer's efforts to maintain a drug-free workplace, the cost in time, money and human misery is insupportable. If the union "wins," the employee simply goes on with his or her self-destructive behavior. The costs of impairment continue in absenteeism, tardiness, poor productivity, accidents, increased use of health care benefits—and personal and family pain, suffering, and financial ruin.

Although unions may feel obliged to resist all management efforts to control employee behavior on political grounds, the reality is that considerable union resources are expended in substance-abuse-related grievances; in some settings, 50% of grievances are substance abuse related. Substance-abusing employees are costly to both management and the union. Forward-thinking unions see that their role in representing the interests of employees should go beyond knee-jerk negativism at every employer incentive. It makes sense, then, to move toward joint programs, in which employees with substance abuse or other problems get a clear message from the union that it will no more tolerate self-destructive behavior on the part of its members than will management tolerate poor job performance. Joint EAPs are simply more effective than management-only or union-only programs.

External Programs

Rather than provide an internal EAP, a sponsor (whether the sponsorship is management, union, or joint) may elect an *external program*, purchasing EAP services from an *independent contractor*—such as a not-for-profit mental health/social service agency, a hospital outpatient program, or a for-profit individual or group practice. The external contract may call for the independent EAP to service clients at its own offices, on the sponsor's premises, or at a separate location provided by either the sponsor or the contractor. For the most part, from the perspective of clinical care, whether the EAP is internal or external is irrelevant; in either case, clients are entitled to the same standard of care, and the relevant law is the same.

EAP Staffing

An EAP may be staffed by professional mental health counselors, such as social workers, psychologists, or nurses. Sometimes other employees, chosen for their apparent interest, intelligence, and talent, may be assigned to EAP functions. EAPs invariably have a strong substance abuse prevention and treatment component, and EAP professionals have specific training in that area. Many EAPs are partially or entirely staffed by volunteers—often themselves recovering substance abusers. Volunteer programs have much to commend them, but they can also create liability problems for their sponsors if they are not carefully monitored. A common model for jointly sponsored EAPs employs professionals to administer the program and provide direct client care, while trained volunteers appointed by management, the union, or both act as casefinders and peer counselors.

An EAP is always presented to potential service users as part of a benefits package, along with medical insurance and a retirement plan. In fact, it is a rare sponsor that is entirely altruistic. Employers sponsor EAPs in an effort to contain the huge cost of employee substance abuse and other social, emotional, and mental health problems. Employees and unions may perceive the EAP as: a health-related personal benefit to employees; a help in promoting safety and improving working conditions; a protection against the employer's disciplinary system; a nefarious social control mechanism; or any combination of the above. The EAP can be any or all of these, depending on the motivation and ethical position of the sponsor.

Legal Issues

The first issue in analyzing the legal implications for an EAP is: Who is the EAP's client? Is it the sponsor that is paying for the service and expects certain results? Is it the employee, who shows a need for service because of a problem he or she is experiencing—whether specifically job related or personal? When there is a clear conflict of interest between the sponsor and the employee, to whom does the EAP owe its loyalty? Who is liable if the EAP makes a clinical error and someone is harmed as a result? Who owns the EAP's records? Who has access to them under what circumstances, and to what use can they be put? Who is liable to a client who suffers loss or damages because of EAP error?

The answers to these questions are to be found in the specifics of the relationships among the sponsor, the EAP, and the person being served ("client"). The three primary relationships inherent in every EAP are: EAP/sponsor, sponsor/client, and EAP/client.

EAP-Sponsor Relationship

The parameters of the EAP-sponsor relationship should always be clearly stated in a written memorandum or contract. Whether the EAP is internal or external, sponsor and EAP must understand and agree upon the scope of the program:

- Types of service to be provided;
- Eligibility;
- Cost;
- Methods of entry;
- Interface with the employer disciplinary system; and
- Confidentiality rules.

These issues must be thoroughly explored and decided upon, preferably prior to commencement of the program, or as soon thereafter as possible.

Every EAP should be established with a full set of documentation: for an external program, a contract with the independent contractor; for an in-house program, a memorandum; and for either, detailed policies and procedures. The most important and obvious issues to be addressed by the contract or memorandum are:

- Control over the program;
- Funding methods and sources;
- Program service parameters;
- Staffing;
- Accountability;
- Liability;
- Interface with the medical and personnel departments of the employer; and
- Client confidentiality.

Sponsor-Client Relationship

The sponsor-client relationship in the context of EAP participation should be defined by the employer in written policies for EAP participation, in personnel policies, and in the collective bargaining agreement, if any. Policies and procedures should establish:

- Eligibility for EAP services;
- Method of access or referral to the EAP;
- Voluntariness of client participation;
- Interface between the EAP and the employer's disciplinary system;
- Use of health benefits, vacation, and sick time or released time for EAP participation;

- Confidentiality; and
- Career consequences of EAP participation.

An EAP brochure or manual spelling out policies and procedures should be given to potential EAP clients. The employer's lawyer should be closely consulted for advice on statutes and regulations to be considered, as well as the impact on program development of any collective bargaining agreements.

EAP-Client Relationship

The EAP-client relationship is essentially a contractual relationship for clinical care, governed by a complex set of legal rules described in detail in the next chapter. It differs from the ordinary clinical care contract in that the EAP-sponsor contract will define the EAP-client relationship to a great extent. Whether the EAP is internal or external, the employer is always a third party, either specifically or by implication, to the EAP's contract with the client. EAP clients must be fully advised prior to service delivery about the parameters of the employer's involvement in their care, as well as the scope of services, confidentiality, consequences of accepting or refusing service, treatment alternatives, cost, and so forth.

Oral or written representations about the EAP and what the client can expect, including such material as employer personnel policies and handbooks, memoranda, EAP brochures, and publicity, will create "terms" of the EAP-client contract. These should be well thought out and coordinated, so that sponsor and client have a consistent and clear understanding of their respective rights and responsibilities. A major source of legal trouble for employers is alleged discriminatory treatment of employees in the disciplinary process. Clear policies and procedures, scrupulously and consistently applied, will go a long way toward protecting the employer from such charges.

In the usual clinical care relationship, the provider owes primary loyalty to the client. This may not be the case in an EAP, and it is absolutely essential that all parties—sponsor, client, and EAP—are clearly aware of the EAP's position. The handling of conflicts of interests between sponsor and client should be addressed in EAP policies and procedures, which must be made known to clients.

The general rule in clinical care law is that the provider owns the clinical record, although the client has certain rights with respect to record access and disclosure. Similarly, the EAP owns its records—but who owns the EAP? The sponsor owns the records of an internal program, so the rights of the client and the sponsor vis-à-vis the record must be clearly established and made known to everyone involved. EAP professional standards require that client clinical records be kept confidential by the EAP, and not disclosed to the employer except when safety is an issue. The rights of a sponsor to access or use of the records of an external EAP should similarly be spelled out. Without a contractual arrangement to the contrary, the external EAP owns its client records, and the sponsor's access will be confined to that provided for in local or federal law.

In an internal program, the sponsor has the right to hire, direct, and fire the EAP personnel, who are its employees and agents. The in-house sponsor is legally responsible (liable) for its EAP staff's negligence in carrying out the program functions. The use of volunteers complicates the liability question. A client is entitled to rely upon the competence of the EAP. When any part of the service is provided by volunteers, the EAP is responsible for screening, training, and monitoring them. Careful definition of the scope of the volunteers' role and supervision of their activities are particularly important. Untrained persons who involve themselves in clinical activities for which they lack knowledge and skill are potentially dangerous to clients and thereby create a liability risk for sponsors.

When the EAP is an external program, the contractor will be responsible for its employees' negligence, and in theory, at least, the sponsor is shielded from liability. There are exceptions to this general rule, however. For example, if an employer requires an employee to participate in an EAP and specifies the service to be received, it is possible to argue that the employer is liable for any injury to the employee arising out of the services, even though the EAP is an outside provider. The issue is: Who controls the service delivery? Liability will follow control.

In summary, there is no specifically defined, integrated body of EAP law, as such, but statutes and regulations governing labor and employment, substance abuse, mental health care, and related fields apply to EAPs. As with any new concept, as employee assistance develops and legal problems arise in EAPs, common law precedents from related fields are adapted to define relationships, rights, and responsibilities of programs, sponsors, and clients. For example, general contract law will regulate the relationships of the sponsor and an external EAP. Labor law will affect the rights and responsibilities of the employer or union to form an EAP in the context of a collective bargaining agreement. Employment law will determine the rights of an employer and an employee when the EAP and the employer's disciplinary system interface. This book brings these seemingly disparate bodies of law into relationship with each other.

Chapter 2

Policy and Procedure Issues for EAPs

The development and implementation of policies and procedures are key factors in the success of an EAP. The nature of policies, their legal significance, and how they are developed within the context of various sponsor and EAP organizations are addressed in this chapter.

Q. 2:1 What are EAP policies and procedures?

A policy is a statement of philosophy that defines a position and is the basis for decision making and action. A procedure is a set of instructions for carrying out an operation. Policies tell the reader why, what, with whom, and under what circumstances. Procedures tell how and by whom.

Every organization has policies and procedures—some informal and unarticulated, others formal and memorialized. Either way, they have the force of rules. The larger and more complex the organization, the more formal and written policies there tend to be. A variety of subjects may be addressed by administrative and clinical care policies and procedures.

EAP policies and procedures govern the operation of the EAP and its interface with its sponsor. (See A-1: Sample Policy: Establishment of an EAP.)

In EAP service delivery, clinical care and personnel policies and procedures define program activities and direct staff in client care operations. They are presumably the result of thoughtful consideration in an atmosphere conducive to decision making. Difficult clients or situations may require quick response, but in the context of a crisis, staff judgment may be less than optimal. Clearly written policies and procedures provide a matrix for staff activity, limit the number of decisions to be made, reduce opportunity for errors of judgment, and increase consistency of care.

Q. 2:2 What constitutional law and statutory principles govern application of EAP policies and procedures?

The U.S. Constitution, federal law, and, often, state constitutions and statutes forbid employer discrimination against certain "protected categories" of employees: minorities, women, persons of certain ages, and handicapped persons. Employers are obliged to apply their policies and procedures in a consistent and nondiscriminatory fashion—not arbitrarily favoring or disfavoring one employee over another because of race, ethnic background, age, or handicap. Federal and state laws governing health care, particularly substance abuse services, apply to EAPs under certain circumstances. Legal consultation is essential in developing EAP policies and procedures that are consistent with both applicable law and any relevant collective bargaining agreement. Policies and procedures contrary to or inconsistent with laws and regulations will be legally unenforceable and expose the EAP and employer organizations and staff to civil and criminal liability.

Kinds of Policies and Procedures

Q. 2:3 What are personnel policies?

Personnel policies state the philosophy of the company with respect to its treatment, management, promotion, and discipline of workers.

Q. 2:4 What kinds of policies and procedures does an EAP need?

Policies and procedures are needed to:

- Define the program and the relationships among sponsor, EAP, and client;
- Facilitate program administration;
- Assure fiscal soundness and accountability;
- Set parameters of service; and
- Direct client care.

(For a list of policy and procedure topics and an outline for their development, see A-2: Policy and Procedure Checklist.)

Q. 2:5 How do EAP policies and procedures interface with the employment contract?

The employment contract establishes work rules and a disciplinary system. The employer's administrative policies and procedures must dovetail precisely with those of the EAP. Referral to the EAP may be a recommended or mandated step in the event of a work rule infraction. Acceptance of EAP services and EAP recommendations may be mandatory or voluntary. A "last chance contract" administered by the EAP may be an option for an employee under prescribed circumstances. (See Ch. 10, "EAPs and Employment and Labor Law," Qs. 10:71 and 10:72.) EAP participation may or may not be an alternative to discipline. Released time may be permitted for participation in the EAP, or the employee may be required to use sick leave or vacation time. If there is a fitness-for-duty policy or a drug-screening program, the EAP may or may not be involved in it. (See A-3: Sample Form: Supervisory Referral to the EAP and A-4: Sample Intake Form: Application for EAP Services.)

Developing Policies and Procedures

Q. 2:6 Who should be involved in policy and procedure development?

The style of the sponsor organization will determine how policies and procedures are developed. Some organizations operate with broad employee participation in management decisions; others exclude all but highest-level management from the process. There are a great number of positions between these poles. Even organizations that ordinarily do not include employees in management may find it to their advantage to do so in developing EAP policies.

Organization theory suggests that resistance to innovation, and particularly to the establishment of rules and procedures, can be reduced by involvement of the people affected. At the very least, the sponsor's EAP liaison and the EAP director or contractor should collaborate in the development process.

Both sponsor and EAP should be legally advised and represented at all stages of policy development about such issues as the impact of any collective bargaining agreement on the EAP, relevant employment and clinical law and regulations, and minimization of liability. EAP consultants may be helpful. Consultation with the relevant sponsor managers is also necessary at every stage of the process. Whether draft policies and procedures are to be submitted for approval one at a time or all at once as an integrated product will depend upon the circumstances. There are advantages and disadvantages to each alternative. If the development group is moving in a direction contrary to the sponsor's, a lot of time will be wasted unless this is cleared up early in the process. On the other hand, a policy by itself may raise more questions than it answers.

Q. 2:7 What is a suggested process for policy and procedure development?

Step 1: ***Identify the Core Policy-Making Group*** (include the sponsor and EAP legal consultants): A memorandum clearly defining the task of the group and the roles of the various participants and spelling out the sponsor's expectations for the group will be of great help in keeping the development process going smoothly. In any group, participants may develop strong positions. Some of the issues in EAP development have the potential to trigger strong emotional responses. Structuring the group and the process will help to avoid disruption.

Step 2: ***List the Issues and Options to Be Considered:*** Using a hypothetical or real case scenario to experiment with the options is an interesting and useful exercise. Try writing out the alternatives in draft policy form. As a policy begins to take shape, procedures for implementing it will naturally enter the discussion. It is easy to confound procedures with policies at this stage. If this occurs, confusion and frustration are likely to follow. Keep policy and procedure issues and recommendations clearly distinguished.

Step 3: ***Coordinate EAP Draft Policies With Other Policies and Programs of the Sponsor:*** EAP policies should be coordinated with personnel, disciplinary, and benefits policies and work rules.

Q. 2:8 What if the sponsor and the EAP cannot agree on policies and procedures?

The sponsor and the EAP should agree on policies and procedures, but the practical reality is that the sponsor has the final word. If the sponsor's policy position is intolerable for the EAP—whether the program is external or internal—the EAP personnel will be placed in an untenable position. Because of the fiduciary nature of the EAP-client relationship, an EAP professional may be unable to make the compromises necessary to satisfy the sponsor. In such a case, ethical and professional principles require resignation from the program or rejection of the contract. Anything less is dishonest and provides a fertile hotbed for trouble.

Q. 2:9 What labor and employment law concepts should be kept in mind when developing EAP policies and procedures?

The traditional employer-employee relationship was "at will"—the employer hired and fired whomever it pleased based on its criteria of the moment, paid what it chose, and imposed whatever working conditions suited its purpose. In theory, employees had equal rights; they could reject or leave a job if they grew dissatisfied with the employer's terms and conditions. In reality, however, the balance of power and economic conditions were such that employers had almost all the rights and employees had few, if any.

The rise of the labor movement legalized collective bargaining and brought about the development of labor and employment law that constrained the power of employers and created rights and protections for all employees, whether union members or not. Company enactment and enforcement of policies and procedures contrary to or inconsistent with the collective bargaining agreement will be construed as a breach of the agreement. Likewise, anything appearing in materials distributed to employees (for example, an employee handbook) that can be construed as a promise to or agreement with an employee may be used to prove that an employer breached its agreement with an employee in a particular instance.

Q. 2:10 When are EAP policies and procedures required to be in writing?

Accreditation bodies and government agency contracts usually require written policies and procedures, and statutes and regulations often do so also. Even in the absence of external requirements, it is good practice to have written policies and procedures.

In an EAP not constrained by statute, regulation, or contract, the decision about whether to have written policies (and if so, how many and covering what subjects) is probably as much a matter of administrative personality and style as anything else.

Q. 2:11 What are the pros and cons of written policies and procedures?

Some people argue against written policies and procedures on the theory that they curb creativity and restrict staff flexibility. Those arguing in favor of written policies say they help create uniformity of staff behavior and consistency of care. Often, administrators are pro writing, and clinicians against.

There is no doubt that accountability is facilitated and staff behavior is easier to assess when there are articulated standards. If a client sues for malpractice or other legal injury based on staff behavior deviating from EAP policies and procedures, the deviation gives rise to a presumption of negligence. Deviation is obviously more difficult to establish if the policies and procedures are unwritten. On the other hand, if they *are* written and complied with, it is highly probable that the risk of staff error and a subsequent lawsuit are dramatically reduced.

Q. 2:12 How can the EAP make the policy and procedures manual work for the organization?

Policies and procedures are worse than useless if the staff does not know what they are and how to use them. Legally, they will weigh against the EAP, the counselor, and the counselor's supervisor if they exist and are not followed. This risk exposure is compounded by the risk of clinical judgment error and administrative confusion if staff members are not practicing in accordance with the plan and expectations of the sponsor or the EAP.

The EAP can take steps to ensure that policies and procedures are working for the organization. These include distribution of the policy and procedures manual to every EAP staff member—professionals, volunteers, and support staff—mandatory thorough orientation, and regular in-service training. Policies and procedures should be referred to in supervision and consultation and noted in case records and administrative memoranda as the bases for decisions. They should be regularly reviewed and revised as necessary to be certain that they conform to actual practice. A very important policy to state is, "Deviation from policies or procedures is not permitted without prior written permission of administration; violation of this policy will result in discipline."

Q. 2:13 How are policies and procedures promulgated?

Once policies and procedures have been approved and adopted by the sponsor and the EAP, they will be binding upon anyone who is charged with knowledge of them. Thus, they should be "published" or distributed to EAP and sponsor staff and made known or available to clients and potential clients. EAP brochures, posters, and other case-finding publicity are excellent vehicles for client education. Sponsor referrers and EAP staff, including volunteers, must be thoroughly trained in the policies and procedures. Sometimes, what seems to be a good idea turns out to be anything but, or conditions change. Poor policies and procedures help no one and can be the source of trouble for clients and the EAP. Policies and procedures should be regularly reviewed and updated to meet program realities.

Legal Effect of Policies and Procedures

Q. 2:14 What is the legal effect of clinical care policies and procedures?

Clinical care policies and procedures establish standards for client care.

Deviation from clinical policies or procedures will give rise to a presumption of negligence on the part of the clinician if a client claims injury for malpractice, breach of contract, or a deliberate wrongful act by a counselor that is related to the deviation. Unless the EAP can overcome the presumption by establishing either that no negligence occurred or that the deviation was not the direct cause of the client's claimed injury, the breach of policy or procedure will be construed as a breach of the counselor's duty of due care.

Q. 2:15 What is the legal effect of company administrative procedures?

Policies, procedures, and work rules that regulate the administration and operation of a workplace become part of the employment contract between employer and employee. Both are bound to obey them, and either can seek redress through the mechanism of the collective bargaining agreement, if there is one, through the grievance procedure established by the employer, if any, and—depending on the nature of the grievance and who is aggrieved—through government administrative agencies or the courts.

Q. 2:16 Can an EAP be charged with negligence for failing to promulgate written policies and procedures?

The incidence of malpractice claims against mental health and social service providers has increased dramatically in recent years, as reflected in the rise in malpractice insurance costs. Because historically there have been few reported EAP malpractice cases, many EAPs have ignored the possibility until lately. With the expansion and professionalization of the EAP field, the risk of liability is now being taken seriously, and standards for clinical care administration have become increasingly strict and formal. Professional industry standards require written policies and procedures, with the result that failure to promulgate written client care standards may be considered administrative negligence in the event of a malpractice claim against the EAP.

Q. 2:17 How does an EAP counselor's deviation from policies and procedures affect liability?

The EAP is vicariously responsible for negligent wrongful acts of its employees, if performed in the scope and course of employment. In theory, there is no vicarious liability for deliberate wrongful acts, or for acts outside the scope of employment. Malpractice insurance protects only against negligent—that is, nondeliberate—errors and omissions, not against willful wrongdoing.

The EAP and its insurance company may logically argue that a counselor who deliberately breached an EAP policy or procedure was acting outside the scope and course of employment. In that case, the EAP may not be held liable for the wrongful act and its consequences, and the insurance company may deny coverage. Then, unless the counselor has individual malpractice insurance that provides coverage, he or she will be personally responsible for defending the claim and paying any judgment.

Confidentiality Policy

Q. 2:18 What is a workable policy for EAP confidentiality?

Confidentiality is a *sine qua non* in employee assistance; an EAP simply cannot function if its clients cannot be assured that information about their personal affairs will not be divulged. On the other hand, there are situations in which public or personal safety or property rights require an exception to the general rule. The EAP policy should state that, as a general rule, client information is confidential and will not be disclosed without the client's written consent, but that there are exceptions: Information will be disclosed (1) in accordance with law (e.g., child abuse reporting; mandated reporting of substance abuse under federal regulations, such as the Nuclear Regulatory Commission); (2) in the event that the staff, in its discretion, believes the client or another is at risk for harm; and (3) when illegal acts or threats thereof are committed against the EAP, the sponsor, or their employees or premises. (See A-5: Model: Employee (EAP Client) Statement of Understanding and A-6: Sample Form: Consent for Disclosure of Information to Supervisor or for Referral.)

Fitness-for-Duty Policy

Q. 2:19 What is a fitness-for-duty policy?

A fitness-for-duty policy establishes criteria for employee fitness to be at work, a method for assessing fitness, and the company's response to employee unfitness. A fitness-for-duty policy is used in conjunction with work rules prohibiting the use of mood-altering substances for a period of time before the work shift (the so-called hourly rule) or during the work shift; or their use, possession, or sale on the employer's premises. Scrupulously followed, it eliminates myriad problems for supervisors who are confronted with impaired employees and provides fair and uniform standards for the employees' protection. (See A-7: Sample Policy: Fitness for Duty.)

Q. 2:20 Is an employer legally obliged to have a fitness-for-duty policy?

Since passage of the Drug-Free Workplace Act of 1988 (as part of the Anti-Drug Abuse Act of 1988, Pub. L. No. 100-690, 41 U.S.C. §701 et seq.), employers with federal government contracts in excess of $25,000, or that are federal grantees, are required to establish policies to maintain drug-free workplaces, including fitness-for-duty policies. The fitness-for-duty policy must address, at a minimum:

- A prohibition against the use of illegal drugs and abuse of legal drugs (including alcohol and prescription or over-the-counter drugs);
- An hourly rule (no less than five hours);
- Other conditions that could affect fitness, such as mental stress, fatigue, and illness;
- A description of programs available to aid employees who have drug or other problems (i.e., an EAP);
- Procedures for testing for chemicals; and
- A description of the actions the employer will take in the event of a finding of unfitness. (See, e.g., 10 C.F.R. §26.20 (1989).)

Companies with federal contracts are advised to keep up-to-date with developments in this area, which are occurring almost daily.

Q. 2:21 If an employee refuses to cooperate with a fitness-for-duty evaluation, what is the employer's recourse?

Fitness for duty is a condition of employment. An employee who refuses to cooperate with the fitness-for-duty policy and procedures is insubordinate and may be disciplined in accordance with the employer's disciplinary program.

Q. 2:22 Are employees who are referred to the EAP following fitness-for-duty procedures exempt from discipline for possession and/or use of drugs?

This depends upon the employer's work rules and disciplinary system. If an employee is guilty of a work rule infraction, he or she is disciplined because of the infraction, not because of the fitness-for-duty policy. An employee who voluntarily seeks help with a problem, drug or otherwise, and who is not referred for cause for a fitness-for-duty evaluation, has not violated a work rule and should not be disciplined. The EAP policies should cover this eventuality.

Most employers take the position that agreeing to EAP assistance will not exempt an employee from discipline, including discharge, for deficiencies in performance, such as excessive unavailability for work, disruptive or insubordinate behavior, unsatisfactory work performance (e.g., errors), and violation of work rules—regardless of the reason for the deficiencies.

Q. 2:23 What are the indicators for referral for a fitness-for-duty evaluation?

Any observable sign of impairment in work capacity is a basis for referral for evaluation. Common signs include, but are not limited to:

- Drowsiness or sleepiness;
- Odor of alcohol on the breath;
- Bloodshot eyes;
- Frequent trips to the washroom;
- Inability to concentrate or lack of attention;
- Slurred, incoherent speech;
- Unusually aggressive behavior;

- Unexplained work errors;
- Lack of manual dexterity;
- Lack of coordination in walking;
- Unexplained work-related accident or injury; and
- Unexplained changes in mood.

Chapter 3

The Clinical Care Contract

EAPs are clinical care providers whose relationships with clients are governed by principles of law related to health care delivery. The nature of the clinical care contract—how it is initiated and how it may be terminated—and the concepts of informed consent and incapacity are discussed in this chapter. The issues of when a client may be given treatment against his or her will and common conflicts of interest that can affect the clinical relationship are also covered.

Q. 3:1 What is the legal basis of the EAP clinical care relationship?

The legal basis of the relationship between the EAP provider and the client is a contract formed when the therapist agrees to provide treatment and the client agrees to be treated. The term "contract" need not be used by the parties. Whether the client seeks services voluntarily or is required to get help (for example, by a court or an employer), and whether the service is paid for and by whom, are not relevant. When clinical services are being provided, a professional relationship is created between the therapist and the care recipient. The fact that the EAP also owes a legal duty to the sponsor will not lessen or otherwise alter the clinical/legal responsibilities of the EAP to the client.

Q. 3:2 What are counseling and psychotherapy?

Psychotherapy is:

> a method or system of alleviating or curing certain forms of disease, particularly diseases of the nervous system, or such as are traceable to nervous disorders, by suggestion, persuasion, encouragement, the inspiration of hope or confidence, the discouragement of morbid memories, associations, or beliefs, and other similar means addressed to the mental state of the patient, without (or sometimes in conjunction with) the administration of drugs or other physical remedies.

Black's Law Dictionary (5th ed., 1979).

Counseling is a process of advising. Neither of these definitions is adequate to describe treatment activities of mental health and social service providers today. Both counseling and psychotherapy require an assessment or diagnosis as the basis for treatment. There are literally hundreds of modalities of psychotherapy; some utilize words alone, and others employ touch, art, music, drama, or body manipulation or exercises.

Q. 3:3 Can a client be harmed by psychotherapy?

For a period of time, there was debate about whether "mere talking" can harm a client. Research on the question has clearly demonstrated that the answer is yes. (See, for example, Stone, "Suicide Precipitated by Psychotherapy: A Clinical Contribution," 25 *Am. J. Psychotherapy* (1971): 18.) For example, injury may result from unskilled tampering with the client's psychological defense system; improper handling of the transference or countertransference phenomena; use of psychotherapy alone, instead of medical or pharmacological treatment, when the latter are indicated; use of a modality of therapy that is known to be relatively ineffective for the condition being treated; or psychological exploitation or abuse of the client.

Q. 3:4 What is the nature of the therapeutic relationship, according to the law?

The law recognizes two realities inherent in the psychotherapy or counseling relationship: the profound influence and power of the therapist and the dependence and vulnerability of the client. Therapy can take place only when the client is free to reveal to the counselor his or her most secret, intimate, and important confessions, hopes, fears, feelings, and thoughts. Because of the therapist's special training and knowledge, the client's lack of information and of independence, and the special trust the client is assumed to have in the therapist, the law characterizes the counseling or psychotherapy relationship as a fiduciary relationship. The powerful party, the therapist, is the fiduciary—that is, he or she is required always to place the client's interests first and to act for the client's benefit. The law's approach to the therapeutic relationship is entirely consistent with clinical theory and ethical principles. The law requires of the care provider precisely what is required by good clinical practice concepts.

Terms and Warranties: What to Include

Q. 3:5 What types of terms are found in an EAP clinical service contract?

The contract consists of terms that are either expressly agreed upon by the parties or imposed by law.

- Express terms are articulated orally or in writing between the EAP and the client (for example, cost, duration, place and type of service, and the parameters of confidentiality). They may be found in EAP or sponsor documents, such as policies and procedures, personnel handbooks, memoranda, and EAP publicity.
- Implied terms are not articulated, but are built into the contract as warranties by operation of law unless there has been an express agreement between the EAP and the client to the contrary.

Q. 3:6 What warranties are implied by law in the counseling contract?

The client is entitled by law to assume and rely upon the following implied warranties:

Competence: The EAP counselor is possessed of that degree of skill and knowledge that the ordinary professional in the community performing the same functions would be expected to have.

Due Care: The EAP counselor will perform his or her functions in the manner of a duly careful professional; he or she will not commit negligent errors nor omit to do what ought to be done for the client.

Confidentiality: EAP personnel will not disclose the client's private, confidential communications without his or her informed consent, except as is permitted or required by law.

Q. 3:7 What remedies are available to the EAP client in case of a breach of warranty?

Both the EAP and the individual staff member who breaches an express or implied warranty are at risk for a breach of contract lawsuit if the client suffers injury as a result of that breach. If the breach is negligent, there may also be a cause of action for malpractice.

Q. 3:8 How does the law define treatment?

Treatment has been broadly defined to cover all steps necessary to effect a cure of an injury or disease—including examination and diagnosis—as well as application of remedies. (*Kirschner v. Equitable Life Assurance Society*, 284 N.Y.S. 506 (1935)) Behavior or activities by a therapist with a client that do not fit this definition will not be considered treatment. For example, socializing or having sexual relations with a client are not considered treatment by recognized therapies. If a client complains of injury by reason of such activities, the therapist's malpractice insurance carrier is likely to try to refuse to pay damages. (*Roy v. Hartogs*, 381 N.Y.S.2d 587 (Sup. Ct. 1976))

Q. 3:9 If there are so many modalities of treatment, how can a standard of care and liability be assessed?

The standard of care in psychotherapy must be assessed in terms of the specific modality or combination of modalities being used. In evaluating a case for liability, a review of the clinical literature and a consultation with an expert in both the condition being treated and the modality of treatment are necessary.

Q. 3:10 Is there an implied warranty of cure?

The law does *not* create an implied warranty of cure; the law *does* require that the EAP provide services properly and without negligence. Unless the provider has expressly guaranteed an outcome, there is no cause of action for failure to achieve a cure or favorable result. (*Rogala v. Silva*, 305 N.E.2d 571 (1973)) The implication is clear: Clinical care providers should scrupulously avoid any language that could be construed by a client or family as a guarantee of result. (*Guilmet v. Campbell*, 188 N.W.2d 601 (1971)) Inexperienced providers are particularly vulnerable in this regard because they are likely to be less skilled in offering reassurance and encouragement without promising more than they can deliver.

Q. 3:11 What clinical care standards apply to EAPs and where are they to be found?

Since every clinical care contract contains a warranty that the care provider will exercise "due care," it is important to know the standard by which the provider will be judged. The law looks to each professional field to determine its own practice standards. EAPs are a recent clinical care concept and, as such, have adopted and adapted standards from the traditional clinical professions and programs. The Association of Labor-Management Consultants on Alcoholism (ALMACA) and the Employee Assistance Society of North America (EASNA) are national organizations of employee assistance providers active in standards development.

EAP practitioners who are members of professional associations are also governed by the practice standards of their own disciplines. Other sources for clinical practice standards are state licensing acts and state and federal statutes and regulations governing mental health and substance abuse treatment and general health care delivery; standard textbooks and professional and trade journals; accrediting body standards; and institutional and program policies and procedures. When there are no standards for a group of practitioners, the courts will apply existing principles for related fields and establish a standard. (P.C. Kissam, "Physician's Assistant and Nurse-Practitioner Laws," 24 *Kans. L. Rev.* (Fall 1975))

How to Initiate a Contract

Q. 3:12 When is the clinical care contract formed?

The EAP and its staff have clinical responsibility to employees (or other eligible persons) once they become EAP clients by participating in or agreeing to accept EAP services. Ordinarily, the contract begins at the moment when the employee agrees to accept the offered EAP service. The terms of the contract are determined by the law, the parameters of the program, and the EAP staff member and client themselves.

Q. 3:13 Can a clinical care contract be formed without an express oral or written agreement?

Sometimes (usually in a crisis), no express agreement is made; service simply begins. Mere behavior can create a duty of care. For example, an EAP staff member may respond to a supervisor's urgent call by immediately assessing an employee, organizing an emergency referral and transportation to an inpatient facility, notifying and counseling the employee's family, and making arrangements with the employer for sick leave. In this case, the contract is formed by implication, and the employee becomes a client when the counselor starts providing service, although there has been no formal offer and acceptance of a counseling contract. (*O'Neill v. Montefiore Hospital,* 202 N.Y.S.2d 436 (1960))

Q. 3:14 What is an implied contract?

An implied contract is not an explicit agreement, but one inferred by the law as a matter of reason and justice, based on the acts of the parties involved and the circumstances in which they occurred. Overall, the circumstances and behavior of the parties would call for a reasonable or necessary assumption that a contract existed between them by tacit understanding. (*Cameron v. Eynon,* 3 A.2d 423 (1939))

Q. 3:15 Can clinical responsibility begin before a potential client is seen?

Contractual responsibility can arise from a phone conversation without the client being seen by an EAP staff member at all. If a potential client calls and discloses information that would lead a competent, duly careful EAP professional to know that immediate service is necessary to prevent harm, failure to act in an appropriate and timely fashion is a breach of due care. The more involvement with the client on the phone, the more responsible the EAP will be.

Clearly, the program should give careful consideration to intake procedures. If a nonprofessional receives calls and does anything more than take a name and phone number, he or she must be trained to recognize an emergency and have immediate access to a clinician for crisis intervention. If emergency service is offered but not accepted, the counselor will have to decide whether such risk of harm exists that police assistance, emergency medical services, or some other legal intervention is indicated. In any event, emergencies merit very detailed recording, including the clinician's rationale for what he or she has or has not done.

> **Example.** On a Friday evening, an EAP counselor receives an emergency phone call from a supervisor, asking him to phone an employee who is in crisis. The employee's wife describes the symptoms, which sound like delirium tremens. The counselor arranges admission to an inpatient alcoholism treatment program, where the staff begins routine detoxification treatment. The employee dies of an undiagnosed brain abscess a few days later, and the widow sues. The issue is: Was the EAP professional negligent in making the telephone diagnosis? In this case, there will probably be no liability to the EAP or the counselor because once the referral was made, a physician at the inpatient program was responsible for the medical diagnosis. The EAP counselor may be at risk because he "prescribed" alcoholism treatment. He would be safer had he simply referred the client to emergency care at a hospital or other medical facility.

Some EAPs provide all of their services on the phone—sometimes across the country—and never see any of their clients in person. A sufficient treatment relationship can exist via telephone contact to support a malpractice suit if the client claims injury by reason of negligence. (*Giallanza v. Sands*, 316 So.2d 77 (1975))

Good Samaritan Protection

Q. 3:16 Do Good Samaritan laws apply to EAPs?

Yes. Because clinicians are concerned with liability risk if they voluntarily help out in an emergency, most states have enacted "Good Samaritan" laws. Under most such laws, the clinician who renders aid in an emergency, has not been grossly negligent, and receives no payment for the services is immune from liability. A clinician is not *obliged* by law to render aid to anyone who is not a client. If the clinician does intervene, he or she is obliged to exercise ordinary care and not abandon the victim until other aid arrives.

How to Terminate a Contract

Q. 3:17 When does the clinical contract end?

When an orderly, planned termination of the counseling relationship takes place, and both parties express their intention and understanding that termination is to occur, the clinical contract ends by agreement. There may be some residual responsibility for follow-up, depending upon the client's circumstances. When a client simply drops out of treatment, it is not as easy to fix the time of formal termination. Depending upon the clinical condition of the client and the reason for his or her precipitous termination, the therapist may continue to be clinically responsible for some period of time, at least until an attempt has been made to terminate formally.

Q. 3:18 What steps should be taken when the client precipitously withdraws from treatment?

A client may withdraw from treatment at will unless he or she is under commitment or other legal constraint. Often, precipitous termination is symptomatic behavior, and due care requires that the therapist take the necessary clinical steps to encourage the client to reconsider, or at least to assure his or her safety. If there is any question about the client's safety, emergency measures may be necessary. Assuming no emergency, the least a therapist should do is call the client and follow up with a letter stating the therapist's view about what is in the client's best interests. The legally appropriate response to precipitous termination is also the clinically appropriate response. Careful recording should be done, however, to reflect due diligence.

Q. 3:19 What is abandonment?

Abandonment is the precipitous, unilateral termination of the clinical relationship by the therapist while care is still required. (*Stohlman v. Davis,* 220 N.W. 247 (1928)) Abandonment can also occur when a therapist fails to respond to a client's needs in a timely fashion, negligently breaks appointments, or fails to provide a suitable back-up or substitute when he or she is unavailable. (For a more detailed account of abandonment, see Ch. 5, "Professional Liability," Qs. 5:36–5:52.)

Q. 3:20 When is the EAP counselor obliged to initiate termination?

The counselor must initiate termination when it becomes apparent that it is not in the client's best interests to continue in treatment. Such a decision might be appropriate if the treatment has been given a fair chance, but the client is not improving despite consultation. The therapist should also terminate if he or she is personally unable to serve the client's needs because of a conflict of interests or an impairment.

Q. 3:21 Under what circumstances may the EAP counselor initiate termination for administrative purposes or for his or her own convenience?

A therapist may terminate treatment for any reason, even when treatment is still needed, as long as the termination is done in a clinically appropriate manner and substitute treatment is available. In most communities, whether or not there are private resources available, there is a social service or mental health agency to which the client can be referred. If no alternative treatment is available and the client would be clinically jeopardized by termination, the therapist may be required to continue treatment if he or she is able to do so. (Holder, *Medical Malpractice Law,* 2d ed. (New York: 1978), 373)

Q. 3:22 What is a clinically appropriate termination?

The correct termination procedure will depend on the client's clinical condition and needs. Enough time must be allowed to introduce the concept of termination and explore the client's feelings about it and his or her options for the future. The therapist is obliged to provide sufficiently adequate records and information to a successor therapist, to assure continuity of care; offer appropriate referrals, if indicated; and allow enough time to enable the client to locate and transfer to a successor therapist, if care is still required.

Informed Consent and the Right to Refuse Treatment

Q. 3:23 What is informed consent, and how does it apply to EAPs?

Because a contract creates legal obligations for both parties, it cannot be formed unless they have reached a "meeting of the minds" about their respective rights and responsibilities. During the 1960s, the rise of consumerism and the development of expanded rights of freedom and privacy translated the meeting-of-the-minds concept into a requirement of informed consent to treatment in all clinical care contracts. Except in an emergency, consent is required before treatment can be given. It stands to reason that a consent cannot be valid unless the client knows to what he or she is consenting; an uninformed consent is no consent at all.

Informed consent requires that the EAP provider inform the client about:

- The nature of the condition being treated;
- The treatment alternatives available;
- The foreseeable risks of the various alternatives (including the risks of refusing treatment); and
- The potential benefits of the various treatments (but not expressed in terms that could be interpreted as a guarantee or promise of results).

Q. 3:24 How much information is necessary to achieve informed consent?

The client should be given enough information to be able to make a reasonable choice in his or her best interests, as that person perceives them. (*Scaria v. St. Paul Fire and Marine Insurance*, 227 N.W.2d 647 (1975)) Although informed consent requires that the client be told the condition for which he or she is to be treated, it may be preferable not to use a diagnostic label. Substance abuse treatment theory insists that a client be told and acknowledge that he or she is an alcoholic or addict, but some mental health providers would hesitate to tell a client that he or she is "paranoid" or "borderline" or "schizophrenic." When the use of a formal diagnostic term seems to the provider to be clinically contraindicated, the counselor may choose to describe the condition phenomenologically, by using, for example, such phrases as "relationship difficulties," or "a feeling of persecution."

In informing the client of treatment alternatives, the law does not require that the client be given an encyclopedic overview of treatment theory or told of every obscure modality or technique. (*Cobbs v. Grant*, 502 P.2d 1 (1972)) When a provider reasonably believes that an existing alternative would not work for a client, he or she does not have to inform the client of it. (*Downer v. Veilleux*, 322 A.2d 82 (1974)) If a recognized treatment exists for the client's condition, he or she should be informed of it, even if it is not available within the context of the EAP or in the client's home community. Clients sometimes have resources unknown to the provider, as the following example demonstrates.

Example. The client suffered from obsessive compulsive disorder. The therapist was aware that drug trials were being conducted for treatment of this condition, but the medication had not yet been approved for use in the United States except in approved research programs. However, the medication was available in Canada. For a long time, the therapist hesitated to tell the client about this possible resource, thinking that the client could never afford to go to Canada for treatment. When he finally did discuss the matter with the client, it was only a matter of a few days before the client's Aunt Sophie from Schenectady came through with the funding, and the client went to Canada, received the medication, and experienced a seemingly miraculous alleviation of symptoms.

Q. 3:25 What is therapeutic privilege in the context of informed consent?

The law varies from state to state, so legal advice should be obtained when developing consent policies and procedures. In some states, the duty to inform is not absolute. (See, e.g., *Ross v. Hodges,* 234 So.2d 905 (1970).) In these states, the clinician is privileged to use his or her best clinical judgment in determining how much information is in the client's interest and what information, if any, to withhold. The standard will be what the duly careful professional would have done under the circumstances. (*Weiser v. Hampton,* 445 S.W.2d 224 (1969); *Nishi v. Hartwell,* 473 P.2d 116 (1970)) Clinical consultation and a careful note in the client's record will help to minimize risk if information is to be withheld.

Q. 3:26 Under what circumstances is a client incompetent to give informed consent?

A client who has been adjudicated by a court of law to be incompetent may not give a valid consent to treatment. Although a person is presumed competent to give informed consent to treatment until he or she has been declared incompetent, if it is clear from a client's clinical condition that he or she cannot make a responsible, informed decision about care, the provider who proceeds without valid substituted consent is at risk for a later lawsuit by the client on the basis that informed consent was not, and could not have been, obtained. The implications are clear: When in doubt, have the person evaluated for competency and seek legal advice.

Q. 3:27 How is a person adjudicated incompetent?

An incompetency adjudication involves a petition to an appropriate court to have an individual declared incompetent and a personal representative appointed for him or her, with power to make decisions and give substituted consent. The precise form of the proceedings and the title for the personal representative (for example, guardian, trustee, conservator, committee) and the adjudicated person (for example, ward, incompetent), will vary from state to state. In some states, guardianship may be shared: a guardian of the person may be appointed to make decisions about such matters as the ward's residence, education, or training, and to give substituted consent for health care; a guardian of the estate may be appointed to handle the ward's legal and financial affairs.

Q. 3:28 Under what circumstances will informed consent be assumed or waived?

When a patient is unconscious or comatose, informed consent to *medical* treatment is waived on the assumption that the client would wish to be treated for an illness or injury. (*Crouch v. Most,* 432 P.2d 250 (1967)) Some, but not all, states permit designated next of kin to consent to medical treatment when the patient clearly cannot do so. Mental health and substance abuse treatment are generally treated as a separate category, however, because the law is concerned about interference with freedom of thought and expression. In most states, even involuntary inpatient commitment to a mental health facility will not, in itself, deprive a patient of the right to accept or refuse mental health care or substance abuse treatment; a separate adjudication as to incompetency is required. (See Ch. 11, "Mental Health Law," Qs. 11:19–11:24.)

Q. 3:29 When can emergency mental health or substance abuse treatment be given over the client's objection?

If a patient or client is refusing necessary treatment, such as medication or electroconvulsive (shock) therapy, most states will permit the provider to treat over objection only in an emergency and on a short-term basis. For anything but emergency intervention, an adjudication of incompetency will be required. In some states, even a duly appointed guardian must apply specifically to the court for permission to consent to psychotropic (mind-altering) medication or shock treatment.

Q. 3:30 Who has legal capacity to contract for or refuse clinical care?

A person over the age of 18 has legal capacity to make treatment decisions unless he or she has been adjudicated by a court to be incompetent. As a general rule, minors cannot make contracts. The law recognizes an exception for "necessaries": reasonable and necessary food, shelter, clothing, and medical care. Federal and state statutes confer capacity on minors (usually at 12 years of age) to contract for treatment related to substance abuse. Some states permit minors to consent to receive pregnancy and birth control services and mental health care. Minors may be given emergency medical treatment without consent because parental consent is implied. Because state laws vary, legal consultation is mandatory when competency or capacity questions arise.

Q. 3:31 Can a mentally ill person or substance abuser be compelled to accept treatment?

A person who requires treatment for mental illness or substance abuse but, because of his or her condition, lacks judgment and refuses it, may be subject to commitment for involuntary treatment. In some states, general mental health law and substance abuse treatment are governed by separate statutes. Although some civil rights advocates have insisted for years that involuntary psychiatric treatment is unconstitutional and should never be imposed upon an unwilling person, mental health commitment laws exist in every state. In developing statutes and regulations governing substance abuse treatment, however, Congress and state legislatures have been greatly influenced by clinical theory positing that drug addiction, including alcoholism, is a physical—not a mental—illness, and that effective treatment requires the patient's willingness and personal commitment. Depending upon local law, although involuntary commitment for mental health treatment may be possible, commitment for substance abuse treatment may not.

Q. 3:32 May an employee refuse EAP services?

A legally competent person who has not been committed by a court cannot be forced to accept clinical services, even if it is clear that he or she needs care badly and the resistance to treatment is most likely a product of the illness. (*Pratt v. Davis,* 79 N.E. 562 (1906))

Sometimes, an employee who has broken work rules and is thus subject to firing or other discipline may be offered a reprieve or reinstatement if he or she participates in a treatment program. Although an employee cannot be forced to accept EAP services, an employer may not be forced to keep a rule-breaker in its employ. But the employee would be fired for breach of the work rules, not for refusing help from the EAP.

When to Get Consent by Power of Attorney

Q. 3:33 How can a client designate a substitute to make treatment decisions in the event of his or her later incapacity?

There is a device called a power of attorney, which can be used to appoint another person to act on one's behalf. The person who signs the power of attorney is called the grantor or principal. Any competent adult—that is, one over 18 years of age—may grant a power of attorney. The person to whom the power is granted is called an attorney-in-fact. An attorney-in-fact is the agent of the grantor, who is the principal. The attorney-in-fact may be, but need not be, a lawyer (attorney-at-law). The law simply requires that he or she be a competent adult. The grantor or principal may grant a general power to the agent or attorney-in-fact to enter into contracts and perform any and all other legal functions (except marry, divorce, make a will, or vote) on his or her behalf, or a special power to perform only certain specific, designated functions. A principal may revoke a power of attorney at any time.

At common law, a power of attorney ended if the principal later became incompetent. Thus, there was no way to plan in advance to have an agent to act for the principal if the principal became incapacitated by illness or some other condition at some time in the future. In recent years, some states have enacted statutes to create a durable power of attorney, which will endure even after the principal becomes incompetent, or unless or until a court appoints a guardian or conservator for the principal.

In most states that have durable power of attorney laws, the principal may grant to the attorney-in-fact power to make treatment decisions, including the right to consent to, refuse, or terminate medical, mental health, and substance abuse treatment. A durable power of attorney is a great help to clients who may be expected to have periodic bouts of incapacity, such as alcoholics, persons suffering from mental illness, or those who are known to have a progressive condition, such as Alzheimer's disease or cancer. Since local laws vary widely, an attorney must be consulted to determine if such a tool exists in the client's jurisdiction, and how it may be framed to meet the client's needs.

Conflicts of Interest and the EAP-Client Fiduciary Relationship

Q. 3:34 How are transference and countertransference relevant to the EAP-client fiduciary relationship?

Some degree of transference (see Q. 3:35) and countertransference (see Q. 3:36) are expected to occur in the normal course of therapy. The client's judgment and decision-making capacity may be severely impaired in an intense transference, so that he or she may be said to lack the capability to make reasonable, rational, self-interested decisions in matters concerning the therapist.

In light of the fiduciary obligations of the therapist, any business dealings or social or sexual relationships with a client raise an immediate presumption of undue influence, duress, or coercion. Transference may also be said to vitiate a client's consent to any activity that is in the therapist's, rather than the client's, interests.

Transference and countertransference, as such, are to be expected in the course of therapy. Impaired judgment and decision-making capacity may accompany an intense transference, with the result that the client may not be able to make reasonable, self-interested decisions in matters concerning the therapist.

Q. 3:35 What is transference?

Transference is the phenomenon whereby one unconsciously identifies another person as some early figure in his or her life and responds to that person as if he or she were the early figure.

Q. 3:36 What is countertransference?

Countertransference is the primarily unconscious emotional response of the therapist to the client's transference.

Q. 3:37 What part do transference and countertransference play in malpractice?

It is generally accepted by most modalities of psychotherapy that clients have a primarily unconscious tendency to assign to the therapist in the present feelings and attitudes originally connected with significant figures, such as parents, in early life. This transference may be positive (the client experiences affectionate feelings for the therapist, whom he or she identifies with a beloved early figure) or negative (the client experiences hostility toward the therapist, whom he or she identifies with a feared or hated early figure). Sometimes, the transference becomes eroticized (the client becomes sexually obsessed with the therapist).

The therapist is expected to recognize transference and countertransference and to respond to them appropriately. (*Landau v. Werner,* 105 Sol.J. 1008 (England C.A. 1961)) Failure to recognize and properly handle these phenomena is malpractice. (*Corgan v. Muehling,* 176 Ill. App.3d 153, 118 Ill. Dec. 698, 522 N.E.2d 153 (1988)) (See Ch. 5, "Professional Liability," for more on malpractice.)

Q. 3:38 What are some common conflicts of interest in clinical relationships?

Any time a therapist has his or her own agenda in dealing with a client, rather than operating exclusively in the client's interest, there is a risk of conflict of interest. A therapist who seeks self-gratification, business advantage, or professional advancement through the client breaches his or her fiduciary duty to the client. For example, if the therapist is performing forensic evaluation services or evaluation for an employer, he or she should make it very clear to the person being evaluated that this is not treatment.

Not infrequently, a client will seek help for problems stemming from a divorce and custody battle, or sexual abuse by a former therapist. The therapist may have to choose between a treatment and an advocacy role, informing the client carefully about the distinctions.

What is important is that the therapist does not force his or her wishes on the client by taking on a role that the client would rather not have the therapist play.

Q. 3:39 May client information or case material be used in professional publications or presentations?

Client information cannot be used for a purpose other than the client's treatment without his or her consent, because the therapist's fiduciary duty to the client prohibits exploitation of the client or the clinical relationship. As a result of the transference phenomenon, a client may not feel free to refuse his or her therapist's request, so even if the client has consented, there is a possible presumption of undue influence on the part of the therapist. Most authorities agree that client material may not be used for publication or demonstration unless it can be done entirely anonymously and without exploitation. When possible, composite cases are preferred and will usually serve the same purpose as actual cases.

Q. 3:40 May a therapist enter into an extratherapeutic business transaction or relationship with a client?

Again, the fiduciary duty of the therapist, and the strong possibility that the client cannot make entirely reasonable judgments when the therapist is involved, mitigate strongly against doing business with a client. If a therapist is considering such activity, he or she must be absolutely certain that the transaction is conducted at "arm's length," and that the client is well represented by an attorney. Consultation to discuss the clinical ramifications of the transaction are in order. It also seems wise, if the client has a family, to be sure that the family is aware of the transaction and agrees to its fairness. Professional ethics forbid exploitation of a client, and psychologists are expressly forbidden to engage in dual relationships with clients.

Q. 3:41 Is sex between counselor and client ever permissible?

In a word, *never!* Every professional code of ethics forbids sexual contact between therapist and client, and some states have enacted laws classifying such behavior as a crime. Courts have found that such activity is unconscionable and deceptive. (*Roy v. Hartogs,* 381 N.Y.S.2d 587 (1976)) The law takes the position that a client is unable to give consent for sex with his or her therapist because it is impossible to determine whether the client's sexual feelings are the product of transference. (*Decker v. Fink,* 422 A.2d 389 (1980)) Furthermore, legal experts agree that sex therapists cannot engage in sex or have "surrogates" engage in sex with clients as a so-called therapy. Sex with a client is always exploitation of the therapeutic relationship and a breach of fiduciary duty. (*Omer v. Edgren,* 685 P.2d 635 (1984)) (See Ch. 5, "Professional Liability," Qs. 5:74–5:83 for more on sexual misconduct.)

Q. 3:42 May a counselor have a social relationship with a client?

Although some modalities of psychotherapy take the opposite view, the better answer is *no.* Social relationships with clients are fraught with danger for both client and therapist. The client-therapist relationship is a professional one, in which the therapist's entire interest is the well-being of the client. The therapist who engages in social relationships with clients usually does so out of isolation and loneliness, using clients to meet his or her own needs. A therapist with a rich and rewarding personal life does not have time for socializing with clients. Breakdown of the boundaries of the professional relationship interferes with therapy by compounding any existing transference.

> **Example.** A former counselor in a day treatment program telephones a client who is still involved in group therapy in the program, and enters into a social relationship with her. The client quite reasonably talks about the relationship in the group. This information so upsets other group members—who feel rejected and left out because they were not singled out for the therapist's favors—that the main focus of the whole group is now on this issue, and other group members' therapy is seriously derailed. The entire group is at risk: clinically, administratively, and legally.

The social relationship may gratify the client's fantasies and wishes, but it in no way helps the client to understand his or her problems. The result is confusion, anxiety, and upset, particularly when the social relationship does not fulfill the client's expectations. One court has stated that the therapist "made a most tragic mistake by introducing social contact into therapy." (*Landau v. Werner,* 105 Sol.J. 1008 (England C.A. 1961))

Q. 3:43 Once the treatment relationship is terminated, is a social or sexual relationship with the former client allowed?

Authorities generally agree that, "Once a client, always a client." (T. Gutheil, "Borderline Personality Disorder, Boundary Violations and Patient-Therapist Sex: Medico-Legal Pitfalls," 146 *Am. J. Psychiatry* (May 1989):5; Simon, *Clinical Psychiatry and the Law* (Washington: 1987), 21) Some states have passed statutes essentially forbidding sex between a therapist and client for a period of time after termination. In Illinois, there is an assumption of abuse if sex occurs within a year. (Ill. Rev. Stat.

ch. 70, par. 801 et seq.) In Minnesota, the period is two years. (Minn. Stat. ch. 148A (1988))

Because it cannot be assumed that transference issues have been resolved simply because treatment has ended, the fiduciary duty of the therapist must extend beyond the treatment period. Theoretically, the further away from termination in time, the less risk there is of a malpractice or other proceeding against the therapist if the former client becomes disappointed in the relationship. There is no guarantee, however, that the former client will not file a lawsuit, taking the position that the social relationship is an extension of the therapeutic relationship.

Example. The client was in brief crisis-centered counseling for three months. A month after termination, she called the therapist in a panic, saying she had no money and was having trouble getting a job. He hired her as office manager and, a year later, during a period of marital difficulties with his wife, entered into a six-month affair with her. When he confessed this in marital therapy, the wife insisted that he end the affair and the employment. The former client/mistress/employee sued for malpractice on the theory that the treatment relationship had never ended, and she still considered the man to be her therapist. The case was settled for a large sum. She also filed charges against him with the state licensing authorities, who found him guilty of unprofessional conduct. The case is presently in the appeal stage.

Q. 3:44 What rules apply to relationships between a counselor and a client's "significant other"?

The rules for relationships between therapist and client apply as well to the client's significant other. A business, social, or sexual relationship with a client's significant other cannot help but interfere in the therapist's fiduciary duty to maintain therapeutic objectivity and neutrality toward the client. Sex with a client's significant other is abandonment of the client. (*Mazza v. Huffaker,* 300 S.E.2d 833 (1983))

Example. The client has sought therapy and counseling for marital as well as other problems, and his wife has participated in some marital therapy sessions. One day, the client comes home to find his therapist in bed with his wife. Despite the client's rage response and his commission of several serious criminal acts against the therapist, the therapist is found guilty of malpractice, on the theory that his relationship with the wife constitutes abandonment of the husband.

Q. 3:45 What is the legal relationship between a consultant and a client?

The terms "consultant" and "supervisor" are often used interchangeably in the mental health and social service world. In fact, a supervisor has control over the management of a case; a consultant does not. If the consultant actually sees the client, he or she is assisting in the client's care, and a direct duty to the client will arise to conform to the standard of care. There is no ongoing duty to treat, however, so long as the client is clearly informed of the consultant's limited undertaking. (*Tomer v. Aiken*, 101 N.W. 769 (1904)) If the consultation is for teaching purposes only, and not a participation in the client's treatment, no duty to the client arises. (*Gielski v. New York*, 200 N.Y.S.2d 691 (1960))

A supervisor has a direct duty of due care to the client and may be either directly or vicariously liable in the event that the client prevails in a claim of negligence.

Chapter 4

Confidentiality Requirements

A counseling program cannot exist without assurance of strict confidentiality and privacy, and ethical and legal principles of confidentiality must exist in the context of community and personal safety. Federal and state laws are complex and often contradictory. This chapter defines the ethical and legal duties with regard to confidentiality. Issues that are addressed include when a counselor must be required to disclose confidential information; the special confidentiality problems created by conjoint and group therapy; therapist duty to report crimes, contagious diseases (to those in danger), and child abuse, or to warn potential victims; and when the law recognizes communication as "privileged."

Q. 4:1 What is confidentiality?

Confidentiality refers to the right of a client to have confidential information that he or she gave in the course of evaluation or treatment protected from disclosure to third parties except in accordance with his or her express consent. Confidentiality refers also to the ethical and legal duty of a therapist not to disclose the client's information.

Ethical and Legal Bases for Confidentiality

Q. 4:2 What is the ethical basis for confidentiality?

Since the adoption of the Hippocratic Oath by physicians in the early days of medicine, every health and social service profession has imposed an ethical duty of confidentiality upon its members. Codes of professional conduct express the duty in various terms, but they are unanimous in requiring professionals not to disclose confidential client information without the client's consent, except as required or permitted by law. The codes establish confidentiality as a practice standard for their respective professions.

Q. 4:3 How do professional associations enforce the ethical duty of confidentiality?

Each professional association has unique procedures for investigating, trying, and sanctioning members who are accused of committing ethics violations. A member who is found guilty may be counseled, warned, reprimanded, censured, suspended, or expelled. Often, the societies publicize ethics sanctions to their memberships, creating significant social pressure for other members to comply. A breach of ethics is considered unprofessional conduct. Many states have laws requiring professional associations to report sanctioned members to licensing authorities for disciplinary proceedings. Breach of confidentiality can result in sanctions as severe as license suspension or revocation.

Q. 4:4 What is the public policy basis for confidentiality statutes?

Recognizing the tremendous economic and social cost of mental illness and substance abuse, national and state public policy encourage prevention and treatment. But the stigma attached to these conditions creates a barrier to treatment. Therefore, confidentiality laws are intended to eradicate fear of exposure as a barrier to treatment.

Q. 4:5 What is the statutory basis for confidentiality?

Federal and state statutes and regulations protect the confidentiality of recipients of mental health and substance abuse services under specific circumstances. Federal law and statutes in many states put a duty on the provider not to disclose client information. Some states have also enacted privilege laws to protect client information and records from compulsory production in judicial, administrative, or legislative proceedings. For cases brought in the federal courts, federal law generally looks to the state in which the court is sitting to determine whether a communications privilege exists. Because state laws vary widely, legal consultation is necessary in developing confidentiality policies and procedures. Multistate EAP programs will require separate policies and procedures for each state of operation.

Q. 4:6 What federal law covers confidentiality of alcohol and drug abuse treatment records?

Alcohol abuse treatment records are protected by 42 U.S.C. §290dd-3; 42 U.S.C §290ee-3 applies to drug abuse treatment records. Regulations in 42 C.F.R. Part 2, effective August 10, 1987, implement both statutory provisions. These statutes and regulations cover any program that is federally assisted, directly or indirectly, and claims to provide and actually provides alcohol or drug abuse diagnosis, treatment, or referral for treatment. Some, but not all, EAPs are subject to federal regulation.

Q. 4:7 Which EAPs are covered by the federal statutes and regulations on confidentiality of drug and alcohol abuse treatment?

An EAP will be covered by the federal regulations if it is operated by an agency of the federal government or is federally assisted, directly or indirectly, and claims to provide—and actually does provide—substance abuse treatment. (42 C.F.R. ch.1, §§2.12(a) and 2.12(b)) Thus, most internal EAPs of unions or private-sector for-profit companies will not be covered by the federal regulations. Nor will external EAPs operated for profit and providing services to employees of for-profit companies. An external EAP operated by a not-for-profit (and, therefore, federally assisted—see Q. 4:8) agency (for example, a community mental health center, family service agency, or not-for-profit hospital) will be covered by the federal regulations, even if it serves the employees of a for-profit company.

Q. 4:8 What does "federal assistance" mean for the purposes of the law?

An EAP is federally assisted if it is:

- Conducted in whole or in part, directly or by contract, by any department or agency of the federal government, with certain exceptions for the Veterans' Administration and the Armed Forces.
- Carried out by license, certification, registration, or other authorization granted by any department of the federal government, including but not limited to, certification of Medicare provider status; authorization to conduct methadone treatment; and registration to dispense a controlled substance, if it is used in treatment of substance abuse.
- Supported by federal assistance in any form, including financial assistance, whether or not the federal money is spent directly on the substance abuse services.
- Conducted by a state or local government unit that receives through revenue sharing federal funds that could be (but are not necessarily) used for the substance abuse program.
- Operated by a not-for-profit corporation (exempt from income taxes, and to which contributions are tax-deductible).

Q. 4:9 What is covered by the federal regulations?

The regulations apply to any information, whether recorded or not, that is received by a covered program for the purpose of diagnosis, referral, or treatment for substance abuse and that would identify a patient as an alcohol or drug abuser. (See Ch. 9, "Substance Abuse Laws," Qs. 9:17–9:50, for detailed coverage of the federal regulations on confidentiality of alcohol and drug abuse patient records.)

Q. 4:10 How do courts view the duty of psychotherapeutic confidentiality?

The common law of mental health and social service delivery has developed largely from cases involving psychiatrists, who were, after all, the first mental health professionals on the scene. Courts recognize that:

> The [therapy client] confides more utterly than anyone else in the world. He exposes to the therapist not only what his words directly express, he lays bare his entire self, his dreams, his fantasies, his sins, and his shame. Most [clients] who undergo psychotherapy know that this is what will be expected of them, and they cannot get help except on that condition.

Taylor v. United States, 222 F.2d 398 (1955).

In the New York case of *Doe v. Roe* (93 Misc.2d 201, 400 N.Y.S.2d 668 (Sup. Ct. 1977)), the court awarded money damages to a client for her therapist's breach of the implied warranty of confidentiality and prohibited distribution of a book written by the therapist about her treatment. The client had given oral consent and then changed her mind. Although the therapist had disguised the client and her family, relied upon the consent, and invested a great deal of effort in the book, the court took the position that the consent was suspect because of the influence over the client inherent in the therapy process. The client's right to confidentiality was held to outweigh the constitutional guarantees of freedom of expression.

Q. 4:11 What is the contractual basis of confidentiality?

The implied warranty of confidentiality is part of every contract for psychotherapy or counseling. To the extent that the counselor and client have expressly agreed to conditions of confidentiality, these will supervene over warranties implied in law. Strict protection of client confidentiality is one of the fiduciary duties of the therapist. Deliberate breach of confidentiality is a breach of contract. Negligent breach is malpractice.

Q. 4:12 How does the implied warranty of confidentiality apply in the EAP practice setting?

The implied warranty of confidentiality is made a part of every treatment contract unless the provider and client have expressly contracted otherwise. If the policies of the EAP require or permit disclosures other than by consent of the client (except as required or permitted by law), it is absolutely essential that these conditions of disclosure be made known to the client. The policies then become part of the EAP-client contract to which the client agrees by accepting them as a precondition of services. For this reason, written confidentiality terms are strongly recommended. EAP and employer confidentiality policies and procedures, and especially exceptions to confidentiality, should be circulated to clients and potential clients and stated in brochures and publicity. Any discussion with a client about confidentiality should be noted in the client's record. A breach of the implied or any express warranties of confidentiality will give rise to a cause of action against the EAP and counselor for breach of contract.

Consent to Disclose Client Information

Q. 4:13 When is a consent required for disclosure of client information?

Consent is always required for disclosure of client information except as otherwise provided by contract or by law.

Q. 4:14 What is a valid consent to disclose information?

Most statutes governing consent require that the consent be in writing. Some statutes put a time limit on the validity of a consent and may require that the client be allowed access to the record. Whether or not it is mandated by statute, for the protection of the counselor and the program, the EAP policy should require a written consent under all circumstances in which client authorization is required for disclosure. To be valid, a consent must be informed. Every consent should include:

- The date;
- The person or agency to whom the material is to be disclosed;
- The purpose for disclosure;
- A prohibition against redisclosure without client consent; and
- The length of time for which the consent is valid.

(See B-1: Sample Form: Consent to Disclose Information.)

Q. 4:15 Can a consent be revoked?

A consent is revocable at the client's will. The revocation should be written if the original consent was written. Disclosures made prior to revocation will not be affected. The EAP is not bound by a revocation until it has actual notice of it.

Q. 4:16 When does the law require disclosure without consent?

A counselor may be required by statute to disclose client information without consent under specific circumstances. A common example is child abuse reporting, which is required in all states, and reporting of abuse of other "vulnerable persons," such as the elderly or handicapped, which is required in some states. A state may require or permit disclosure in cases involving juveniles; in homicide or other felony cases; when disclosure is required in commitment or competency proceedings against the client, and in other cases in which the client has himself or herself raised his or her mental condition as an element in a lawsuit; or to warn an intended victim of a client's violent intentions.

Q. 4:17 Is the duty of confidentiality absolute?

The duty of confidentiality specifies certain exceptions, chief among which is a bona fide emergency in which disclosure is necessary to attempt to prevent a clear, imminent danger of injury, disease, or death. Otherwise, a counselor has discretion to disclose client information without consent only if the client has agreed to this as part of the contract, and the law otherwise allows. An attorney should be consulted to determine what state and federal law require under particular circumstances. If federal law applies, certain procedures are required before disclosure can be made.

Q. 4:18 Under what conditions is consent to disclosure of confidential information implied?

If the EAP has policies in place stating the exceptions to confidentiality, and these are represented to the client as the basis upon which the EAP and client will work together, the exceptions become part of the EAP-client contract. By participating in the program after being made clearly aware, through EAP and employer policies, brochures, and other material, of circumstances under which the counselor would disclose without consent, the client has given his or her "implied consent" to those disclosures.

Q. 4:19 Is consent required to refer an employee to the EAP?

No consent is required for referral to the EAP by the employer, peers, or others, because there is no legal duty of confidentiality in the employer-employee or peer relationship.

Q. 4:20 May parents have access to therapy information about their minor children?

At common law, the parents of a minor child have the right to consent to treatment for the child, as well as the right of access to the child's treatment information. In states where the minor has statutory capacity to consent to a treatment, the law usually prohibits disclosure of treatment information to the parents unless the minor consents, except when the counselor believes the minor to be endangered and disclosure to the parents to be in the minor's best interests. Some states have statutes permitting minors to consent to their own treatment for certain conditions, (for example, substance abuse, venereal disease, or pregnancy). Federal law, and some state laws, mandate confidentiality for clients who are 12 years old or older and who receive treatment relating to venereal disease and substance abuse.

Using Third-Party Information

Q. 4:21 What information may the EAP receive without client consent?

A referral source, family member, or other person may share with the EAP any information about a client or potential client that appears to be germane to the client's apparent needs. A counselor may listen to anything anyone has to say but, of course, may not respond or share information with that person unless the client has given consent.

Q. 4:22 Should the counselor inform the client about third-party information?

It is a good general rule to take the position that anything told to the counselor about the client by third parties will be shared with the client. The EAP owes a duty of loyalty to the client, not to third parties who intervene in the client's treatment. Failure to inform the client of third-party activity in the treatment may be considered a breach of the counselor's fiduciary duty to the client.

Information Sharing Between Employers and EAPs

Q. 4:23 Can the EAP share information with the employer or vice versa?

The employer may disclose any information about an employee to the EAP, but the EAP provider may disclose client information to the employer only in accordance with the client's informed express consent and the policies, procedures, and representations that have been made part of the client's contract. Policies and procedures must therefore provide a mechanism for feedback to employer referral sources, including a clear statement about exactly what is to be shared under what circumstances and with whom. Typically, unless the client agrees to additional sharing, only the fact that the employee has sought assistance at the EAP and, if applicable, the fact of a referral for treatment, will be shared.

Policy should provide for sharing of information necessary to attempt to avert danger (for example, informing an employer hospital of an employee nurse's drug use; informing an employer airline of an employee pilot's suicidal ideation). Policy may also require the EAP to inform the employer of criminal acts against it or its premises or customers (for example, informing an employer hospital of an employee nurse's diversion of patient medication; informing an employer of employee thefts from the premises). Needless to say, exceptions to confidentiality procedures for information sharing should be clearly explained to clients.

Q. 4:24 Are the rules about sharing information with employers different for internal and external EAPs?

Essentially, the confidentiality of employee-clients should be equally protected whether the EAP is internal or external. However, the rules for internal EAPs will be determined by the employer-sponsor's written policies and procedures, and by the representations the company has made to employees about program confidentiality, on the basis of which the client has been induced to accept EAP services. The rules for an external EAP on the other hand, will be determined by the contract between the EAP and the sponsor. In both internal and external EAP models, state law may regulate disclosure to the sponsor. If the external EAP is operated by a not-for-profit organization, disclosures to employers will also be governed by federal regulations.

Employing Confidentiality in Family or Group Therapy Situations

Q. 4:25 How is confidentiality handled in couple or family treatment?

Any information disclosed in the context of couple or family treatment is obviously known to everyone present at the session. If the therapist meets with anyone individually, he or she must decide what is to be communicated to the other parties. This is partly determined by the clinical orientation of the therapist. Some therapists believe that conjoint treatment cannot succeed if there are secrets; others feel able to manage exclusive information and maintain the trust of the entire client group. If the therapist agrees to keep a secret with one member of a conjoint group, the other(s) may have a legitimate complaint that the therapist is disloyal to him or her. Whatever the intention of the therapist, it must be clearly communicated to and agreed to by the clients.

Q. 4:26 How is confidentiality handled in group therapy?

It is the therapist's duty to establish the confidentiality contract for a therapy group. All members of the group must understand that they are responsible for maintaining the confidentiality of the others, and that breach by one group member of the confidentiality of another is a breach of contract, privacy, and trust. The wronged group member could even sue the one who breached.

Q. 4:27 Who has access to couple, family, and group records?

Any client who attended a recorded session should have access to records, but no one who was not present during a session should have access unless the other(s) agree. Similarly, history and other individual information may not be shared without express permission. A simple, efficient method of record maintenance to avoid access problems among members of conjoint therapy arrangements is to record any individual information on paper of a different color. Then, when access is requested, it is easy to restrict it to what is pertinent to each individual.

Q. 4:28 Can confidentiality be assured in conjoint or group therapy?

Obviously, the therapist cannot control disclosures of information by clients who choose not to abide by the confidentiality contract to which they have agreed. Conjoint or group therapy clients create a pool of potential witnesses against one member of the group who may have disclosed compromising information in therapy. Most states do *not* extend a communications privilege to conjoint or group therapy, on the theory that the disclosing client had no expectation of privacy when he or she disclosed in the presence of others.

Q. 4:29 What are the confidentiality ramifications in selecting clients for conjoint and group therapy?

Since a therapist cannot guarantee confidentiality of conjoint or group information, clients should be selected for these modalities with this in mind. A client with a legal problem could have his or her legal interests compromised by coclients. Such a client may be better off in individual treatment. Local law should be checked to ascertain the confidentiality and privileged status of conjoint and group therapy disclosures. Clients should be informed in this regard, so that they can make choices about disclosure in accordance with their legal, as well as clinical, situations.

Employing Confidentiality After Termination of Treatment

Q. 4:30 Does the duty of confidentiality survive the clinical care contract?

The duty to maintain the client's confidentiality continues after termination of the treatment relationship. For confidentiality purposes, "Once a client, always a client."

Q. 4:31 Does the duty of confidentiality end with the client's death?

Even after the death of a client, the therapist continues to owe him or her a duty of confidentiality. Unless there is a statute or judicial ruling permitting disclosure, the therapist is obliged to protect the confidentiality of the client's information and records to the same degree as when the client was alive. This rule is intended to enable people, perhaps especially suicidal or terminally ill patients, to seek therapy without fear of disclosure after death. Sometimes, a local statute will provide a mechanism for access under certain circumstances (for example, in a proceeding to determine the validity of a will or insurance policy; by beneficiaries claiming under a will or insurance policy of the decedent (but not by persons contesting the will); by the court-appointed personal representative of the decedent—the administrator or executor). At least one state, Illinois, requires therapist approval for disclosure of mental health records after a client's death.

Special Problems in Confidentiality

Q. 4:32 Does the duty of confidentiality prevent an EAP from collecting unpaid bills?

An EAP is not precluded by confidentiality law from collecting an unpaid bill—by either turning it over to a collection agency or suing directly. The collection process, however, must be handled in the context of the fiduciary responsibility of the therapist to the client. Only the fact that service was rendered and the dates and cost of service should be disclosed in the collection process. Envelopes, stationery, and billing forms should not disclose the nature of the services provided. The use of post cards in collections is inappropriate. The best approach to collection—which can be used only if the jurisdiction permits—is to sue alleging an "account stated," rather than the terms of the contract.

Q. 4:33 What are the legal and ethical dilemmas of confidentiality for EAPs and employers?

Legal and ethical dilemmas of confidentiality arise when there is a conflict between the confidentiality rights of a client and the legitimate rights and needs of the community to maintain public peace and safety and of other individuals to protect their personal safety and property.

Q. 4:34 How should the EAP handle a conflict between the client's right to confidentiality and the employer's right to know?

Although the EAP is intended as a resource for aiding troubled employees, it does not make clinical or economic sense for a client to be allowed to exploit the EAP at the employer's expense. Confidentiality dilemmas should be clearly defined and thought through in the policy-making process. Policies on disclosure should be in place to direct both the EAP and the employer when the employer is legally at risk or in danger of losing property as a result of an employee's impairment or illegal acts.

A policy to disclose illegal acts against the employer and other liability risks is legally and clinically sound. When services are being provided by an external EAP, the contract must reflect the policy and clearly establish the rights and duties of both employer and EAP with respect to this issue. When the policy is communicated to potential clients as a precondition of EAP service, it becomes part of the clinical care contract between the EAP and the client when service is accepted by the client.

Illegal or Unsafe Activities to Avoid

Q. 4:35 What is the clinical significance of a client's disclosing illegal activities to the counselor?

The clinician uses the client's productions (disclosures in the context of treatment) diagnostically. When a client discloses illegal activities against the employer, the clinical question is, "Why are you telling me this?" Disclosure that is against the client's apparent interests and likely to provoke a negative response is generally interpreted as transference behavior—a plea to the therapist as "good parent" for approval of the acting-out behavior; a "cry for help" to the "parent" to intervene and stop the "naughty child" from continuing to act out; a cry for punishment to relieve the burden of guilt; or an attempt to intimidate, taunt, and torment the parental figure in an expression of rebellion against authority. Talking about misdeeds in counseling allows the client to pass on his or her "hot potato" to the therapist and get temporary relief from anxiety and guilt. Most clinicians agree that healing cannot take place in the context of deception or intimidation, so the appropriate clinical response to such productions is a confrontation of the client and interpretation of the behavior.

Q. 4:36 What are the clinical and legal rationales for a policy in favor of disclosing a client's illegal acts against the employer?

Clients are well aware that employers directly or indirectly sponsor the EAP. Unless there is a stated exception in the EAP-client contractual relationship, the EAP will not have a right to disclose illegal acts against the employer. Those EAPs that are subject to the federal substance abuse treatment confidentiality law (see Ch. 9, "Substance Abuse Laws") can make such disclosures if a client commits a crime against an EAP. Although the law permits disclosure for protection of the EAP, it does not allow disclosure of criminal acts against the EAP sponsor.

On the psychological level, the clinical result of not disclosing is that the counselor becomes an unwilling conspirator or accomplice of the client against the employer. It is generally accepted that allowing the client to get away with illegal acts against the employer or the EAP would compromise the integrity of the EAP and would not serve the client's clinical needs.

Thus, the EAP sponsor's policy representation to clients should include an exception to confidentiality by permitting disclosure of criminal acts against the employer. Such an exception should be stated in the policies and promulgated to employees.

Q. 4:37 Is there a clinical argument for disclosure to the employer of other information that may be required under certain circumstances to minimize employer liability?

The same clinical argument applies when a client discloses to the EAP counselor information about circumstances or events that create liability risk for the employer (for example, conditions that create a severe safety risk to employees or others using the employer's premises or products, or behavior of other employees that constitutes a hazard).

> **Example.** The client, an airline stewardess, discloses to the EAP counselor that a pilot friend of hers has blackouts, which are probably caused by a form of epilepsy. He is afraid to tell his doctor about this because he does not want to be grounded, so he is not receiving treatment. The client is afraid for her own life and safety, as well as that of others—including her friend—but she feels that "ratting" on him is immoral. Her anxiety and guilt over the situation are what bring her to the EAP. She refuses to allow the EAP counselor to disclose the information to the company, even if he promises not to use her name.

In the above example, absent a policy or contract providing for disclosure, the EAP counselor will be breaching the client's confidentiality if he discloses. Further, if the EAP is operated by a community mental health center, federal regulations require application to a court for permission to disclose. In some states, there is a duty to protect, which may require disclosure. One way or another, it is clear that the EAP counselor cannot simply allow a tragedy to occur. He should seek local legal advice and clinical consultation about how best to handle the situation and take the steps necessary to make the disclosure.

Q. 4:38 Should the EAP report a client's prior criminal behavior to the police?

As a general rule, absent a statute to the contrary, a counselor is neither obliged nor allowed to breach the client's confidentiality by reporting his or her prior criminal behavior to the police. Therapists are not expected to be police informants. This view is encompassed in the federal regulations on confidentiality of drug and alcohol treatment records, as well as some state laws.

Q. 4:39 Is there an exception to the rule against reporting of prior criminal acts?

If the counselor becomes concerned about his or her own safety as a result of the client's disclosure of a criminal act, reporting to the authorities may be indicated—not for the purpose of aiding law enforcement agencies, but for the purpose of self-protection. A diagnostic assessment is necessary: Why has the client made this "confession" to the therapist, and why now? Careful exploration of the client's psychological needs and expectations is required to assess for danger to the therapist, the client, and others. Consultation with a senior clinician is necessary in any such case, and the matter should be thoroughly documented. If the EAP is subject to the federal regulations, disclosure may require application to a court for an order permitting this disclosure.

Q. 4:40 Does the EAP have a duty to report future intended criminal acts?

Common law holds that every citizen has an affirmative duty to prevent the commission of a felony. Recent case law in some states, followed by statutory enactments, requires that a therapist act to prevent anticipated harm to an identified third person—by warning either the intended victim or the police, or both. Under the federal substance abuse regulations and some state laws, a counselor must apply to a court for permission to make such a disclosure, except in an emergency when delay for purposes of obtaining a court order would result in grievous harm. EAP policies and representations to clients, providing that the EAP will disclose intended criminal or harmful acts, will avoid trouble for the EAP and its staff and eliminate the apparent conflict between the client's right to confidentiality and the community's need to protect itself.

When There Is a Duty to Warn Third Parties

Q. 4:41 Is there a duty to warn an identified, intended victim of a client's contemplated harmful acts?

The California case of *Tarasoff v. Regents* (17 Cal.3d 425, 131 Cal.Rptr. 14, 551 P.2d 334 (1976)) is generally interpreted as establishing a duty of a psychotherapist to warn an intended victim of a client's contemplated harmful act. In fact, *Tarasoff* actually establishes a duty to *protect* endangered third persons who are foreseeable victims of the client from violence. Warning the potential victim may be the first step, but it may not be all that is required. An additional step, such as committing the client to an institution or notifying law enforcement authorities, may be indicated. Some, but not all, states have adopted a duty-to-warn position. (See, e.g., *McIntosh v. Milano,* 168 N.J. Spec. 466, 403 A.2d 500 (1979).) Local law should be consulted. Again, the dilemma of whether to warn will be avoided by having an appropriate policy and representations.

Q. 4:42 Does a counselor have a right or duty to warn of AIDS or other communicable diseases?

Controversy rages over whether AIDS or other communicable diseases create an exception to confidentiality and a right or duty of a therapist to warn or otherwise act to protect against it. At common law, a physician has a duty to warn others to prevent the spread of contagious diseases (for example, tuberculosis and venereal disease). In one early case, a doctor was found not to have breached the confidentiality of his patient when he notified the patient's rooming house landlord that the patient had syphilis and should not be allowed to share a bathroom with others. This concept has been cited as the basis of the modern "duty to warn."

Many people feel that even in those states that have not adopted the *Tarasoff* case, a therapist has a moral, if not a legal, duty to warn a client's significant other if the client suffers from a communicable disease and refuses to disclose it. The argument may have special merit in AIDS cases, because AIDS is invariably fatal, but it should apply for other contagious diseases as well.

Q. 4:43 Is a counselor at greater legal risk by disclosing or not disclosing the client's contagious disease to the significant other?

A therapist who discloses a client's contagious disease to that person's significant other is at risk for a lawsuit by the client. A therapist who is aware of the disease and the intimate relationship, but fails to disclose to the significant other, is at risk for a lawsuit by the significant other. The courts will assess the therapist's behavior in terms of what a duly careful practitioner in the community would do under the circumstances. As a practical matter, it would appear that disclosure is the less risky course for the therapist. It seems unlikely that the outraged client would prevail in a lawsuit arising out of the good-faith disclosure to the significant other; it seems extremely likely that the significant other who contracted the disease would prevail against the therapist who knew of the danger and did not disclose.

Q. 4:44 How can the EAP avoid the communicable-disease dilemma?

The dilemma can be avoided from the outset if the EAP policies and representations to the client make it clear that the counselor will disclose client information when, in the counselor's sole discretion, the disclosure is necessary to attempt to prevent imminent risk of disease or death to another person. If the client knows this from the beginning, his or her consent to the disclosure is implied by agreeing to participate in the program.

When There Is a Duty to Report Child Abuse

Q. 4:45 Are EAPs subject to child abuse reporting laws?

Like other professionals, EAP staff members are covered by child abuse reporting laws if they are "mandated reporters" under state law. (A mandated reporter is usually a professional person in the health, social service, education, law enforcement, or child welfare fields.) Child abuse reporting is an exception to the duty of confidentiality and will not constitute a breach of the client's rights or the therapist's fiduciary duty. Every state mandates reporting of child abuse and neglect, although state laws vary on the definition of abuse and neglect and on who is a mandated reporter. Some states require mandated reporters to report any suspicion of abuse or neglect; others require a report only if the professional is "reasonably certain." A statute may require reporting only if the child is known to the professional in his or her professional capacity. EAP staff should be well grounded in local reporting laws.

Until 1987, the federal regulations on confidentiality of alcohol and drug treatment did not contain a provision for reporting. This created a dilemma for those EAP professionals who were subject to the federal regulations and were mandated reporters under state laws. The 1987 regulations eliminated the conflict by providing for reporting when required by state law.

Q. 4:46 Must an EAP professional testify against a client in a child abuse proceeding?

Child abuse cases are usually an exception to communications privileges. Even states that provide a testimonial privilege that would otherwise excuse an EAP professional from disclosing client information and records in judicial proceedings ordinarily required therapists to testify if they have any information about child abuse.

Q. 4:47 How should EAP staff go about child abuse and neglect reporting?

State statutes and child protection regulations establish the procedure for child abuse and neglect reporting. Good clinical practice dictates that the client, whether the alleged abuser, victim, or other family member, be informed prior to reporting that the report will be made—unless informing the client is likely to create a danger for the counselor, the abused or neglected child, or another person. The local state statute and regulations will dictate the reporting procedure.

Q. 4:48 Should the perpetrator of child abuse or neglect be encouraged to self-report?

It may make clinical sense to encourage the child-abusing client to self-report, but from a legal point of view, self-reporting may not be indicated. There are varying philosophies about the management of child abusers. Some people believe that prosecution under criminal law is necessary and just; others prefer a nonpunitive therapeutic approach coupled with affirmative steps to protect the child. There are situations in which child protection proceedings in a juvenile court may be possible, but criminal prosecution may not be viable or successful because there is no competent witness against the alleged perpetrator. It is not the clinician's role to manipulate the evidence in a legal proceeding, but if the therapist encourages the client to self-report, both therapist and client should be aware that the self-report is an admission of guilt that can and will be used against the client in a criminal proceeding, if one is brought.

The therapist's fiduciary duty to the client requires advising the client to seek immediate legal advice.

How to Handle Privileged Communication

Q. 4:49 What is a privileged communication?

A communication is privileged when, by reason of a statutorily created rule of evidence, one person has the right to prevent another person from disclosing confidential information in a judicial proceeding. This right is referred to in the context of confidentiality as testimonial privilege—the privilege not to give testimony or evidence. Testimonial privilege applies only in a situation in which a person would otherwise be required to give evidence in court or before an administrative tribunal or legislative hearing.

Q. 4:50 Why does the law provide a privilege?

Privilege is a derivative of the right to privacy—the right to have one's personal information kept private. The law recognizes that trust is the essence of the therapeutic relationship, and if clients are unable to freely express their thoughts and feelings without fear of compelled disclosure, the benefit of therapy will be diminished or lost. A few relationships that depend upon trust to survive are recognized as so important to the community that maintaining them is considered more important than the outcome of a legal case. (Marriage and the attorney-client relationship are two examples.) Some states perceive the counseling or psychotherapeutic relationship in the same light. Those states have enacted a privilege for psychotherapy information, but the privilege may take as many forms as there are states. Every EAP professional should consult with local counsel to ascertain in detail the state privilege laws governing his or her practice.

Q. 4:51 What elements does the law require for the creation of a privilege?

"The law abhors a privilege," because cases cannot be fairly litigated unless all relevant and material facts are known to the trier of fact. For this reason, courts are loath to allow evidence to be limited. States vary in their criteria for the establishment of a communications privilege. A prominent legal authority on rules of evidence sets down four essential conditions for a testimonial privilege (8 Wigmore, *Evidence* §2285 *(Chadbourn rev. 1985):*

1. The communication must originate in a confidence that it will not be disclosed.
2. Confidentiality must be essential to the full and satisfactory maintenance of the trust relationship between the parties.
3. The relationship must be one that is so important to the community that it ought to be fostered.
4. The injury to the relationship by disclosure of the confidential communication would be greater than the benefit gained by the disposition of a case in litigation.

Q. 4:52 Are EAP clients' communications privileged?

There is no question that they *should* be, but the most accurate answer is: They *may* be. Every state has its own privilege laws, which will be very strictly construed. Many states confer privilege on communications given to certain professionals, but not others. Some states confer a privilege based on the type of information given, not on the discipline of the person to whom it was given. Depending upon the specific state law and the discipline of the therapist, communications in the EAP-client relationship may be privileged. It is possible, however, that within the same EAP, clients of some therapists will be protected by a privilege, but clients of another therapist will not.

Q. 4:53 What are the ramifications of privilege law for EAP staffing and assignment of clients?

It is absolutely essential that the local state privilege and confidentiality laws be thoroughly understood in the context of staffing the EAP and assigning clients to staff. For example, in one state, communications to a licensed psychologist or social worker are privileged, but communications to a master's-prepared psychiatric nurse or guidance counselor are not, even if all are certified substance abuse counselors. In another state, communications in the course of substance abuse treatment are privileged, but other mental health counseling information is not. The scrupulously careful EAP will hire only those professionals whose clients are protected by a communications privilege. If there are members of the EAP staff already working who are not covered by privilege, care must be taken not to assign them clients who are known to have legal problems. If legal problems emerge for a client in the course of treatment, transfer to a covered therapist is indicated. Clients must be informed, as part of informed consent, of the risks of compelled disclosure in litigation.

Q. 4:54 Is there a communications privilege for couple, family, or group therapy information?

In most states, there is a privilege only for information given by a client individually to the therapist. If another person is present, even for the purpose of the therapy, the law traditionally holds that the privilege is "polluted." Even the intentional or unintentional presence of an eavesdropper (such as a supervisor observing through a two-way mirror or listening to a tape, whether or not this is known to the client), can pollute the privilege. In some states, the presence of a child will not affect the communications privilege; in other states, it will. Privilege law is extremely complex. Consultation with a clinically knowledgeable lawyer is essential to establish policies and procedures in accordance with local privilege law, and the staff must be well trained to protect clients in this area. The absence of a communications privilege may make couple, family, or group treatment undesirable or impossible for clients with legal issues. This issue should be explored with the client, and the choice of modality of treatment should be made with this in mind.

Q. 4:55 Who holds the privilege in the therapist-client relationship?

Generally, it is the client, not the therapist, who has the power to assert the privilege. In a very few states, the privilege statute provides that either the client or the therapist, on behalf of and in the interest of the client, may assert the privilege and prevent the disclosure.

Q. 4:56 What type of information can be privileged?

Privilege statutes vary widely from state to state, but typically, when a communications privilege for counseling information exists, any private, confidential information communicated in the context of treatment between therapist and client, as well as the therapist's diagnosis, conclusions, and observations, will be protected. Some states exclude the mere information that a person is a client, on the basis that this is not private or confidential information—anyone can see the person coming to or from the therapist's office. The frequency, duration, and cost of treatment may also be excluded, particularly if a third-party payor has been involved.

Q. 4:57 Is there a communications privilege in federal law?

There is no general testimonial privilege in federal civil law for psychotherapy or counseling communications. Rule 501 of the Federal Rules of Civil Procedure provides that the federal courts may apply the privilege laws of the state in which the case is being litigated. This results in considerable variance among federal jurisdictions, and sometimes even within the same jurisdiction, as to what will be protected from disclosure. For communications made in the course of substance abuse treatment, however, a privilege does exist: it is created by 42 U.S.C. §§290dd-3 and 290ee-3 and 42 C.F.R. Part 2, if the treatment is provided by a program covered by the statute. (42 C.F.R. ch.1, §2.13(a))

Chapter 5

Professional Liability

This chapter presents an overview of professional liability in the context of EAP practice. General concepts of liability are introduced, together with common precautions individuals and organizations can take to shield themselves from lawsuits. The focus is on the kinds of behaviors that are unlawful; pitfalls therapists can unwittingly fall into; elements plaintiffs must prove to establish a claim; errors that may be excusable; and defenses against various kinds of charges. Categories of professional liability that are covered include malpractice (negligent diagnosis, negligent treatment, and abandonment); intentional torts (including assault and battery, defamation, invasion of privacy, fraud, false imprisonment, and sexual exploitation); breach of contract; and premises/equipment liability.

Q. 5:1 What is professional liability?

Professional liability refers to legal responsibility for damages arising out of one's professional practice.

Q. 5:2 What are the major categories of professional liability?

There are five major categories of professional liability:

1. Malpractice;
2. Intentional torts;
3. Breach of contract;
4. Premises liability; and
5. Equipment liability.

Q. 5:3 Who is liable for professional wrongful acts?

Any person, program, or company that has contracted with a client to provide clinical care, invited a person onto the professional practice premises for professional or business purposes, or provided or used equipment in delivering care, will be liable for injuries resulting from:

- Breach of the contract or negligent or deliberate wrongful acts committed in the course of service delivery;
- Dangerous conditions on the practice premises; or
- Dangerous or faulty equipment.

A therapist is individually responsible for his or her professional wrongful acts, whether as a private practitioner or an employee. If the therapist is an employee, his or her employer may also be liable under the theory of vicarious liability.

Vicarious Liability

Q. 5:4 What is vicarious liability?

Vicarious liability is the legal responsibility of one person (or entity, such as a company) for the wrongful conduct or negligence of another. Vicarious liability arises out of the laws of agency. An agent is a person (or entity) who acts for, and under the direction and control of, a principal (another person or entity). Because the principal has the right to control the activities of the agent, the principal is responsible for compensating a plaintiff who is injured by the agent. In an employer-employee relationship, the employer is the "master" or principal, and the employee is the "servant" or agent. Under the legal doctrine of *respondeat superior* ("let the master answer"), the employer must answer for the negligent acts of employees under its supervision.

Q. 5:5 Under what circumstances can the EAP or sponsor be liable for the wrongful acts of the staff?

Under the theory of vicarious liability, an employer is legally responsible for the negligent, wrongful acts of an employee, if they are committed within the scope and course of employment. The employer of the EAP staff—the person or entity having the right of supervision and control over staff activities—will be vicariously liable for staff misfeasance or malfeasance. In an internal program, therefore, the sponsor will be vicariously liable. In an external program, the principal of the program will be liable.

Q. 5:6 Will a sponsor ever be vicariously liable for the wrongful acts of an external EAP?

Vicarious liability arises out of control. If the sponsor controls the activities of the external EAP staff (for example, by specifying the treatment modalities, treatment facility, or professional to be used), the sponsor may be held vicariously liable for harm arising therefrom.

Example. The employer-sponsor directs the external EAP that every client who is diagnosed as a substance abuser must be referred for treatment to Rosy Future Pavilion for a 27-day inpatient program employing behavior modification with aversive conditioning, including the use of Antabuse. The client wishes, instead, to go to Happy Harbor for a 14-day program employing Transactional Analysis and Gestalt techniques. The EAP, following the sponsor's directive, insists upon Rosy Future. While there, the client decompensates (into an acute psychotic state) and is rushed to a psychiatric facility, where he is diagnosed as suffering from manic-depressive illness. The client sues Rosy Future, the EAP, and the sponsor for malpractice, alleging negligent misdiagnosis and negligent treatment. Rosy Future is held directly liable. The EAP and sponsor are held vicariously liable, on the basis that they specified the treater and treatment modality.

Q. 5:7 Is the EAP vicariously liable for the malpractice of a provider to whom it refers a client?

If the EAP is not negligent in its referral, it will not be liable for the negligence of the professional or program to which it refers a client. (*Tramutola v. Bortone*, 304 A.2d 197 (1973)) If, however, the referring clinician continues to participate actively in the care of the client, he or she may be jointly liable for the malpractice of the treater to which he or she referred the client. (*Arshansky v. Royal Concourse Co.*, 283 N.Y.S.2d 646 (1967)) If the EAP does not participate actively, but specifies the treatment to be provided, vicarious liability is possible.

Q. 5:8 How can the sponsor of an external EAP shield itself from vicarious liability?

If the contract between the sponsor and the external EAP specifies that the EAP, and not the sponsor, has clinical control and professional responsibility, and in fact the sponsor does not direct the professional activities of the EAP, the sponsor has little risk of vicarious liability.

Bases for Wrongful Act Suits

Q. 5:9 Who can sue for professional wrongful acts?

Any person who is harmed by breach of contract, a deliberate or negligent wrongful act committed by a professional in the course of his or her practice, a dangerous condition in the practice premises, or dangerous or faulty equipment has a cause of action (basis for a lawsuit) for compensation. An injured client's spouse may sue for loss of consortium. In the event of a client's death by reason of professional liability, the surviving spouse (or if there is no spouse, the client's surviving children, siblings, or parents), may sue for wrongful death.

Q. 5:10 What is loss of consortium?

Consortium is traditionally the conjugal fellowship of spouses, and the right of each to have the companionship, society, cooperation, affection, and aid of each other in every aspect of their relationship. Spouses commonly seek damages for loss of consortium in cases of wrongful death or injury arising out of the negligence of another. (*Black's Law Dictionary,* (5th ed., 1983)) In recent years, if there is no surviving spouse, the children, parents, or siblings of the deceased person have been permitted to bring loss-of-consortium claims.

Q. 5:11 What is a wrongful death action?

When death is caused by the willful or negligent wrongful act of another, either the heirs at law or anyone relying upon the deceased person for support may bring a lawsuit for damages. Wrongful death is a statutory cause of action and will vary from state to state in terms of which survivors may sue, and for how much in damages. The estate of the decedent may sue for the direct costs of the alleged wrongful act (for example, hospital bills). Persons to whom the decedent contributed support or other services may be entitled to compensation for their monetary losses. (Grief, however, is not compensable.)

Malpractice

Q. 5:12 What is malpractice?

Malpractice is the failure of a professional to exercise the degree of skill and knowledge in diagnosis or treatment that may be reasonably expected from a member of the profession under the circumstances of a particular case, which causes or aggravates an injury to the client or those who are entitled to rely upon him or her. It is any professional misconduct, unreasonable lack of skill or fidelity in professional or fiduciary duties, evil practice, or illegal or immoral conduct. (*Black's Law Dictionary,* (5th ed. 1979)) Literally translated, the word "malpractice" means bad practice. In fact, as the term is usually used, malpractice does not refer to deliberate wrongful acts of a professional, but to unintentional errors and omissions.

Q. 5:13 Should EAP professionals carry individual malpractice insurance?

Every professional should carry his or her own errors and omissions policy (malpractice insurance), whether or not the EAP carries insurance for its staff. Most EAPs do carry malpractice insurance, but the carrier may take the position that a particular staff member's activities were not covered (for example, they were outside the scope of his or her employment or were deliberate). Occasionally, a professional will feel himself or herself scapegoated in a professional liability case, or may disagree with the employer's or its carrier's strategy or position. Having one's own policy and lawyer can be a great comfort to a clinician.

Sometimes employers think their policies cover their employees when in fact they do not. The EAP should ascertain whether the carrier requires the names of insureds to be listed. Any named insured will be covered personally against a liability claim. Unnamed insureds are not personally covered for their own risk; the coverage for unnamed insureds is for the benefit of the employer. In addition to being covered by his or her own insurance, every professional should be a named insured on the agency's policy. The employment contract should clearly specify that the employer carries insurance for the protection of the professional and will hold the professional harmless in the event that he or she turns out not to be insured under the employer's policy. If the professional is not an employee, but an independent contractor, the EAP should require that the professional provide evidence of current insurance for errors and omissions in the face amount of at least $100,000–$300,000. (Under current conditions, even higher amounts are preferable.)

Q. 5:14 What are the common areas of malpractice risk for EAPs?

Risk of a malpractice claim against an EAP is most likely to occur in the following areas: lack of informed consent; omission or inadequate description of risks of treatment; negligent evaluation, including failure to refer for physical examination and medical care; negligent treatment; abandonment; wrongful disclosure of confidential information; failure to prevent suicide or harm to a third party; abuse of the therapeutic process; and negligent supervision or vicarious liability.

Q. 5:15 How does malpractice arise?

Malpractice may arise from inadvertence, negligence, ignorance, or lack of skill. It may also arise when a professional is trained and skillful, but willfully or maliciously fails to exercise the skill he or she possesses.

Q. 5:16 What are errors and omissions?

An error is an act that a reasonable, duly careful professional would not commit under the circumstances. It may be a careless mistake or the result of poor execution. An omission is the failure to do what a reasonable, duly careful professional would do under the circumstances.

Q. 5:17 What is the basis for a client's right to sue for malpractice?

The basis of the client's right to compensation for harm suffered in the course of clinical care is the contractual relationship between him or her and the therapist. The clinical care contract includes the implied warranties of competency (possessing adequate skill and knowledge) and due care (appropriately and nonnegligently exercising that skill and knowledge).

Q. 5:18 What elements must a plaintiff prove to establish a malpractice claim?

To support a claim of malpractice, the plaintiff (the person who files the lawsuit) must prove all four elements of malpractice; if the plaintiff fails to prove any one of these necessary elements, the case will be dismissed.

Duty: The plaintiff must prove that the therapist owed a duty to the person whom he or she allegedly harmed. To establish duty, the plaintiff must prove that a clinical care relationship had been created and existed at the time of the alleged wrongful act. If there was no contract, there was no duty. Without duty, there can be no malpractice.

Breach of Duty: The plaintiff must prove that the therapist failed to exercise the requisite duty of care owed the client—that he or she omitted to do that which the duly careful professional in the community would have done under the same circumstances, or that he or she did something that a duly careful professional would not have done. If the professional's behavior does not deviate from the standard of care in the community, there is no breach of duty.

Injury: The plaintiff must establish that the client suffered some harm. The harm might be physical, emotional, or financial. It might include aggravation of the client's condition, prolongation of the client's illness or disability, and so forth. The harm need not be severe, debilitating, or permanent, but as a practical matter, the worse the harm, the more money the client is likely to receive in compensation.

Proximate Cause: The plaintiff must establish that the harm suffered by the client was directly caused by the therapist's breach of duty—that but for the therapist's breach, the harm would not have occurred.

Q. 5:19 What is proximate cause?

Proximate cause is:

> that which, in a natural or continuous sequence, produces injury and without which the injury would not have occurred. It need not be the last act nor the sole cause, but it must be a concurring cause. And the injury resulting from the alleged negligent act must be such that a reasonably prudent person would have anticipated it.

Castillo v. United States, 552 F.2d 1385 (10th Cir. 1977).

Example 1. An EAP client turns up at a follow-up group in an obviously inebriated condition, which is against the rules. The counselor tells him to go home immediately because he is disrupting the group. The client gets in his car and drives off. When his wife arrives home four hours later, she finds his car in the closed garage, ignition on and out of gas, driver's door open. Her husband is dead in the front seat, slumped over the wheel. No suicide note is found, and she will never know if he deliberately killed himself or passed out and died accidentally.

In this example, negligent treatment (the therapist should have acted to see that he got home safely) was the proximate cause of the death, whether the client committed suicide or died accidentally.

> **Example 2.** Picture the same scenario as in Example 1, but this time the client leaves the group and walks to the bus stop, where he passes out on a bench while waiting for the bus. A stolen car being driven at high speed by an adolescent, who is high on marijuana and attempting to elude the police, jumps the curb, rams the bench, and kills the client.

In this example, the counselor may have been negligent, but his treatment was not the proximate cause of the client's death. The therapist would not be liable for wrongful death in Example 2, although he would be liable in Example 1.

Q. 5:20 What are the major types of malpractice?

Malpractice may consist of wrongful diagnosis, wrongful treatment, abandonment (wrongful withdrawal of treatment), or any combination of these.

Q. 5:21 Is diagnostic error per se malpractice?

A good-faith error is not malpractice. The law does not require perfection; it requires due care—that is, nonnegligent care. For example, although a diagnosis might turn out to be incorrect, if the clinician did not deviate from the standard of care in arriving at the diagnosis, or if the error occurred notwithstanding an absence of negligence, there is no liability. (*Cameron v. State,* 37 A.D.2d 46, 322 N.Y.S.2d 562 (1971))

Q. 5:22 Is treatment error per se malpractice?

A good-faith error in judgment—that is, one that occurred in spite of compliance with acceptable standards for treatment—is not a basis for civil liability. (*Holton v. Pfingst,* 534 S.W.2d 786 (1976))

Q. 5:23 If alternative treatments are available, is it negligence not to choose the one used most frequently by the majority of practitioners in the vicinity?

A clinician is in charge of his or her practice and has the right to choose among apparently appropriate techniques or modalities. Even though it may turn out, in retrospect, that another treatment choice would have been more efficacious, the treatment used will not be considered malpractice as long as it was one that would have been acceptable to a "respectable minority of the profession." (*Chamber v. McClure*, 505 F.2d 489 (6th Cir. 1974); *Leech v. Bralliar*, 175 F. Supp. 897 (D. Ariz. 1967)) The law does not prefer one form of treatment over another, but this issue must be considered in the context of the duty to obtain informed consent.

Q. 5:24 What is the test for malpractice?

One may test for malpractice by asking, "Did the professional know, or should he or she have known, the risk factors in the case?" "What would the duly careful, competent professional have done under the same circumstances?" If the condition that is the subject of inquiry is esoteric—that is, a duly careful, competent professional would no more have recognized the danger than did this therapist—there will be no culpability for the harm (because there was no negligence). Put another way, a therapist will not be held liable for harm that was not foreseeable and thus could not be guarded against. (*Palsgraf v. Long Island RR*, 248 N.Y. 339, 162 N.E. 99 (1928))

Negligent Treatment and Standards of Care

Q. 5:25 Is failure to cure a basis for malpractice?

The law does not impose a duty or warranty of good result or cure. When a therapist undertakes to provide care, he or she is not an insurer held to a promise of cure, but is held only to a promise to provide diligent and skillful treatment. (*Ray v. AmeriCare Hospital*, 400 So.2d 1127 (La. Ct. App. 1981))

Q. 5:26 What is "standard of care?"

Standard of care refers to the degree of care and level of performance that a reasonably prudent professional would exercise under the same circumstances. It has been otherwise described as the minimum performance that would be considered acceptable and nonnegligent by the profession. The traditional standard is the exercise of the "average" degree of skill, care, and diligence exercised by members of the same profession in the same or similar locality.

Q. 5:27 Is the standard of care the same for all clinical care professionals?

There is a general standard of care for all clinicians: ordinary and reasonable knowledge, skill, diligence, care, and judgment under the circumstances. No lesser standard will be acceptable. The standard to which any clinician will be held will depend upon the level of education, skill, and training he or she possesses.

When a clinician represents himself or herself to be a "specialist," the public is entitled to assume and rely upon the fact that he or she is more than ordinarily skilled, so the standard to which he or she will be held will be that of other specialists—higher than that of the "ordinary practitioner." (J. Smith, *Medical Malpractice—Psychiatric Care* (Colorado Springs, Col.: 1986), 15) A therapist will be held to the standard of care exercised by other professionals in his or her field of expertise who are similarly situated. (*McCarthy v. Boston City Hosp.*, 266 NH.E.2d 191 (1971)) For example, a clinical social worker who claims to be a specialist in treating substance abuse would be held to a higher standard of care in treating it than would another clinical social worker who does not claim such expertise.

Q. 5:28 Where does one find the standard?

Professional standards are found in a variety of places. Textbooks, treatises, professional journals, statutes, and institutional or group policies and procedures all contain practice standards. Some professional societies have published standards for practice that set the standard not only for their own members, but for all professionals of that discipline, whether or not they belong to the society. Standards may apply to practitioners or to programs. Standards for institutions, agencies, and programs are also found in accreditation guidelines and manuals.

Q. 5:29 How is the standard of care established in a malpractice trial?

In a malpractice case, expert witnesses are usually required to testify on the standard of care and whether or not the defendant professional has deviated from it. In some states, an expert witness may not be required if a "learned text" can be introduced into evidence to establish the standard.

Q. 5:30 How is the standard of care being developed for EAPs?

Because the EAP field is so new, standards must be borrowed and adapted from allied professional fields. The law develops by applying previous court decisions, known as precedents, to later cases with similar or identical facts and questions of law. Thus, medical malpractice cases provide the primary source of law for healing and related professions. Many of the cases cited as examples in this book are medical or psychiatric cases. The principles set forth in those cases will be applied to other, newer professions involved in providing clinical care to clients or patients.

Q. 5:31 What are the problems in developing the standard of care for EAPs?

In psychiatric and other medical malpractice cases, identifying a standard is difficult because physicians do not always agree, notwithstanding the fact that medicine is an established profession with centuries of acquired knowledge and experience. For EAPs, it is even more difficult because of the lack of history and the variety of professionals involved in the field. A large part of the work of EAPs is mental health and social service counseling or psychotherapy, with an emphasis on substance abuse. There is wide disagreement on the nature and treatment of mental and emotional disorders generally, and perhaps even more in the case of addictive disorders. This creates problems for sponsors and EAP professionals, who are trying to determine what the law considers "the right thing." This state of the law is a two-edged sword; if the standard is difficult to ascertain, it is equally difficult to establish that a professional has deviated from it!

Q. 5:32 To what standard will EAP professionals be held?

EAP professionals will be held to the standards of their respective disciplines (that is, what the duly careful, competent nurse, clinical social worker, psychologist, or counselor would consider acceptable). (*Thompson v. United States,* 368 F. Supp. 466 (D. La. 1973)) Professional standards apply whenever practice takes place, but care is assessed in terms of what is reasonable in light of the surrounding circumstances. There is as yet very little direct experience with malpractice cases against EAPs, or even against addiction specialists per se, but as more malpractice cases are brought, the standards of the various disciplines will be defined specifically in terms of what the duly careful professional in an EAP would do. In fact, the standard will be defined by EAP professionals. To qualify as an expert witness for the standard of care in a malpractice case against a professional, the witness must be of the same school as the defendant professional or of a school that espouses substantially the same theories and methods. (*Dolan v. Galluzo,* 396 N.E.2d 13 (1979); R. Slovenko, "Malpractice in Psychiatry and Related Fields," *J. of Psychiatry and Law,* Spring, 1981:5–63)

Q. 5:33 What types of statutes establish professional standards?

Licensing acts of the various professions involved in EAPs establish some practice standards for the respective professions, including minimum credentials for licensure and the grounds for discipline of the licensee. Standards of care for individual practitioners and inpatient or outpatient programs or facilities might be found in program or facility licensing acts, mental health and substance abuse treatment acts, statutes mandating the reporting of abuse of vulnerable persons, and—with respect to confidentiality and privileged communications—sometimes in evidence codes.

Q. 5:34 Can an EAP or practitioner contract with a client for a waiver of liability or a standard of less than ordinary care?

Public policy prohibits any contract whereby a clinical care professional is excused from liability in the face of negligence or other fault. (*Meiman v. Rehabilitation Center,* 444 S.W.2d 78 (1969))

Negligent Diagnosis

Q. 5:35 What are some specific duties to clients that the EAP provider should be aware to avoid negligent diagnosis?

Listen to the Client's Complaints: Don't assume a client is malingering or "merely somatizing." Take the client's complaints seriously, and follow up on them.

> **Example.** A client comes to the EAP complaining of vague and puzzling symptoms. The EAP counselor sends the client away with an appointment several days hence. The client commits suicide. The therapist is at risk for a wrongful death action on the basis of failure to properly evaluate for significant depression and suicidal tendencies.

Refer to Other Professionals or Specialists as Needed: i.e., stay within the parameters of one's professional capability and credentials. Only a physician should make a diagnosis when a client has physical symptoms. If a client does not respond to treatment within a reasonable period of time, the client must be referred for consultation. (*Akins v. Novinger,* 322 F. Supp. 1205 (D. Tenn. 1970))

> **Example.** The client's present complaint is relationship problems, especially an inability to connect with women. After a period of psychotherapy, he confides to his therapist one day that he is experiencing an unrelenting burning sensation in his penis. The therapist interprets this symptom as psychosomatic, having to do with the client's fear of sexual rejection. After weeks of therapy spent discussing and analyzing it, the client finally seeks consultation on his own with another psychotherapist, who refers him to a urologist. The diagnosis is venereal warts, requiring surgical treatment. The client sues the first therapist, alleging negligent diagnosis and treatment and breach of the implied warranty of competence.

A client with apparent psychotic symptoms should always be referred to a psychiatrist for evaluation. Never undertake to treat physical or psychotic symptoms by psychotherapy unless a physician has ruled out the need for medical treatment. (R. Slovenko, "Malpractice in Psychiatry and Related Fields," *J. of Psychiatry and Law,* Spring, 1981:5–63, 12; see also *Larson v. Yelle,* 246 N.W.2d 841 (1976).)

Example. Although the client continues to work on a daily basis, she complains to her therapist over a long period of time about weakness, fatigue, nervousness, palpitations, and slowing down on the job. The therapist diagnoses subclinical depression and continues psychotherapy to treat it. One day, the client is passed over for promotion because of her marginal work performance. She is so distraught that night that her husband becomes alarmed and takes her to the emergency room. A psychiatric consultation yields a diagnosis of panic disorder, and the client is placed on medication. In a matter of days, her symptoms begin to abate. The therapist is at risk for a negligence claim for misdiagnosis and failing to consult or refer for consultation.

Verify Facts: Before making a diagnosis or treatment decision, a therapist is under a duty to verify facts, as indicated by the circumstances of the case. This might include asking the client's permission to contact family members or others to confirm data that seem questionable. If the client is referred to the EAP by a supervisor or other person, the referrer may be requested to produce corroboration or additional information. (*Merchants National Bank v. United States,* 272 F. Supp. 409 (D. N.D. 1967))

If the client refuses permission to consult others, the therapist must assess the case for dangerousness and make a determination on whether he or she has some affirmative duty to take further action in the case. When action without verification is negligent, the therapist will be liable for any harm that results.

Example. The client's wife tells the EAP counselor that her husband is furious with his supervisor for picking on him, has purchased a gun, is threatening to shoot the supervisor, and has become increasingly violent at home. She fears he will harm her or the supervisor, and she wants him hospitalized. She further states that the husband has made these threats in the presence of his brother and a neighbor, and that she is planning to file for divorce. When asked by the counselor, the client denies having bought a gun or ever having made the threats. The therapist decides that the client seems like a "pretty nice guy,'' and that the wife is hysterical and trying to get the husband in trouble to gain leverage in the divorce; he offers the husband supportive counseling to help deal with the vicious wife. The husband in fact shoots the wife and the supervisor. The therapist is sued by the survivors of the deceased for negligent diagnosis and treatment.

Respond in a Timely Manner: A therapist has a duty to respond to a client's phone calls in a timely manner. What ''timely'' is will be determined by the facts in a given case. With some clients, limit setting is appropriate, and a therapist may limit contacts between sessions. This usually occurs in the context of treating clients with personality disorders. When considering limitations on extrasession calls, the diagnostic condition and treatment needs of the client—not the convenience of the treater—must be considered. If the client's needs exceed the capacities of the treater, the client should be referred to someone else. Any limitations on client contacts should be checked with a consultant or supervisor, clearly communicated to the client, and noted in the client's record along with the rationale for them. The client must be given an emergency alternative, which may be a local community crisis line or emergency room. If the therapist has been unreasonable in failing to respond to calls, he or she will be at risk for an accusation of abandonment.

Abandonment and Treatment Termination

Q. 5:36 Is abandonment a form of malpractice?

Yes. (*Magana v. Elie,* 108 Ill. App.3d 1028, 64 Ill. Dec. 511, 439 N.E.2d 1319 (1982)) As with other forms of malpractice, unless the client suffers harm by reason of the therapist's unreasonable or incompetent behavior, there will be no liability.

Q. 5:37 What is the legal basis for the theory of abandonment?

Once a practitioner or program has undertaken to provide care and a therapist-client relationship contract has been formed, the provider owes an implied continued duty of care to the client until the relationship has been properly terminated. (*Collins v. Meeker,* 424 P.2d 488 (1967)) If the provider unilaterally and improperly withdraws care, he or she has breached the implied terms of the contract.

Q. 5:38 What are the elements of a legal claim for abandonment?

The plaintiff must establish that:

- A clinical care relationship existed;
- The provider unilaterally terminated the relationship without sufficient notice, appropriate clinical procedures, and referral to or assistance in finding a successor therapist; and
- The client suffered injury as a direct result of the abandonment.

Q. 5:39 What are the forms of intentional abandonment?

Intentional abandonment may be overt, as when a therapist whose client still needs care precipitously ends the clinical relationship without sufficient notice, a clinically proper termination process, and referral to or assistance in finding a successor therapist.

Example. A borderline client (see Q. 5:76) abuses the therapist for weeks, calling numerous times daily, leaving shouted profanities on the answering machine when the therapist does not answer personally, coming to the office between sessions, and refusing to leave when the therapist states that he cannot see her. The therapist recognizes the behavior as pathological and responds to it empathetically, continuing to tolerate the acting out on the theory that it will cease with additional treatment. One day, in the throes of a borderline rage, the client grabs a book from the therapist's desk and throws it across the room. The therapist loses control and shouts at the client to leave immediately and never come back. He refuses to return the client's calls and sends back several notes from her unopened. She takes an overdose and then calls an ambulance. After discharge from the hospital, she sues the therapist for mishandling the transference/countertransference and for abandonment.

Intentional abandonment may also be covert, as when the therapist consciously fails to provide emergency care for a client, or coverage or a means of contact when the therapist is unavailable. It may be difficult to distinguish this deliberate, willful failure to provide necessary care from a negligent failure to diligently attend a client. The practitioner's motivation may be the key here, but as a practical matter, in a malpractice case, it will be pleaded as negligence so as to ensure access to the provider's professional liability insurance.

Example. The client is doing well and is not in the habit of calling between appointments or demanding extra sessions. On the Friday afternoon of a three-day Christmas weekend, the client's cat is run over by a car. It is nearly midnight when she telephones her counselor who, in his haste to get out of town, did not provide emergency therapist coverage for his clients, and leaves a sobbing message on his answering machine. The next day, her adult children arrive for Christmas dinner and find her lying in bed exhausted and unable to talk. They call an ambulance, and she is admitted to the psychiatric unit in an acute depressive state. The therapist attempts to return her call as soon as he takes his messages from the machine—on Tuesday, when he returns to the office. After two weeks in the hospital, the client is discharged in the care of another therapist. The client is encouraged by her outraged children to sue for abandonment.

In this instance, the theoretical basis for the lawsuit might be that the therapist abandoned the client by not providing alternative care while he was out of town for the three-day weekend.

Q. 5:40 What is implied abandonment?

Abandonment may be implied if a therapist exercises poor judgment in terminating treatment, unintentionally neglects to arrange coverage for a period of time, makes a good-faith error in refusing an extra appointment to a client, or negligently fails to diligently attend a client. Implied abandonment is a form of negligence.

Q. 5:41 Must a therapist be available at all times?

A program may determine the hours of practice, and a therapist is not obliged to be at the other end of the telephone 24 hours a day, every day of the year. (*Dabney v. Briggs,* 121 So. 394 (1929)) However, a provider undertaking to care for clients who are likely to have emergencies makes a commitment to be available when those emergencies occur, or to provide an adequate substitute. (Holder, *Medical Malpractice Law,* 2d ed. (New York: 1978), 30)

Q. 5:42 Is it abandonment for a therapist to restrict access by having an unlisted home phone number?

Some authorities suggest that an unlisted phone number without some means of contact outside the therapy hour constitutes abandonment. (Van Hoose and Kotler, *Ethical and Legal Issues in Counseling and Psychotherapy* (1977)) This is an ultracareful view, which has been moderated in recent years as a result of the proliferation of community mental health centers; telephone answering services, machines, and paging devices; and the use of hospital emergency rooms as crisis intervention facilities. The current view is that a therapist is entitled to the privacy of an unlisted phone number, but he or she *must* have a method for dealing with after-hours emergencies.

Q. 5:43 How can an EAP reduce the risk of liability for implied abandonment?

Clients, referral sources, and community contacts should be informed of the EAP's after-hours emergency resources. Some form of after-hours contact should be provided, preferably an answering service that has access to an on-call professional who can respond in a crisis. If this is not possible, the program should have an answering machine with an announcement of an emergency phone number, or at the very least, an announcement instructing the client to go to the nearest emergency room.

Q. 5:44 How can a therapist who will be temporarily unavailable avoid abandoning his or her clients?

The EAP should have a policy and procedures for emergency appointments and time limits in returning client calls. A therapist has a right to take reasonable days off and vacations, and may sometimes be ill or otherwise unable to attend his or her clients. Every EAP must have arrangements in place for such contingencies. A competent substitute, who has been provided with adequate information to enable care, must be available. (*Dashiell v. Griffith*, 35 A. 1094 (1896); *Browning v. Hoffman*, 111 S.E. 492 (1922)) When a protracted absence is expected, the therapist is obliged to notify the client in advance so that the client can make his or her choices about substitute care. For some clients, transfer to another therapist may be indicated. The absence of a therapist creates clinical issues that should be addressed before and after the therapist leaves. When clinically appropriate, the therapist and client may agree that the client take a vacation from therapy while the therapist is away. In the event of an emergency, the substitute therapist can fill the breach.

Q. 5:45 Who is an appropriate substitute therapist?

The substitute therapist should have credentials and experience equivalent, or as similar as possible, to those of the therapist whose place he or she is taking. (*Miller v. Dore,* 148 A.2d 692 (1959)) The client has contracted for care based on the background of the regular therapist and is entitled to be treated by a substitute of equal skill.

Q. 5:46 What are the therapist's obligations when arranging for a substitute?

The therapist should inform the client as early as possible of the impending absence and should address the issue in terms of its clinical significance to the client. The substitute should be described to the client and, if indicated, introduced—perhaps in the client's regular therapy session—so that the client can decide whether to accept the proffered substitute or to make other arrangements. The substitute should be familiarized with the practice and the clients. If a client is particularly vulnerable to regression or fragmentation, thought should be given to possible hospitalization or other protective measures. The substitution procedures and process should be documented as a protection against a claim for abandonment. (J. Smith, *Medical Malpractice—Psychiatric Care* (Colorado Springs, Col.: 1986), 51)

Q. 5:47 Under what circumstances may a provider have a right to withdraw from a case while care is still needed?

A provider may withdraw for personal or professional reasons, or because the client is either not cooperating or, despite everyone's best efforts, not progressing in or benefiting from treatment. Some programs have a built-in time limit, but the client may still require care at the end of the prescribed time. Clients may owe money and refuse or be unable to pay. Some clients may be threatening and present a risk of harm to the therapist. (*Harold v. State,* 449 A.2d 429 (1982)) In all such cases, as long as sufficient notice is given, the clinical issues surrounding the termination are addressed, and a referral is offered, there will be no abandonment.

Q. 5:48 Can an EAP build into its treatment contract conditions for termination under certain circumstances while treatment may still be needed?

The initial therapist-client contract may specify certain conditions under which termination will occur (for example, coming to treatment while intoxicated; committing violent acts during treatment, or threatening EAP personnel or other clients), but even then, the clinical condition of the client may create a circumstance under which termination is not appropriate. (*Boxberger v. Martin*, 552 P.2d 370 (1976))

> **Example.** A substance abuse program contract provides that a client will be terminated immediately if he or she comes to the session while impaired by alcohol or other drugs. The client appears one day in a clearly drunken condition. The therapist may not simply eject him from the office; he or she must take some action to see that the client is protected in his vulnerable state. Although termination is called for under the contract, and is clinically correct under some treatment theories, the therapist cannot simply refuse to see the client again. He or she is obliged to offer a referral to another suitable program or therapist.

Q. 5:49 Are there circumstances in which a provider may not be able to terminate a case?

There are rare circumstances in which a provider may be legally and ethically constrained to retain a case. This could occur if the client would be endangered or caused to suffer if care were not available and there was no appropriate program or individual provider to whom he or she could reasonably be transferred. If there really was no alternative care available, the therapist might be legally and ethically obliged to continue treatment until the client's condition had improved to the point where treatment could be terminated. (Holder, *Medical Malpractice Law* 2d ed. (New York: 1978), 373) If, on the other hand, there is appropriate substitute care available, but the client rejects it for his or her own reasons, the provider may terminate over the client's objection, as long as the termination has been handled in a clinically appropriate manner. The need for extremely thorough documentation in such a situation cannot be overemphasized.

Q. 5:50 To what abandonment risks are EAPs particularly vulnerable, and how can these be avoided?

EAPs share the same programmatic or administrative risks for abandonment of clients as any social service or mental health agency. There are times when program changes require making alternative plans for clients. Clients may become ineligible for service because of termination or suspension of employment, sometimes arising out of the very conditions for which the client was obtaining EAP services. EAP and sponsor policies should be in place to deal with such situations. In no case should the client simply be eliminated from the program; in all cases, a clinically appropriate termination and transfer are required. Anything less is malpractice. Programs using student interns must be scrupulous in informing clients at the start that their therapists will be available only for a limited period. Clinical supervisors must monitor the termination process with the student-therapist; unless termination of the treatment is clinically appropriate, an orderly transfer of the case is mandatory.

Q. 5:51 Under what circumstances may a client terminate treatment?

Unless a client is under court order, such as commitment for involuntary treatment, he or she may terminate treatment at will. A client may have chosen to accept treatment instead of a less palatable alternative (for example, job discipline or firing, jail, divorce, or loss of custody or visitation). Such a client always has the option to change his or her mind, leave treatment, and accept the consequences.

Q. 5:52 Does the EAP have any legal obligation to the employer or legal authority when a client accepts EAP services as an alternative to job or legal sanctions?

The EAP will not generally have an obligation to the employer or court that required a client to accept EAP services unless the EAP has represented to that referring entity that it will be notified if the client drops out. There are situations in which a court may approve probation or parole, or some third party is entitled to assume that a person is not a danger to himself or herself or others, on the basis that he or she is in treatment. When a court or other third party acts in reliance on the EAP's monitoring a client and informing it of a change in the client's condition that would cause the third party to change its position or actions, the EAP owes a duty to communicate. In any case in which a third party may be harmed by reliance on the EAP, the EAP should insist at the outset that the client provide a consent to disclose treatment termination or disruption to the referrer. If the consent is not supplied, the EAP should refuse to undertake the case. If the consent is later withdrawn, notice of the withdrawal should be given to the party relying on the information.

> **Example.** After a meeting with the employee and the EAP, the employer permits an employee to return to his high-risk job following inpatient alcoholism treatment only on the condition that the employee stays in treatment under the direction of the EAP. The EAP counselor agrees to closely monitor the employee because of the high-risk nature of the work, and the employee signs a consent for the EAP to communicate with the employer. The client begins missing sessions with his counselor, always with some more or less plausible excuse. The employer has no reason to suspect that all is not well. After three weeks of sporadic attendance, the client has an accident, causing an explosion that injures himself and kills two fellow employees. Blood tests indicate that he was legally intoxicated at the time of the explosion. Workers' compensation claims are filed, and the client's family, the families of the two dead men, and the employer all sue the EAP.

Intentional Wrongful Acts (Torts)

Q. 5:53 How does an intentional wrongful act differ from malpractice?

Malpractice is generally considered the result of a negligent, accidental, or unintended error or omission. When a clinician deliberately—with design, resolve, or determination—and knowing or actually desiring that untoward consequences are likely to result from it, commits a private wrongful act against his or her client (other than breach of contract), he or she has committed an intentional tort. Note that any time a clinician commits an intentional tort against a client, he or she has also committed a breach of fiduciary duty.

Q. 5:54 What is the practical effect of the distinction between malpractice and intentional torts?

If a therapist commits a deliberate wrongful act against a client, he or she will have a cause of action against the therapist, but it will not be for malpractice. Rather it will be for an intentional tort. To the client who has been wronged, this may seem to be a distinction without a difference. In fact, it is of considerable importance, because malpractice insurance covers a therapist for *negligent errors and omissions,* not deliberate wrongdoing. Thus, in some instances, the client may actually have less recourse if he or she brings the action for an intentional tort. As a result, plaintiffs' attorneys will ordinarily make every effort to frame their cases in terms of malpractice unless they have reason to believe that the clinician has some other form of insurance to cover the claim or has a sufficiently large estate to make a case of intentional tort worthwhile.

Procedurally, the difference is also significant, because an expert witness is necessary to establish malpractice liability, but not liability for deliberate tortious conduct. If, therefore, an expert is not available, the plaintiff's attorney will attempt to frame the case as an intentional tort. The clinician, thus personally exposed, will resist this approach.

Another difference between a tort and malpractice is that in some states, the statute of limitations for malpractice may be shorter than for intentional tort. If the case has not been brought within the statutory time for negligence, the attorney may frame it in terms of intentional tort so that the case can still be tried.

Assault and Battery

Q. 5:55 What is assault and battery?

Assault is any willful attempt or threat to inflict injury upon the person of another, when coupled with an apparent present ability to do so, and any intentional display of force such as would give the victim reason to fear or expect immediate bodily harm. Assault can be committed without an actual touching of or physical injury to the person of the other. Battery is the culmination of an unlawful assault. Assault and battery is any unlawful touching of another that is without justification or excuse.

Q. 5:56 When may therapy be assault and battery?

Any inappropriate, nonconsensual touching of a client by a therapist may be considered assault and battery. There are so-called nontraditional therapy modalities that employ touch (for example, "body therapies," such as Rolfing, bioenergetics, some techniques used in Gestalt therapy or reparenting, and others). Many authorities describe these as "wild" or "unconventional." When these are employed, specific informed consent will be required. Lawsuits may arise against therapists who employ these techniques—essentially for failure to obtain the informed consent of the client for their use.

Even with informed consent, courts have not been ready to permit therapies that utilize beating or punishment. In the well-known case of *Hammer v. Rosen* (165 N.E.2d 756 (1960)), a schizophrenic client was treated over a period of time by Dr. Rosen, a well-known psychiatrist, who employed striking and beating as a response to her inappropriate or psychotic productions. The therapist claimed that the beatings were treatment, not assault and battery, and had been consented to by the client. The court held that they were by their nature improper and malpractice.

In *Abraham v. Zaslow* (San Francisco County Sup. Ct., 1972; reported in *The New York Times,* July 5, 1972), perhaps the first reported case against a psychologist, a 22-year-old client was awarded $170,000. She was being treated by Dr. Zaslow, who had pioneered a controversial modality called Rage Reduction Therapy to treat autistic children. For this adult client, it involved a 13-hour session in which she was choked, beaten, held down, tied down, and had fingers stuck into her mouth.

Q. 5:57 Is it assault and battery to physically restrain a violent client to prevent personal injury or property damage?

A violent client may be restrained to prevent him or her from assaulting another person, harming himself or herself, or destroying property. However, only the degree of force that is reasonable under the circumstances may be employed. Any undue force will be considered assault and battery. (*Bellandi v. Park Sanitarium Association*, 6 P.2d 508 (1931))

Example. A voluntary patient wished to leave a private mental hospital. The therapist and members of the staff garotted him with a towel and drugged him with ether. He died as a result of either strangulation or an overdose of ether. His family sued for wrongful death and won.

Defamation

Q. 5:58 What is defamation?

Defamation is the holding up of another to ridicule, scorn, or contempt in a respectable and considerable part of the community. It includes libel and slander. Libel is written, printed or broadcast defamation; slander is spoken defamation. Slander per se occurs when a statement is falsely made that charges the commission of a crime, imputes some offensive or loathsome disease that would tend to deprive a person of society, charges a woman with "unchastity," or tends to injure a person in his trade, business, office, or occupation. (*Restatement (Second) of Torts* §570)

A communication is defamatory if it tends to so harm the reputation of another as to lower that person in the estimation of the community or to stop third persons from associating with him or her. (*Restatement (Second) of Torts* §570)

Q. 5:59 What elements must a plaintiff prove to establish a case for defamation?

There are five elements to a defamation action, all of which must be proved to establish a prima facie case of defamation:

1. The communication by the defendant of defamatory language is adverse to the reputation of the plaintiff.
2. The plaintiff is reasonably identifiable to the recipient.
3. The defendant has publicized the defamatory material to a third party (the recipient).
4. There has been injury to the plaintiff's reputation.
5. The defendant intended malice. (Malice will be presumed when

a private person is injured; it must be proved if the plaintiff is a public figure.)

If the material is libelous on its face, i.e., the defamatory intent is clear without reference to any extrinsic facts; it is libel per se, and damages are presumed. That is, the plaintiff need not prove specific injury or loss. If the material is communicated orally, slander is not presumed, but damages must be proved.

Q. 5:60 How might defamation occur in the context of an EAP?

In *Berry v. Moench* (331 P.2d 814 (1958)), the landmark case on defamation by mental health providers, a young couple fell in love and wished to marry. The girl was from a wealthy family, and her father did not like the fiance. The father asked his family physician to inquire about the young man's background. The physician contacted a psychiatrist who had treated the young man briefly seven years previously. The psychiatrist responded by letter, stating that the young man was "manic depressive in a psychopathic personality." He stated his opinion that the man was irresponsible, a troublemaker, and a poor provider who would give a wife trouble; he also released information about the young man's family. Despite being given the information, the girl married the man and was promptly disinherited.

The young man sued the psychiatrist for libel and invasion of privacy. The psychiatrist defended on the basis that what he had said was true and he made the disclosures under conditional privilege. The court rejected his arguments, stating that the disclosures were inappropriate and a violation of the physician-patient relationship, and that the doctor had disseminated partial untruths, which displayed a failure to use reasonable diligence in ascertaining facts and communicating information fairly. The fact that the doctor was not acting out of spite was irrelevant. He disclosed the information intentionally, from which the court inferred malice.

A therapist who makes a negligent diagnosis and then communicates it to the detriment of the client is at risk for a defamation action. Calling a client alcoholic, addicted, character disordered, or psychotic is defamatory when there is not sufficient evidence to back up the diagnosis. (*Moyer v. Phillips,* 341 A.2d 441 (1975)) A client who consents to disclosure cannot later complain if he or she is adversely affected by it. A clinician who discloses information upon which a third person is expected to act is obliged to make full and fair disclosure, so as not to mislead the person receiving it. (*Clark v. Geraci*, 208 N.Y.S.2d 564 (1960)) Much difficulty of this sort can be avoided if the therapist first discloses to the client whatever will be disclosed to others, so the client can make an informed choice before consenting.

Invasion of Privacy

Q. 5:61 What is the right of privacy?

The right of privacy, in its constitutional context, is the right of an individual to be free of unwarranted intrusion in his or her life by the government. The right to refuse treatment, to control one's own body, and to be free of unwarranted storage, dissemination, and use of data about one's personal affairs are examples of the constitutional right of privacy. The private right of privacy protects individuals from nongovernmental intrusion into their private affairs and has several aspects: to be let alone; to control the use of one's name and likeness; and to have one's private facts kept private. (*Black's Law Dictionary,* (5th ed., 1979))

Q. 5:62 What is invasion of privacy?

Breach or *invasion of privacy* falls into four general classes:

1. *Appropriation:* Appropriating the plaintiff's name or likeness for the defendant's benefit.
2. *Intrusion:* Intruding upon a person's solitude or seclusion, as by invading his or her home; eavesdropping; or persistent unwanted telephone calls.
3. *Public disclosure of private facts:* Publicly disclosing private information of a highly objectionable kind about the plaintiff, even though it is true and an action for defamation could not be brought.
4. *False light in the public eye:* Publicizing facts about the plaintiff that would place him or her in a false light to the public.

(*Black's Law Dictionary,* (5th ed., 1979))

Q. 5:63 How is invasion of privacy likely to occur in the EAP setting?

Any breach of confidentiality is also breach of privacy. When a client's private information is deliberately disclosed by a clinician or other employee of the EAP, the client will have a cause of action for breach of fiduciary duty and invasion of privacy. There is no excuse for gossip, but it frequently occurs. Cocktail party conversation about EAP clients is a direct source of liability. If the private information is of such a nature that the client's professional status is impaired, or he or she is held up to ridicule or opprobrium, a defamation action may also be brought. Professional and support personnel should be adequately trained and regularly reminded that disclosure of information about a client is absolutely forbidden.

A client is entitled to the privacy of his or her treatment. Observers, such as students or other professionals not involved in the care of the client, may not be permitted to hear or view sessions or tapes of sessions without the client's informed consent. Some authorities suggest that use of clients for training purposes is exploitation, and the transference phenomenon renders a client's consent void. The classic invasion of privacy case in a patient care setting is the venerable case of *DeMay v. Roberts* (9 N.W. 146 (1881)), in which a physician brought a drinking companion along when he attended a delivery at a farmhouse. He introduced the man as another doctor, although, in fact, he was a salesman who was curious to see a birth. The woman sued successfully for invasion of privacy.

Q. 5:64 Is it invasion of privacy to use client case material for teaching or publication?

The use of client information, case material, photographs, audiotapes, or videotapes for teaching, demonstration, or presentation at professional meetings or for commercial purposes, without the client's written informed consent is invasion of privacy. (*Feeney v. Young,* 191 A.D. 501 (1920))

Example. A therapist used a case record, including verbatim statements of the patient, to write a book. She claimed to have received verbal consent from the client, who was partially disguised. The client succeeded in obtaining an injunction against further sale of the book—

a most unusual occurrence, given the First Amendment prohibition against prior restraint of expression—and was awarded damages. (*Doe v. Roe,* 345 N.Y.S.2d 569 (1973))

Fraud and Misrepresentation

Q. 5:65 What is fraud?

Fraud is the intentional perversion of truth for the purpose of obtaining something valuable from another or inducing another to surrender a legal right. Fraud may be committed by words or conduct; false or misleading allegations (either deliberately or as a result of a reckless disregard for the truth); or concealment, with the intention of deceiving another so that a person acts to his or her own detriment. Actual fraud consists of the intentional and successful use of deceit, cunning, or artifice to circumvent or cheat another. Constructive fraud is an act, statement, or omission that operates as a virtual fraud upon another, or which, if generally permitted, would be prejudicial to the public welfare, and yet may have been unconnected with any selfish or evil design. (*Black's Law Dictionary,* (5th ed., 1979))

Q. 5:66 What is fraud or deceit of treatment?

Transference and dependency render EAP clients particularly vulnerable to fraud at the hands of an unscrupulous therapist. Any intentional misrepresentation to induce a client to undergo treatment is fraud. Examples are: misrepresenting the nature of a treatment; stating that a procedure was administered when it was not (*Allison v. Hewlitt,* 348 S.W.2d 182 (1961)); giving a warranty or guarantee of result when the therapist knows that no guarantee is possible; and lying to a client about the risks of a treatment. (*Bowers v. Talmadge,* 159 So.2d 888 (1963))

Inducing a client to undergo either unneeded treatment or the more expensive of equally suitable alternatives, for the purpose of the therapist's financial gain, is also fraud. (*Nork v. Superior Court,* 33 Cal. App. 3d 997 (1973)) This charge can be extremely difficult to prove, because clinicians may have honestly differing opinions about clients' needs. If it can be established, however, that personal profit was the motive for the treatment choice, fraud may be implied. For example, insisting that long-term inpatient treatment for substance abuse is the only possible course for a client will open the therapist to a charge of fraud if it can be shown that outpatient day treatment or short-term treatment were clinically appropriate alternatives and that the therapist received some money or other reward for the referral.

Misrepresenting the legal possibilities or consequences of a treatment decision is fraud. Inducing a client to enter an inpatient facility by telling him that he will otherwise be involuntarily hospitalized, when the therapist knows that the client is not subject to commitment, will expose the therapist to a civil suit no only for fraud, but also for false imprisonment. In some states, it is also a crime.

Q. 5:67 Is it fraud for a therapist to conceal a treatment error?

When a treatment error has been made, and the client's condition has worsened as a result, the clinician is under a fiduciary duty to be honest with the client. An attempt at cover up will add an action for deceit to a malpractice case. Further, the statute of limitations does not begin to run until the fraud is discovered. (*van Bronckhorst v. Taube,* 341 N.E.2d 791 (1976)) Any clinician has an absolute obligation to tell his or her client the truth and not to misrepresent the client's condition or what is to be done. Furthermore, in the relationship between clinician and client, silence alone may be sufficient to constitute actionable fraud. (Holder, *Medical Malpractice Law,* 2d ed. (New York: 1978) 286)

Q. 5:68 Is it fraud to have a psychiatrist or psychologist "sign off" on insurance claims for services provided to a client by other EAP staff?

Any action taken to mislead another for purposes of inducing him or her to do something he or she would not otherwise be obliged to do is fraud. In situations in which third-party payors are not required to reimburse for services provided by other than approved professionals, it has become common practice to set up arrangements whereby an approved provider submits claims under his or her name and number for services provided by noncovered providers, receives the reimbursement, and splits the fee in some manner. If the third-party payor pays the claim under the misapprehension that an approved provider has actually provided the service, fraud has been committed. It is no defense that the approved provider has "supervised" the care. (*Eisenberg v. Meyers,* 148 Cal. App. 3d 814 (1983))

Some third-party payors will approve claims for services provided by professionals other than physicians, even though this is not readily apparent from the plan documents provided to the insured. Others may approve claims for services prescribed or rendered under supervision of a physician. (California Medicaid does not do so, as the defendants in *Eisenberg* found out to their financial discomfiture.) The important thing is not to mislead the payor in filing claims. A telephone call to the company will ascertain the scope of coverage, and it is essential that a note be made of the date and time of the call and the name of the person at the payor's office who gave the information. Careful practitioners and programs may wish to follow up the phone call with a confirmatory letter. Since sponsors contract for insurance benefits, they are in a position to dictate that EAP services and providers be covered. If this has not been arranged, EAP administration should work with benefits administration toward that end.

Another common form of insurance fraud is misrepresentation of the number and length of sessions provided, and the fee per session. Many health insurance plans require a sizable deductible or coinsurance payment. Providers will often make arrangements with clients whereby they will accept the maximum insurance reimbursement as full payment and not require the client to pay the balance. If the payor has contracted to pay a percentage of the fee on condition that the client pay the remainder, this practice is obviously fraudulent. If the insurance plan provides a fixed amount per session, rather than a percentage reimbursement, there is no such problem.

Example. The therapist charges on a sliding scale, with a maximum of $70 per 45-minute session. The client's insurance reimburses 50% of the fee per session, up to $50. The therapist agrees to bill at $100 per session, accept the insurance reimbursement of $50 as full payment, show a running balance of $50 per session on the client's account ledger, but not require payment or attempt to collect it from the client. This is insurance fraud.

Insurance fraud is civilly actionable; it is also a crime. If the claims and payments have been sent by mail, it is a federal offense. Programs or professionals with such arrangements in existence should seek immediate legal counsel.

False Imprisonment

Q. 5:69 What is false imprisonment?

False imprisonment or arrest involves the detention of an individual or the restraint of his or her personal liberty or freedom of movement without legal authority. This unlawful restraint may be effected by words alone, by acts alone, or by both. Under some conditions, it may also be a crime.

Q. 5:70 How can an EAP be guilty of false imprisonment or arrest?

Occasionally, an EAP professional is asked to participate in the commitment of a client under dubious circumstances, or trickery is employed to facilitate hospitalization. Under no circumstances should a therapist cooperate with misrepresentation or sign certification papers without having personally examined the client. Most mental health codes require that an examination for certification be conducted within a specified time prior to the actual certification. Any deviation from the strict statutory rules and requirements could result in an action for false imprisonment and, in some states, criminal prosecution. A clinician who cooperates with the false imprisonment activities of another may also be guilty of false imprisonment.

It is illegal to detain a person without due process of law. Sometimes, a client's mental or physical state is such that he or she is in no condition to be allowed to leave the EAP office. Although reasonable restraint is permitted and required to prevent a client from harming himself or herself or another or destroying property, one who does so runs the risk of a charge of false imprisonment. This is a "devil or the deep" dilemma; the clinician must try, under emergency conditions, to take the action best calculated to protect the client and the community. As long as the action taken is reasonable under the circumstances, the risk of lawsuit is contained.

A threat to commit a client to a state hospital as a ploy to induce him or her to agree to inpatient hospitalization, if it creates a fear that actually induces him or her to enter the hospital, constitutes an unlawful restraint of personal liberty. To sustain a suit for false imprisonment, the plaintiff must establish that he or she was threatened and reasonably feared force if he or she did not submit. The threat of commitment and confinement is "restraint" within the context of the tort of false imprisonment. (*Marcus v. Liebman,* 375 N.E.2d 486 (1978))

Outrageous Conduct

Q. 5:71 What is the tort of outrage?

Outrageous conduct is deliberate conduct intended to inflict emotional distress or reckless conduct that the perpetrator knows or ought to know would inflict distress, and that is so atrocious and intolerable that a recitation of the facts to an average person would arouse his or her resentment against the perpetrator and lead him or her to exclaim "outrageous!" (*Johnson v. Williams Hospital,* 527 S.W.2d 133 (1975)) To prevail in a lawsuit for outrage, the plaintiff would have to prove that (1) the behavior was intentional or reckless; (2) it was outrageous, intolerable, and shocking or offensive to all generally accepted standards of decency and morality; (3) the defendant knew or should have known that it would cause great distress; and (4) the outrageous conduct was the proximate cause of the plaintiff's deep distress.

Historically, the law did not permit recovery of damages for emotional distress unless it accompanied physical injury, on the theory that emotional harm was too subjective and difficult to assess. A few cases were so blatant, however, that the concept of "outrage" developed to provide a remedy that would otherwise be unavailable. Hurt feelings by reason of bad manners or unpleasantness will not be sufficient to sustain a suit for outrage. For example, recovery was denied to two employees who were fired as a result of a false accusation that they had sex in the women's bathroom. (*Dowling v. Blue Cross of Florida, Inc.,* 338 So.2d 88 (Fla. App. 1976)) For behavior to be considered outrageous, it must be "atrocious" or "intolerable." (*Goldfarb v. Baker,* 547 S.W.2d 567 (1977))

Q. 5:72 How might a charge of outrage arise in EAP practice?

Conduct that would not be viewed as outrageous if directed to persons of normal sensibilities might be actionable if knowingly and deliberately directed against a particularly vulnerable individual. (*Nickerson v. Hodges,* 84 So. 37 (1920)) Recklessness in diagnosis might result in an action for outrage, along with an action for malpractice (*Molien v. Kaiser Foundation Hospital,* 616 P.2d 813 (1980)) Sadistic behavior against a vulnerable client, spreading a false diagnosis, a particularly blatant breach of privacy, and sexual exploitation of a client could all be bases for actions in outrage.

> **Example.** A female employee is referred to the EAP by her supervisor, who is concerned about her generally sad demeanor and intermittent lack of concentration on the job. The client reports to the EAP counselor that she has been seeing a psychiatrist and takes a minor tranquilizer prescribed by him, but that it makes her lethargic, so that her husband accuses her of being lazy. She suffers from anxiety, guilt, and low self-esteem. The counselor ends the intake session by telling her that he is disgusted by her, that it is clear that she is a "junkie" who is denying her drug dependency, and that the only hope for her is inpatient treatment in a substance abuse program. On the spot, he telephones the client's husband and conveys the same message, telling him he had better see to it that she gets treatment for her own sake and that of the children. The husband files for divorce and custody of the children, citing her "unfitness" and "drug habit." It is established by her psychiatrist and consultants that the substance abuse diagnosis was totally without foundation and she was, in fact, a battered wife too terrified, ashamed, and depressed to tell anyone.

The therapist in this example is certainly guilty of malpractice and unethical conduct. The facts in this case would probably support an action for outrage.

Undue Familiarity

Q. 5:73 What is undue familiarity?

Undue is defined as more than necessary, not proper, or illegal. It denotes something wrong, according to the standard of morals that the law enforces in human relations. Familiarity is closeness or intimacy. *Black's Law Dictionary,* (5th ed. (1979)) Undue familiarity, in the context of human services delivery, then, may be defined as improper, unnecessary, or illegal closeness or intimacy between therapist and client. Opinions may differ about what is proper and necessary closeness. Intimacy is an element in any psychotherapy and, to some extent, counseling activity. Only the degree and form of intimacy that are appropriate to the work being done are therapeutic and proper. Since the fiduciary nature of the therapy contract places the management and control of the relationship squarely in the hands of the therapist, any undue familiarity is entirely his or her responsibility.

The ethical code of every helping profession strictly and without exception prohibits sexual contact between therapist and client. Implicitly or explicitly, they all prohibit exploitation of clients. The code of conduct of the American Psychological Association specifically forbids "dual relationships" between its members and their clients. (*Amer. Psychologist* 36:6 (June 1981): 633–638) Undue familiarity can take forms other than actual sexual relations, but a lawsuit in those cases will generally be pleaded as malpractice based on negligent mishandling of transference. (*Landau v. Werner,* 105 Sol.J. 1008 (England C.A. 1961))

Sexual Exploitation

Q. 5:74 What is sexual misconduct in the context of EAPs?

Sexual contact of any kind with a client is sexual misconduct. In addition to any overt, physical manifestations of sexual behavior between client and therapist—however slight (for example *any* touching at all with sexual overtones)—"sexual contact" is defined to include *requests* by the therapist for sexual conduct.

Q. 5:75 Are some therapists particularly at risk for sexual exploitation?

One author reported his conclusions after studying the characteristics of defendants in sexual exploitation cases. (A. Stone, *Law, Psychiatry and Morality* (1976) The following are descriptions of "types" of therapists he found to be particularly prone to this kind of difficulty:

The Middle-Aged Depressed Psychotherapist With Problems in His Own Marriage Who Becomes Involved With a Younger Woman Patient: Typically, he exploits a positive transference, not seducing the patient by charm, but rather by telling her his troubles. Often, he talks of divorcing his wife and marrying the patient. The activity is not confined to the therapist's office.

The Therapist Who Is Character Disordered—"Bad" in the Old-Fashioned Sense: He is manipulative and sociopathic not only in sexual involvements, but in other aspects of life as well. His sexual exploitation of patients is only one aspect of his exploitation of position and the opportunities presented for self-gratification.

The Therapist Who Has a Perverse Sexual Fixation: The perverse impulses are repeatedly acted out with patients. There is no exploitation of transference in these cases, but rather an exploitation of the therapeutic situation.

The "Sexually Liberated" Therapist: He believes that sexual liberation includes sex with patients and is quite open about it. He uses his professional position to actualize his sexual ideology.

The "Grandiose Lover": He grandiosely loves his patients and wants to be loved by them, particularly if they are young and attractive. He wants the intimacy of the therapy to be real. He often begins by hugging and kissing his patients, but does not stop there. Unlike the depressed type, he is expansive, charming, and aggressively seductive.

The Therapist Who Is Withdrawn, Introverted, and Uncomfortable With Human Intimacy: When confronted with a patient who has an intense positive eroticized transference, he succumbs. In a sense, he believes he has been seduced, but he feels very guilty nonetheless, and is quite apt to confess.

Q. 5:76 Are some clients particularly likely to present a risk to therapists for sexual acting out?

Clients with borderline personality disorders are particularly likely to evoke an inappropriate response from a therapist. Those features of clients with this disorder that are most relevant here are borderline rage, neediness and/or dependency, boundary confusion, and manipulativeness and entitlement. (E. Gutheil, "Borderline Personality Disorder, Boundary Violations, and Patient-Therapist Sex: Medicolegal Pitfalls," *Am. J. Psychiatry* 146:5 (May 1989): 597, 598–599)

Borderline Rage: These clients, when they feel thwarted or confronted, are given to intense, volcanic rage attacks that are so intimidating that therapists give in, through fear, to their inordinate demands and wishes. They are capable of vicious, violent, and vengeful behavior, including the filing of specious lawsuits.

Neediness and/or Dependency: These clients are needy and dependent. The difference is that borderlines manifest these features in the extreme. They often appear helpless and waif-like, appealing to the therapist's rescue fantasies. They wish the therapist to gratify *all* their needs, not merely the therapeutic ones. The therapist's countertransference response may be a reciprocal narcissistic fantasy: to be everything to the client.

Boundary Confusion: These clients cannot differentiate themselves from others. They perceive others not as independent humans with needs of their own, but rather as extensions of themselves and instrumentalities for gratifying their needs. Borderlines interpret the behavior of others only in terms of what it does or does not do for themselves. They long to merge with the therapist, fantasizing being made part of the therapist's idealized family or becoming his or her eternal lover.

Manipulativeness and Entitlement: Borderlines exhibit an intense narcissistic entitlement and sense of specialness, which they seem to seduce vulnerable therapists into sharing. There is a fascination about these people, which can result in a therapist's deviation from the standard of care notwithstanding an awareness that something is radically wrong. The countertransference seems to interfere with the therapist's judgment to the point of taking any self-protective measures, such as consultation.

Q. 5:77 Are there criminal implications for sexual misconduct?

Sexual misconduct is both tortious and criminal behavior. Masturbation and fellatio have been held to be aggravated felonious sexual assault when committed by a psychologist on a 14-year-old client. (*State v. Von Klock,* 433 A.2d 1299 (1981)) The use by the therapist of any sedative or tranquilizing medication to prevent the client from resisting sexual advances was the basis for a charge of rape against a physician. (*Ballard v. Superior Court,* 410 P.2d 838 (1966)) Sexual intercourse with a 16-year-old girl who had been referred for treatment of her promiscuity was held to be statutory rape. (*People v. Bernstein,* 340 P.2d 299 (1949))

Wisconsin, Michigan, and Minnesota make sexual activity with a psychotherapy patient a crime. (Wis. Stat. Ann. §940.22 (West Supp. 1984–1985); Mich. Stat. Ann. §28,285 (Callaghan 1981)) Other states are considering legislation to specifically criminalize such behavior. Some states (e.g., New Hampshire) still criminalize adultery, sodomy, and fornication. (N.H. Rev. Stat. Ann. §632-A:2 (VII) (Supp. 1983)) Many states have adopted Section 213(1)(2)(b) of the Model Penal Code, which characterizes sexual contact as rape when consent is defective and one "knows that she suffers from a mental disease or defect which renders her incapable of appraising the nature of her conduct."

Q. 5:78 What are the civil liability implications for sexual misconduct?

A client who claims injury by reason of a therapist's misconduct has several avenues of redress other than criminal prosecution. The client may sue for breach of contract. In *Anclote Manor v. Wilkinson*, 263 So.2d 256 (1972), a widower brought suit against a psychiatric hospital after his deceased former wife, who had filed for divorce while a patient there, committed suicide a year after discharge. A psychiatrist at the hospital had professed love for her and told her he would divorce his wife to marry her. The court awarded damages to the ex-husband for breach of contract, allowing recovery of all sums paid by him during the entire course of her treatment, on the theory that the physician's breach of contract destroyed the possibility of any benefit that could have been anticipated under skillful treatment in the first instance.

In *Zipkin v. Freeman* (436 S.W.2d 753 (1968)), the plaintiff was awarded damages for malpractice on the theory of mishandling of the transference. The behavior complained of included sexual relations. In *Roy v. Hartogs* (381 N.Y.S.2d 587 (1976)), sexual relations in the guise of therapy was held to be malpractice. (See also *Andrews v. United States*, 732 F.2d 366 (4th Cir. 1984) in which a professional working for a government-owned facility convinced a patient that having sex with him was therapy for depression.)

Q. 5:79 What are the elements of an action for sexual misconduct?

To sustain a case for sexual exploitation, a plaintiff must establish that the sexual activity:

- Was presented to the client as treatment;
- Took place in the context of therapy or as a consequence and outgrowth of the therapeutic relationship (unresolved transference); and
- Resulted in injury to the client (causation).

It is often difficult to prove damages in sexual exploitation cases, but injury to reputation, emotional deterioration, marital disruption, development or exacerbation of physical ailments, depression, anxiety, and suicidality are evidences of trauma. Causality may also be difficult to establish because it may be claimed that the client had problems before the sexual activities. To overcome these difficulties, sexual misconduct has been held to be malpractice per se; that is, no special damages need be proven to support a verdict, and no expert witness will be required to establish deviation from the standard of care. (*Omer v. Edgren*, 638 P.2d 635 (1984))

Q. 5:80 Is client consent a defense to an action for sexual misconduct?

One cannot consent to a crime, so in those states in which sexual exploitation of a therapy client is a criminal act, there is absolutely no question that consent is *not* a defense. In civil cases, the defense of consent has also been rejected, on the theory that transference makes consent impossible. "Inherent in the transference neurosis is the development of a strong dependence by the patient upon the analyst and an extraordinary faith and trust in him which may frequently develop into a love relationship and which can deprive the patient of her independent judgment and ability to distinguish the reality of her interaction with the analyst and vice versa." (*Decker v. Fink*, 422 A.2d 189 (1980))

Q. 5:81 Is it malpractice for a therapist to engage in sex with a client's significant other?

A sexual relationship with the spouse or significant other of a client is malpractice. Specifically, it has been held to be abandonment of the client. (*Mazza v. Huffaker*, 300 S.E.2d 833 (1983)) Other cases have allowed recovery on a general malpractice theory. For example, in *Horak v. Biris*, (474 N.E.2d 13 (1985)) malpractice was found when a therapist had an affair with a client's wife. In this instance, the therapist had initially been treating the wife and then requested the husband to enter in therapy. The wife eventually divorced the husband.

At least one court has found liability when the female therapist engaged in sexual relations with the lesbian lover of a client. (*Rowe v. Bennett*, 514 A.2d 802 (1986))

Q. 5:82 Does the spouse of a client with whom a therapist engages in sexual relations have a cause of action against the therapist?

In most of the cases in which a cause of action has been allowed by a spouse of a client with whom a therapist has engaged in sexual relations, the plaintiff spouse has also at one point been a client of the therapist. In *Anclote Manor v. Wilkinson* (263 So.2d 256 (1972)) damages were allowed to a nonclient husband on a breach-of-contract theory. Given an emerging trend to find liability against therapists for failing to protect third-party victims of their clients from foreseeable emotional distress (*Hedlund v. Superior Court of Orange County,* 669 P.2d 41 (1983)), it is logical for a court to use the same reasoning in finding that a wronged spouse has a cause of action.

Q. 5:83 Is sexual misconduct a basis for license discipline?

There have been numerous cases of license discipline, including revocation and suspension, of mental health and social service professionals found guilty of sexual misconduct with clients and patients. Licensing acts sometimes specifically prohibit sexual contact with clients; sometimes, the prohibition is against "moral turpitude," "unprofessional conduct," "dishonorable conduct," or some similar term. (See, e.g., *Bernstein v. Board of Medical Examiners,* 22 Cal.Rptr. 419 (1962); *Texas State Board of Medical Examiners v. Koepsel,* 322 S.W.2d 609 (1959); *Solloway v. Department of Professional Regulations,* 421 So.2d 573 (1982).)

Breach of Contract

Q. 5:84 What is a contract?

A contract is a mutual agreement between or among two or more competent parties, for valuable consideration, to do or not do a particular thing. Valuable consideration usually implies payment or exchange between parties. It is the basis of the therapist-client, employer-employee, and EAP-sponsor relationships, so contract principles will apply in determining the rights and responsibilities of the parties in any of these relationships. The law enforces contracts by either requiring specific performance or awarding damages. Specific performance is a remedy whereby a party is required by the court to perform the duties required by the contract. It cannot be used to require personal service (including therapy) under most circumstances, because of the constitutional ban against involuntary servitude. Damages are compensation for breach of contract or torts.

Q. 5:85 What is breach of contract?

Breach of contract is the failure, without legal excuse, to perform any promise that forms the whole or a part of a contract. A breach may be of express terms of the contract or of terms implied in law. In the EAP context, any act of the therapist that breaches his or her fiduciary duty to the client will be a breach of contract. Often, an act of malpractice is also a breach of implied warranty. Any behavior that makes it impossible for the purpose of the contract to be carried out is breach of the contract. (*Anclote Manor Foundation v. Wilkinson*, 263 So.2d 256 (1972))

Premises/Equipment Liability

Q. 5:86 What is premises liability?

Premises liability will result if a client or other business invitee is injured on EAP premises by reason of an unsafe condition. Examples are a ceiling that collapses and a broken stair or railing or a torn carpet that results in someone falling. Injuries caused by unsafe furniture or equipment will give rise to a cause of action for equipment liability.

Q. 5:87 Who bears the liability when a client or other person is injured as a result of a premises hazard?

Ordinarily, the entity having control over the premises will be liable for injuries resulting from unsafe conditions. If the EAP is owned and operated by the sponsor, the sponsor will be liable. An external EAP will bear liability for injuries on its premises. Common areas of a rental building that are in the control of the landlord, such as hallways, elevators, stairwells, and parking lots, are the landlord's responsibility. Some states make property owners liable for falls caused by ice or snow accumulation on parking lots, driveways, sidewalks, and stairs. Other states do not impose liability for injuries resulting from natural accumulation of precipitation unless an effort is made to clear it away. The theory behind this apparent contradiction is that property holders have no duty to clear the precipitation, but if they do so voluntarily, leading pedestrians or drivers to assume that the area is safe, the clearing must be adequate to prevent injury. Tenants may have little control over unsafe conditions in common areas, but if a business is aware that such conditions exist and does nothing to warn or protect its invitees, it seems logical to assume that liability may result.

Q. 5:88 Is the EAP liable if a client's children are hurt while waiting outside during a parent's appointment?

It is possible that the EAP will be held liable for injuries to children left unattended in the waiting room or grounds of the EAP. If the parent-client has any reason to assume that the children are being looked after by EAP personnel, such as a receptionist, and in fact this is not true, there is a strong probability that the EAP will be responsible. In some ways, having toys, books, and so forth for children in the waiting room is a tacit invitation to bring them to the session and leave them outside. If toys or other equipment are provided, they must be absolutely safe (that is, unbroken; free of sharp edges or loose screws, nails, or staples; fire resistant; and nontoxic). It is recommended that EAPs instruct clients not to bring their children unless someone will be specifically responsible for babysitting. If a client arrives with young children and there is no one to tend them, they should be included in the session and not left alone.

Example 1. The six-year-old child of a client was playing in the waiting room with a wooden toy. A staple worked loose, and the child swallowed it. It lodged in one of her bronchi, necessitating surgery. The client sued the EAP and the therapist. The EAP sued the store that sold the toy and the manufacturer's representative. The manufacturer was in Japan and not subject to the jurisdiction of the state court.

Example 2. A teen-aged client became frustrated with a vending machine on the EAP premises. Someone nearby told him that the machine always gave trouble, and that he should shake it to make it work. The lad shook and rocked the machine, whereupon it toppled onto him, causing serious injuries. His parents sued the EAP. The EAP's insurance company asserted the defenses of contributory negligence and assumption of risk. The court held that the EAP knew of the recalcitrant machine, that people regularly shook and rocked it to make it work, that teenagers have a particular propensity for such behavior, and that the lad's injuries were therefore foreseeable. It rejected the EAP's defenses on the basis of the client's age and the nature of the EAP-client relationship.

Q. 5:89 What can an EAP do to insulate itself from premises/equipment liability?

The premises lease should provide for maintenance and repairs; either the EAP should be responsible and therefore able to control safety conditions, or the landlord should be clearly responsible. If it can be negotiated, the best arrangement is a clause giving the EAP the power to make necessary repairs at the landlord's expense. Such a clause would provide for notice to the landlord and give the EAP power to act either in an immediate emergency or if the landlord does not act within a reasonable time. Unfortunately, many landlords will not agree to this sort of flexibility. A fall-back position would be a clause requiring the landlord to indemnify and hold the EAP harmless for any liability arising out of the landlord's failure to maintain and repair. Every business should be adequately insured for liability, with malpractice and premises liability policies coordinated.

Q. 5:90 What are the liability risks of transporting clients in an EAP staff member's car?

Some EAPs have policies forbidding staff members to transport clients in their private cars. If a staff member disobeys this policy and an accident that injurs a client occurs, the EAP should theoretically not be liable. Courts have been known, however, to take the positions that the EAP should have better control over its employees, that the injuries would not have occurred to the client except as a concomitant to the EAP relationship, and that the EAP should thus be responsible for the damages. A strategy for impressing upon EAP employees the folly of disobeying a policy against transporting clients is a requirement that the employees sign an indemnification and hold harmless agreement, protecting the EAP and the sponsor from the consequences of deviating from rules, procedures, and policies. When transporting clients is part of a counselor's work, both the counselor and the EAP will be responsible for any injury arising out of negligence in the transportation. EAP staff should be required to provide the EAP with proof of insurance that will cover injuries to clients in staff members' cars.

Defenses Against Lawsuits

Q. 5:91 How does one defend against a professional liability action?

When a lawsuit is filed, the defendant's attorney first looks for any legal theory that might cause the case to be immediately dismissed. If there is none, the attorney then determines whether the lawsuit as brought, meets the legal criteria upon which a remedy can be based: Does the plaintiff's complaint state a cause of action against the defendant? If it does not, and the plaintiff cannot amend the complaint to make it sufficient, the suit will be dismissed at that point. If the suit seems to be based on sufficient and proper legal grounds, it goes to trial and the plaintiff presents his or her evidence. The plaintiff has the legal burden of establishing by competent evidence all of the elements of the cause of action upon which he or she is suing. Failure to meet that burden will result in the case being dismissed at the close of the plaintiff's presentation. If the plaintiff meets the burden, the defendant must then interpose his or her legal defenses. Defenses to a malpractice claim include: denial ("I did not do what I am accused of, or I did what he says I did, but it was not wrongful"); lack of duty ("he was not my client"); contributory or comparative negligence; assumption of risk; expiration of the statute of limitations; and immunity. (See Qs. 5:92 and 5:96.)

Q. 5:92 What is the statute of limitations, and how does it work?

Every state has a statute of limitations, which bars the bringing of a lawsuit more than a specified time after the incident upon which the case is based. Some states take the position that the statute of limitations for a malpractice case begins to run when the cause of action accrues—that is when there has been an actual injury sustained by the plaintiff (the so-called time-of-damage rule), whether or not the plaintiff was aware of the injury at the time. Some other states take the position that the statute begins to run when the treatment relationship ends, regardless of whether the patient or client has discovered the injury at that time. Most states have adopted the time-of-discovery rule—the statute begins to run when a reasonable person would have discovered the injury. These states may put an outside cap on the time of discovery; for example, two years after a reasonable person would have discovered the injury, but no more than four years after the date of the actual occurrence. The period of time within which a suit may be brought varies from state to state, so every EAP and professional must check with local counsel.

Q. 5:93 Is there any situation that will stop a statute of limitations from running?

A statute of limitations is tolled (stopped temporarily) during the period of a plaintiff's minority (the client is under 18 years of age) or other incapacity (the client is adjudicated incompetent), or while the malpractice is being fraudulently concealed.

> **Example.** The client was 16 years old at the time the alleged negligent misdiagnosis and treatment occurred. The limitation period in his state is 2 years after the malpractice occurs or 2 years after a minor plaintiff has reached majority, whichever is later. The suit will not be barred by the statute of limitations until the client's twentieth birthday.

Q. 5:94 What is the implication of the statute of limitations for retention of client records?

A good clinical record is the best defense tool a clinician has in defending a malpractice suit. Records should, therefore, be retained until the limitation period has passed, taking the matter of a client's minority into consideration.

Q. 5:95 Are there circumstances in which a clinician is immune from suit?

There are a few situations in which a clinician is immune from suit. At common law, a government cannot be sued unless it agrees; this is called sovereign immunity. Thus there are numerous suits on the record in which a plaintiff has been unable to recover damages in spite of clear evidence of fault because, for example, the treatment was rendered by a state hospital. Because Congress enacted the Federal Tort Claims Act, which permits the United States to be sued under certain circumstances, there are many cases against the Veterans' Administration, many of which have been landmark cases that created legal precedents in malpractice law.

Charitable institutions were also immune from suit under common law, but most states have enacted statutes eliminating or modifying this concept in the case of hospitals, mental health centers, and the like that have or can obtain insurance.

Mandated reporters who make good-faith reports are immunized from suit under most child abuse reporting acts and similar statutes; public officials acting in their official capacity are also immune.

Q. 5:96 What are affirmative defenses to malpractice actions?

Affirmative defenses are defenses by reason of which, assuming the facts stated in the plaintiff's complaint to be true, the defendant will be shielded from liability. In malpractice suits, the common affirmative defenses are:

Assumption of Risk: The plaintiff has knowledge of facts constituting a dangerous condition, knows and appreciates the danger, and voluntarily exposes himself or herself to it.

> **Example.** The client is a chronic-stage alcoholic. His wife leaves him and files for divorce. He decides he is going to stop drinking "cold turkey," and asks for two weeks' leave from work to detoxify himself. The EAP counselor warns him strongly that this should be done in a hospital, describing in graphic detail the dangers of delirium tremens. The client refuses hospitalization, stating that if he cannot beat this on his own, he would rather die and get it over with. There is no legal basis on which he can be forced into a hospital, and there is nothing the counselor can do to change his mind. The counselor asks permission to discuss the matter with the client's wife and adult children, but the client refuses and threatens to sue the therapist if he discloses. The EAP is not subject to the federal regulations on confidentiality of alcohol and drug abuse treatment, and there is no state law under which one can petition a court for leave to disclose. The counselor decides that he would rather be sued for breach of confidentiality than be morally responsible for the death of a client. He informs the client's estranged wife, who refuses to get involved. He also informs the client's adult son, who says that his father is a surly

and stubborn man who has never listened and never will, and he does not think there is anything he can do.

The client has assumed the risk of detoxifying on his own; neither he nor his family will have a viable cause of action against the EAP or counselor for the consequences of the client's decision, as long as the counselor has done all that a reasonable professional in his situation would do.

Contributory Negligence: The plaintiff commits an act or omission amounting to want of ordinary care; this act, in concurrence with the defendant's negligence, is a proximate cause of the plaintiff's injury. The law imposes a duty on persons to protect themselves from injury; if a person fails to do so, his or her own negligence is a complete bar to recovery of damages from the defendant. In most states, contributory negligence has been replaced by comparative negligence.

Comparative Negligence: Under this doctrine, negligence is measured in terms of percentages. Any damages allowed to the plaintiff for the negligence of the defendant will be diminished in proportion to the amount of negligence attributable to the plaintiff, as long as the plaintiff's negligence is less than the defendant's and the plaintiff could not have avoided the consequences of the defendant's negligence by exercising due care to protect himself or herself.

Example. The client suffers from alcoholism and manic-depressive illness. He is being managed for his affective disorder by a psychiatrist to whom he was referred by the EAP, and is also being followed by the EAP. He has been warned repeatedly by the EAP counselor and the psychiatrist not to drink while taking lithium. He relapses and has a couple of whiskeys—ordinarily not enough to faze him—and then has an auto crash in which he is seriously injured and the other driver is killed. The client's own negligence in drinking and driving while taking lithium effectively eliminates any cause of action he might have thought he had against his treaters.

Immunity: By law, certain persons or institutions may be immune from lawsuits, regardless of whether they could be held accountable for their actions if not for immunity. Examples of immunity are sovereign (government) immunity, diplomatic immunity, or statutory immunity (see Q. 5:95).

Chapter 6

Malpractice Liability Stemming From Common Clinical Problems

EAPs deal with the same clinical areas that any mental health or social service program handles, but problems related to substance abuse are their major area of concentration. This chapter discusses specific problems and related legal issues and risks that are of particular interest to EAPs and their sponsors: alcoholism, mental impairment, personality disorders, suicide, and dangerousness. Liability in these instances falls under the category of malpractice.

Alcoholism

Q. 6:1 What are "primary," "secondary," and "familial" alcoholism?

Primary alcoholism is a chronic disease of uncertain etiology that has genetic, biological, chemical, and psychological aspects. Its major symptom is loss of control over alcohol or other mood-altering chemicals. It is treatable, but it is thought to be incurable; that is, the symptoms can be controlled, but the alcoholic will never be able to drink without relapsing into addiction.

Secondary or *reactive alcoholism* is an effect, result, or concomitant of another condition—a psychiatric illness or psychological problem, such as depression—in which the sufferer "self-medicates" with alcohol to relieve the symptoms of the primary, underlying illness and becomes addicted. Theoretically, if the primary illness is successfully treated, the secondary alcoholism clears up. (J. Kinney and G. Leaton, *Loosening the Grip* (St. Louis: 1987), 66) Some authorities believe that there is no such thing as secondary alcoholism, that it is useless to treat other symptoms until the addiction is brought under control, and that once that occurs, other problems will clear up. Between these two poles are innumerable permutations and combined theories. Most treaters agree that some form of lifelong attention to the condition is necessary, whether through Alcoholics Anonymous, psychotherapy, or both.

Familial alcoholism is a form of the disease marked by a family history of alcoholism, an earlier age of onset, and more severe symptoms requiring earlier treatment than primary or secondary alcoholism; it is not marked by an increased presence of other psychiatric disorders. (E. Jellinek, *The Disease Concept of Alcoholism* (New Haven: 1960))

Q. 6:2 What special legal risks does alcoholism create for EAPs?

Not all physicians or psychotherapists are trained to recognize substance abuse. There are numerous stories of patients and clients who have been treated for various complaints over a period of years without being asked if they drink or abuse drugs. Negligent failure to diagnose and treat substance abuse will place a treater at risk for lawsuit from the client and, in some jurisdictions, from a victim of an intoxicated client. Not only the client, but also his or her victim and their respective spouses or survivors, might have a cause of action if the intoxicated client has damaged property or caused personal injury or death to a third person as a direct result of substance abuse. On the other hand, if the EAP counselor assumes that the client's physical symptoms are "just alcoholism," and the client relies on this "diagnosis" and neglects to see a physician about a cough that is actually caused by lung cancer, there are grounds for a lawsuit for malpractice and breach of the implied warranties of competence and due care. (*Johnson v. Borland*, 26 N.W.2d 755 (Mich. 1947)) Nonphysician therapists who diagnose and treat physical symptoms by psychotherapy have also been charged with the unauthorized practice of medicine!

Q. 6:3 What is the common course of alcoholism?

Alcoholism is said to be a progressive disease in which symptoms appear to develop in a definite pattern. There are four phases of alcoholism. (E. Jellinek, *The Disease Concept of Alcoholism* (New Haven: 1960); J. Kinney and G. Leaton, *Loosening the Grip* (St. Louis: 1987))

Prealcoholic: Social drinking that leads the drinker to experience tension relief in the drinking situation. When the drinker becomes aware of this, he or she deliberately uses drinking as a stress-reduction device. An increase in tolerance occurs over time. This phase can last from a few months to more than two years.

Prodromal: Drinking marked by sudden onset of blackouts—"alcoholic palimpsests"—during which the drinker appears to be functioning normally but later cannot remember anything that happened. The drinker begins sneaking drinks, gulping the first drinks, and experiencing guilt about his or her drinking. It begins to be difficult for the drinker to act normally. This phase can last from six months to four or five years.

Crucial: Drinking marked by loss of control; the drinker can control whether or not to take the first drink, but once that is taken, the drinker cannot control the amount that will be drunk. The drinker must now account for his or her behavior, and so starts to rationalize and begin a series of unsuccessful strategies to regain control (for example, abstinence for a time, change of drinking patterns, job, or location). He or she alternates among resentment, remorse, and aggressiveness. Family and social life deteriorate. Morning drinking may begin, and alcohol-related hospitalization may occur. Drinker can probably maintain job and social position, but not without effort.

Chronic: Daily, daylong intoxication begins early in the day. The drinker binges more often and begins to frequent "dives" and have questionable associates. Social position and general functioning deteriorate. Alcohol craving is so great that he or she will drink anything. Tolerance drops dramatically; the drinker becomes stuporous after a few drinks. Tremors and paranoia develop. The drinker's rationalization system fails, and he or she is spontaneously ready for treatment.

Q. 6:4 What symptoms should trigger inquiry into alcohol use?

Every individual is unique, of course, but a constellation of traits and symptoms should indicate to the duly careful, competent EAP professional that substance abuse should be explored: mood swings, rationalization, denial, memory distortion, projection (putting the blame on others or assigning one's own negative feelings to others), decreased self-esteem, paranoid ideation, deteriorating functioning, undependability, family disruption, deterioration of relationships, and sexual dysfunction. Job troubles often develop long after other areas of life have deteriorated. The problem is that any one or several of these symptoms are also symptoms of other psychosocial or psychiatric problems, so differential diagnosis is essential. A serious issue in the substance abuse treatment community is the fact that many substance abuse care providers are trained in alcoholism and drug addiction only and are not competent to recognize other pathology. Misdiagnosis and consequent liability are risks.

Q. 6:5 What are the diagnostic criteria for substance abuse?

Substance abuse is a maladaptive pattern of use of a psychoactive substance when the user has a persistent or recurrent social, occupational, or physical problem caused by the substance, or uses it under dangerous conditions (for example, operating machinery). The symptoms are either recurrent or have lasted at least a month, but the sufferer is not an addict.

Q. 6:6 What are common organic factors in alcoholism and drug abuse?

Alcoholism frequently causes serious physical problems, including persistent cough, headaches, malnutrition and its consequences, heart and liver disease, impaired vision, periodontal disease, pancreatitis, hypertension, convulsive disorders, chronic gastritis, and organic brain syndrome. Some research suggests that alcohol increases cancer risk by enhancing the effect of other carcinogens. Little research has been done on the synergistic effect of alcohol with industrial toxins, but some studies suggest that alcohol increases the danger of deleterious effects from certain chemicals commonly used in industry. (Godard, "Alcohol and Occupation," in *Alcohol Problems in Employment* (1981)) In addition to causing illness, alcohol is implicated in accidents causing serious, often fatal, injuries: 5.7 million cases of family violence and 50% of all fires and deaths from falling are directly related to alcohol. Fetal alcohol syndrome is the third leading cause of birth defects. Alcoholism and drug abuse can masquerade as numerous other problems and, undiagnosed, can exacerbate other physical conditions.

Q. 6:7 What is withdrawal?

Withdrawal is the cluster of symptoms that occur after a drug that causes physical dependence is no longer being taken. There are two types of withdrawal; morphine type and alcohol-barbiturate type. Unlike morphine withdrawal, which is not life-threatening and can be accomplished without too much difficulty, alcohol-barbiturate withdrawal is intense and risky. Withdrawal from alcohol dependence has a mortality rate of up to 25% without medical treatment. Hospitalization for 10 to 21 days is necessary to withdraw safely. The initial symptoms of alcohol withdrawal are severe muscle tremors, nausea, weakness, and anxiety. Untreated, alcohol-barbiturate withdrawal can cause severe convulsions and cardiovascular collapse.

Alcohol hallucinosis occurs in 25% of cases, usually within 24 hours of the last drink. The client will experience true auditory and visual hallucinations, illusions, misperceptions or misinterpretation of real environmental stimuli, and horrible nightmares. Because the client believes that the hallucinations are real, he or she is at considerable risk for acting on them, and doing harm to himself or herself or others. Appropriate treatment includes observation in a safe environment. If this condition persists for more than two or three days, antipsychotic medication may be needed.

Delirium tremens (DTs) is the most serious form of alcohol withdrawal syndrome. Even with modern treatment, there is a 1% to 2% mortality rate. The client will experience hallucinations, confusion, disorientation, and mounting attacks of anxiety, accompanied by heightened autonomic nervous activity, marked tremulousness and agitation, elevated blood pressure, and fever. Sedation is required to counteract the agitation, fluid loss, infections, and respiratory problems. There is no sure way to predict who will go into DTs, but there is a profile of most likely candidates: a daily drinker who has consumed over a fifth a day for at least a week prior to abstinence and has been a heavy drinker for 10 years or more.

(J. Kinney and G. Leaton, *Loosening the Grip* (St. Louis: 1987), 142; W. Witter and P. Venturelli, *Drugs and Society,* 2d ed. (Boston: 1988))

Q. 6:8 What legal risks to the therapist accompany withdrawal?

Because alcohol-barbiturate withdrawal is life-threatening, it should always take place in a hospital under skilled medical care. There have been cases in which well-meaning family members or friends or "amateur drug counselors" have undertaken to withdraw alcoholics or addicts with fatal results. A closet alcoholic is at considerable risk when, for example, he or she requires hospitalization or surgery for a medical condition and the attending physician is unaware of the addiction. A secret addict who goes on a family wilderness camping trip intending to just sweat it out may end up in acute withdrawal with the family totally unaware of the situation and the care that will have to be provided. The EAP professional is at risk for liability if he or she has failed to intervene appropriately when a client is contemplating self-withdrawal or embarking on an activity or adventure that could be fatal.

Q. 6:9 What are the common indications that inpatient care is required?

Therapist liability arises from negligent diagnosis and negligent treatment. It is not always easy to know which of several treatment choices to recommend, so that in today's litigious climate, there may be a tendency to overtreat as a risk-management strategy. The following factors are considered indicators for hospitalization:

- History of previous outpatient treatment;
- Potential for withdrawal problems;
- Medical problems;
- Lack of social or family support; and
- Ambivalence about undergoing treatment.

Clients who are first-timers with good family and social support, no medical complications, little risk of withdrawal, and a recognition of need for treatment are good candidates for outpatient care. Informed consent to the treatment choice is mandatory. This requires a thorough discussion with the client of the foreseeable risks of refusal of treatment and the various treatment alternatives (including impact on career, family situation, pending or potential legal problems of the client, and so forth).

Q. 6:10 What are the legal implications of inpatient treatment?

Even when the therapist is absolutely certain that inpatient care is the treatment of choice, it must be recognized that such treatment may have legal or political implications for the client. The client's professional license may be in jeopardy, for example. Some states have a prohibition against issuing a firearms license to persons who have been hospitalized for psychiatric disturbances; an intrepid hunter might find himself unwittingly deprived of his major source of recreational satisfaction. There may also be a negative impact on insurability.

Obviously, the risks of refusal of inpatient care may be far greater than the risks of accepting it, or may be far less than the benefits to be gained by it. Concern for the possible negative implications of inpatient care for one's career, a custody dispute, or security clearance may move some clients to agree to hospitalization in a setting far from home. For some clients in sensitive positions, this option may be the least detrimental alternative, although family involvement in the treatment is obviously hampered by such a choice. Some clients prefer to fund their inpatient treatment privately rather than using insurance benefits; they do not want a permanent record in the insurance companies' data banks that may be accessed at a later date.

Because denial is common among substance abusers, it is easy for a counselor to label as such a client's real concerns about the ramifications of inpatient care. This must be assessed and explored, of course, keeping in mind that a therapist's misplaced "religious zeal" can have tragic consequences for a vulnerable client, and creativity can sometimes produce viable alternatives to what might ordinarily appear to be the "only correct treatment approach." An assessment of risk-benefit ratio, taking into account all the facts, is part of the informed consent process.

Q. 6:11 What are the legal risks of family and group treatment?

Conjoint couple, family, and group therapy are commonly used in substance abuse treatment. There are legal ramifications, however, that should be taken into account in using these modalities. For a client who has legal problems of any kind, and especially for someone involved in litigation, couple, family, or group therapy may not be a good option. Most states, and the federal government, have privilege laws that protect the content of psychotherapy and counseling treatment from discovery in judicial proceedings.

But privilege laws vary widely and dramatically, and some do not protect therapy communications made in the presence of third parties, even those involved in the treatment. The presence of anyone other than a therapist is said to "pollute" the privilege. In some states, there is a spousal privilege, wherein one spouse cannot be required to give testimony against another, but there are numerous exceptions to this, so even marital therapy may be risky in some situations. It is absolutely mandatory that every counselor and therapist be thoroughly grounded in the confidentiality and privilege laws of his or her state. This is often an extremely complex matter, and expert legal consultation should be used in any situation in which a client is at legal risk. (See also Ch. 4, "Confidentiality Requirements.")

Q. 6:12 What are the common symptoms of employee alcohol abuse?

The common symptoms of employee alcohol abuse include:

- Chronic absenteeism (especially notable after weekends and holidays) and partial absences;
- Unexplained changes in behavior; and
- Uneven work pace (for example, lowered productivity, accidents and mistakes, lost time from accidents, lying, avoiding supervisors and co-workers, on-the-job drinking).

Q. 6:13 Are there occupational risk factors in certain work settings for the employee with an alcohol problem?

Yes. Alcohol and work have a peculiar ambivalent relationship. Alcohol use has been expected in connection with employment—the office party, company picnic, customer entertainment, commuter train bar car, martini lunches, celebration drinking, and after-work "happy hours," to name a few. Commonly, however, work rules prohibit on-the-job drug or alcohol use. Whether or not alcohol is apparently part of the culture of a given workplace, there are occupational hazards for persons susceptible to alcoholism or drug abuse that should be taken into account in job placement for those individuals.

An EAP professional who is aware of an existing or incipient substance abuse problem may be faced with a dilemma when promotion or transfer is an issue or possible solution to an employee's problem. Some types of jobs are just not suitable for some types of employees. The EAP counselor's role in such cases may be unclear, posing possible legal, moral, and ethical dilemmas. Whose interests must be served? Who decides what those interests are? A review of such ethical positions as self-determination of the client in light of legal duties to warn and protect may present a framework for attacking the dilemma, even if it does not reveal a solution. Consultation is indicated as a risk-avoidance maneuver.

Q. 6:14 What specific work factors can exacerbate a substance abuse problem?

Employment factors exacerbating substance abuse include:

- Absence of clear career goals;
- Lack of supervision on the job;
- Job isolation, low visibility, and freedom to set one's own work hours and work sites;
- Lack of job structure (for example, sales representatives working away from the business place);
- Work addiction;
- Occupational obsolescence (common in technical and scientific fields);
- Change in work status;
- "Required" job-related drinking (entertaining customers);
- Reduction of social controls;
- Severe role stress;

- Competitive pressure; and
- Presence of illegal drug users (less an issue for alcohol abusers).

(J. Kinney and G. Leaton, *Loosening the Grip* (St. Louis: 1987), 221)

Q. 6:15 Are there risks for the recovering alcoholic working as an EAP professional?

A major risk for the recovering substance abuser working in an EAP is the problem of maintaining objective neutrality with clients and avoiding conflicts of interest. For example, EAP staff members who attend AA meetings with their clients will find themselves supporting the clients rather than taking care of themselves. They run the risk of talking about their cases or clients in meetings, which not only breaches client confidentiality, but also damages the integrity of the treatment process in general (listeners may think, "I don't want any counselor talking about my case that way in some other AA meeting."). Conversely, they run the risk of making disclosures at work of information gained at AA about clients or co-workers. The "specialness" of being a substance abuse counselor may also work to distance one from other AA members and create feelings of low self-esteem or resentment in the others. There is a distinct problem of boundary breakdown unless the recovering EAP professional scrupulously separates his or her work life and private life.

Mental Impairment

Q. 6:16 What are some malpractice-prevention techniques when working with mentally impaired clients?

If possible, the client's significant others should be brought into the treatment-planning process. Although the client (or client's legal guardian, if he or she has been adjudicated incompetent) is usually the only one with legal power to give a valid consent to treatment, if the family has been informed and involved in the decision making, they are less likely to take legal action against the therapist.

The informed consent process should always be well-documented. Some therapists audiotape or videotape consent sessions when there is a possibility of a later claim of lack of informed consent. The client's chart should reflect who was there, what part each played, and an overview of the information conveyed. Informed consent should be dynamic and ongoing, because the client's condition changes during treatment. Consent issues should be thoroughly recorded, and any changes in the treatment contract documented.

Written information, such as one of the many excellent popular books that therapists use as part of the client/family education process, may be given to the client and his or her relatives. The EAP may purchase or develop its own handouts with information about the program, the condition for which the client will be treated, the proposed treatment, and any other information relevant to the decisions to be made. Written material should be carefully reviewed by legal counsel before being used with clients. A written disclaimer should accompany any written material, making it clear to the reader that every therapy experience is unique, and the material is meant to inform generally, not to make warranties or guarantees.

Q. 6:17 What are the legal ramifications of treating a client whose cognition and judgment are impaired?

Substance abuse is a likely culprit in cognitive impairment, but it is not the only possible cause. Anxiety, depression, malnutrition, fatigue, and physical or mental illness can all affect one's capacity to understand and process data and interfere with judgment and decision making. Psychotherapy and substance abuse treatment often (perhaps always) produce anxiety and psychic pain on the way to positive change; not infrequently, clients have periods of regression and temporary negative behavioral change. Relationships with significant others (particularly codependents) will be disrupted, for better or worse. It is not, therefore, surprising that clients and their significant others sometimes scapegoat the treater.

Because the acutely distressed client probably cannot be expected to consent to treatment in a fully independent and reasoned manner, the matter of informed consent is both extremely important and difficult to manage. The law that requires that a therapist ordinarily obtain informed consent before treating a client protects both the client and the therapist. If a client's judgment and memory are impaired, he or she may genuinely not remember the information conveyed by the therapist in obtaining consent to treat, and a lawsuit may ensue.

Personality Disorders

Q. 6:18 Which clients are most likely to present legal issues to an EAP?

The clients who are the most difficult to manage therapeutically and, therefore, the most likely to create liability for the therapist are those with certain personality disorders (also known as character disorders), as described in the Diagnostic and Statistical Manual of Mental Disorders (DSM III-R). (Washington, D.C.: American Psychiatric Association, 1987)) Differential diagnosis of personality disorders is often difficult, because the symptoms often mimic those of other mental disorders, and clients rarely fit a specific mold.

Q. 6:19 What is a personality disorder?

Personality traits are enduring patterns of perceiving, relating to, and thinking about the environment and oneself and are exhibited in a wide range of important social and personal contexts. When personality traits become inflexible and maladaptive and cause either significant functional impairment or subjective stress, they constitute personality disorder. Many features of personality disorders may be manifested during an episode of another mental disorder, so the diagnosis of personality disorder is made only when the characteristic features are typical of the person's long-term functioning and are not limited to discrete episodes of illness. (DSM III-R, 335)

Q. 6:20 Which personality disorders are the most difficult to manage therapeutically?

Antisocial personality disorder, borderline personality disorder, and narcissistic personality disorder are notoriously difficult to manage. Substance abuse is often, but not always, associated with a personality disorder.

Q. 6:21 What are the features of the antisocial personality disorder?

The terms "sociopath" or "psychopath" were formerly used to describe persons with the antisocial personality disorder (APDs). APDs have a lifelong pattern of irresponsible and antisocial behavior, commencing during childhood, when this pattern is known as a conduct disorder. APDs do not conform to social norms and repeatedly perform antisocial acts, such as using violence, lying, destroying property, stealing, harassing others, having an illegal occupation, cheating, and/or failing to pay their bills; they are unable to function as parents or plan ahead and cannot sustain consistent work behavior. APDs tend to be irritable and aggressive, abuse spouses and children, and have a reckless disregard for personal safety. (They frequently speed or drive while intoxicated.) They are typically promiscuous (unable to sustain a monogamous relationship for over a year), generally have no remorse about the effects of their behavior on others, and may even feel justified in having hurt or mistreated others. After age 30, the more flagrant antisocial behavior (sexual promiscuity, fighting, and criminality) may diminish. (DSM III-R, 342)

Q. 6:22 What are the features of the borderline personality disorder?

Borderlines exhibit a pervasive pattern of instability of self-image, interpersonal relationships, and mood. Almost invariably, they show marked, pervasive, and persistent identity disturbance, manifested by uncertainty about several life issues, such as self-image, sexual orientation, long-term goals or career choice, types of friends or lovers, and values. They frequently complain of feelings of emptiness or boredom. They have unstable and intense personal relationships, often characterized by alternation of extremes of idealization and devaluation. They cannot tolerate being alone, and will make frantic efforts to avoid real or imagined abandonment.

Affect (mood) instability is common, evidenced by marked, rapid mood shifts, inappropriately intense and recurrent anger, and physical fights. They tend to be impulsive, particularly in self-damaging behavior such as shopping sprees, substance abuse, reckless driving, casual sex, shoplifting, and binge eating.

Recurrent suicidal threats and gestures and other self-mutilating behavior are common in severe cases. This behavior may be used to manipulate others, or may be the result of intense anger or feelings of "numbness" and depersonalization that arise in periods of stress.

This disorder is frequently accompanied by many features of other personality disorders. Such clients often swing between dependency and self-assertion and exhibit a social contrariness and pessimistic outlook. Social and occupational functioning are often severely impaired. (DSM III-R, 346–347)

Q. 6:23 What are the features of the narcissistic personality disorder?

Persons suffering from the narcissistic personality disorder (NPDs) exhibit a pervasive pattern of grandiosity (in fantasy or behavior), hypersensitivity to the evaluation of others, and lack of empathy (inability to recognize and experience how others are feeling). They have an exaggerated sense of self-importance, often alternating with feelings of special unworthiness. They tend to exaggerate their accomplishments and talents, and expect to be noticed as "special," even without appropriate achievement. They feel that their problems are unique and can be understood only by other special people.

NPDs are preoccupied with fantasies of unlimited power, success, wealth, brilliance, beauty, or ideal love, and have chronic feelings of envy for those they perceive as more successful than they. The fantasies often substitute for realistic activity, but when they do actively pursue their goals, it is with a driven, pleasureless quality.

Self-esteem of NPDs is very fragile; they are often preoccupied with performance and how others regard them. They are frequently exhibitionistic, needing constant admiration and gratification. They can be extremely charming, but respond to criticism or confrontation with intense rage, shame, or humiliation (often masked as cool indifference).

Interpersonal relationships of NPDs are invariably disturbed. They have a sense of entitlement and an unreasonable expectation that they will receive special treatment. They are interpersonally exploitive, taking advantage of others to achieve their own ends or for self-aggrandizement. Friendships are made based on how they might profit from others. In romantic relationships, the partner is treated as an object to be used to bolster the person's self-esteem. Features of other personality disorders are often associated with that of NPDs. (DSM III-R, 349–350)

Q. 6:24 What are the legal problems that personality disorders bring to the EAP?

Borderlines are often difficult to diagnose, because they can make a good impression and often sustain this for a considerable period of time. (R. Simon, *Clinical Psychiatry and the Law* (Washington, D.C., 1987), 204–213) They can regress with frightening rapidity; indulge in outrageous and dangerous acting-out behavior; and provoke intense countertransference reactions, such as abandonment and other ill-advised behavior on the part of the therapist, to which they are likely to respond in outrage with malpractice suits for failure to prevent them from harming themselves or others. They are particularly risky to therapists who are in any way vulnerable to sexual seduction or other boundary violations, and account for a majority of sexual misconduct charges (genuine and false) against therapists. (T. Gutheil, "Borderline Personality Disorder, Boundary Violations, and Patient-Therapist Sex: Medicolegal Pitfalls," *Am. J. Psychiatry* 146 (May 1989):597–602)

Example. A hospital-based EAP professional treated a female health professional for substance abuse, work difficulties, depression, and anxiety. The therapist lived a few blocks from the client. The client took to walking by when the therapist was gardening and insisted upon helping—despite the therapist's protestations—and began to attend the therapist's church. The therapist recognized the client's neediness, felt sorry for her, and felt that modeling social behavior would be useful. One day, the client became aware that the therapist was planning a birthday party for her young daughter and begged to be allowed to attend so that she "could see how a real, normal family behaves." Over her own misgivings, the therapist allowed the client to attend. Some weeks later, as the client's own birthday approached, she became increasingly agitated, saying that if no one took her out to dinner for her birthday, she would commit suicide. The night before her birthday, she telephoned the therapist at 3 a.m. saying she had intravenous equipment and poison that would act immediately, and she planned to use it. The therapist calmed her down, secured a no-suicide promise—and agreed to take her out to dinner the next night with a neighbor known to both of them.

The midnight calls continued for a time, until the therapist and her family became distraught. The therapist felt that medication was necessary to control the client's behavior and attempted to transfer the client to a psychiatrist. The client responded with a drug overdose and a complaint to the ethics committee of the therapist's professional association, charging her with breach of confidentiality, abandonment, and dual relationship. The ethics board found the therapist guilty as charged, suspended her for six months, and required her to be supervised for two years.

Q. 6:25 What preventive measures can an EAP take to minimize legal risk from personality-disordered clients?

Policies and procedures should clearly prohibit any behavior between therapist and client that could be construed as a breakdown of the professional relationship boundary. Social contact with present or former clients should be forbidden, with exceptions allowed only after permission is given by a supervisor or when agreed to by a consultant. Clinical recording for these cases must be particularly careful, clearly revealing the reasoning behind treatment decisions and demonstrating that there was no deviation from the standard of care. When a client shows symptoms of a severe personality disorder, supervision or consultation should be the rule, not the exception. An EAP therapist who is not experienced in dealing with such clients, or cannot devote sufficient time to them, should refer them elsewhere.

Suicide

Q. 6:26 Is the risk of suicide a particular issue for EAPs?

EAPs see a large number of alcoholics and other substance abusers. This population is at much higher risk for suicide than the general population. The risk of suicide in the general population is 10–15 per 100,000; 70%–90% of suicides are committed by people with major psychiatric disorders, including substance abuse. *Psychiatric Diagnosis and Therapy '88/'89*, J. Flaherty, R. Channon, and J. Davis, eds. (Appleton and Lange, Norwalk, CN, San Mateo, CA: 1988) 50–51, 169) Between 1970 and 1980, there were at least 30,000 suicide attempts each year. There is one successful suicide every 20 minutes in the United States; alcohol is involved in 25%–35% of suicides and 50%–70% of all homicides. Suicide is a known risk of alcoholism and, therefore, must be a known risk in the EAP client population. Once alcoholism is a known factor for a client, the issue of suicidal impulses must be explored, particularly if the client is in crisis.

Q. 6:27 Can an EAP be held liable for a client's suicide?

Courts have been slow to impose liability for failure to control the behavior of outpatients. There will be liability, however, if a therapist has failed to meet the standard of care for predicting suicidal impulses or controlling the client's behavior; that is, if it can be shown that negligent misdiagnosis or negligent treatment was the proximate cause of the client's suicide. (*Lange v. United States,* 179 F. Supp. 777 (N.D. N.Y. 1960)) Under the theory of *respondeat superior,* the EAP will also be liable. If negligent supervision has played a part in the tragedy, the supervisor may be held liable, as well.

> **Example.** A client is brought to the EAP office by his supervisor for an emergency appointment. The supervisor is concerned about him because his wife left him following the death of their teenaged son in an auto crash, he has just been fired for drinking on the job, and he has said that he has nothing more to live for and plans to take his own life. The client appears depressed and despairing, and admits to suicidal ideation and a suicide plan. The counselor decides that the client is being melodramatic, tells him to "brace up" and realize that the firing was his own fault for failing to follow the counselor's previous advice to go into a treatment center, and makes an appointment for him to come back the next day to meet with the consulting psychiatrist. The client goes home and immediately carries out the plan he described to the counselor. The widow sues for wrongful death and malpractice, with negligent diagnosis and negligent treatment as the proximate causes.

Q. 6:28 What is an acute suicidal state?

An acute suicidal state seems to be the result of a combination of low self-esteem arising from self-hate or guilt; a state of extreme agitation, so that the client cannot think clearly; and a constriction of intellectual functioning, so that the client cannot see or think beyond the immediate situation. A person caught in this "lethal triangle" who gives evidence of any of the following factors is at dire risk for suicide:

- Significant loss, such as a love relationship, close relative, position, or fortune;
- Adverse change in medical condition, chronic unrelenting pain, recent surgery, tumor, terminal illness, or facial disfigurement;
- Starting or stopping of psychotropic medication;
- Increase in despair;
- Sudden improvement of depressed mood (may be the result of a decision to give up the struggle and end it all);
- Statement of suicidal intent or behavior indicating suicidality;
- A history of suicide attempts; and
- Alcohol or drug intoxication.

Hospitalization is usually indicated for acutely suicidal persons until the self-destructive impulses have passed. The most dangerous period may be when the severely depressed client seems to be improving in mood, and energy is available to carry out a suicide plan. (J. Fawcett and R. Shaughnessy, "The Suicidal Patient," in *Psychiatric Diagnosis and Therapy* '88/'89, J. Flaherty, R. Channon, and J. Davis, eds. (Appleton and Lange, Norwalk, CN and San Mateo, CA: 1988), 50–51)

Q. 6:29 If a client is acutely suicidal and refuses treatment, does the clinician have a duty to commit for involuntary treatment?

Public policy requires self-determination of clients and treatment in the least restrictive manner *consistent with the client's needs and the public safety.* The standard of care requires that steps be taken to guard a suicidal client from foreseeable harm, and if hospitalization is clinically indicated, it would be negligent not to hospitalize. If the client refuses appropriate treatment, and is reasonably expected to commit serious injury to himself or herself in the near future, he or she is subject to involuntary hospitalization; failure to institute commitment proceedings would be a breach of due care.

Q. 6:30 What is a chronic suicidal state?

Some severely personality-disordered clients live their lives in a chronic state of rage, dissatisfaction, and emptiness. They depend on others for self-esteem, are constantly disappointed because their insatiable dependency needs can never be met, require constant reassurance and attention, and never experience real joy, fulfillment, or contentment. This combination of personality traits, combined with depression and alcoholism, often results in a chronic suicidal state as a maladaptive life style; the threat of suicide is used to manipulate others, and the client can soothe himself or herself with the reminder that, if things get any worse, he or she can carry out the threat. These clients are impulsive and prone to suicidal gestures (self-destructive behavior with the intention and expectation of being rescued). The risk here is that the anticipated rescue does not come through.

Clinical intervention with such a client is aimed at enabling that person to face and master conflicts and disappointments rather than avoid them or escape through suicide. Therapists find such clients extremely difficult to manage and, indeed, they require skilled, very well-trained clinicians. Most EAPs do not have the clinical resources to manage these clients, and they should be referred as quickly as possible.

Q. 6:31 Does an EAP clinician have a duty to warn the family of a suicidal client?

There is an argument to be made that a therapist has a duty to inform the family of a suicidal client so that it can take steps to protect the client from himself or herself. That notion has been specifically rejected by a California court in *Bellah v. Greenson,* 81 Cal. App.3d 614 (1978), but *Bellah* is authority in California only, and other states have not ruled on the point. The *Bellah* court ruled that there is no duty to a client's family to breach the client's confidentiality by warning of suicide potential. It is to be noted, however, that this decision came in the wake of a great outcry from mental health providers when California established a highly controversial duty upon mental health providers to warn a potential victim about a dangerous therapy patient. (*Tarasoff v. Regents of the University of California,* 551 P.2d 334 (1976)) The *Bellah* court stated, "We decline to further extend the holding of *Tarasoff.*" (81 Cal. App.3d at 622)

This issue is by no means settled in other states at this time, and it is entirely likely that another court could arrive at a contrary opinion. A pragmatic approach is to consider the liability risks: Is a therapist more likely to be successfully sued for breach of confidentiality for disclosing a client's suicidal state in an effort to help, or for wrongful death for failing to meet the standard of care in involving the family in the treatment process?

Q. 6:32 Is there a duty to involve a suicidal client's family in the treatment?

Bellah v. Greenson, 81 Cal. App.3d 614, 622 (1978), does *not* address the issue of failure to involve the family in the treatment as a breach of the standard of care. There may be a duty to involve the client's family in his or her treatment, a breach of which would be negligent. Some authorities hold, "It is absolutely essential that the therapist involve other members of the patient's family [in the client's psychotherapy]. The therapist should first inquire about the perceived support the patient receives from key family and friends. A family evaluation should be made in order to educate family members about the patient's condition, to assess their support capacity, and to consider the benefits of family therapy." (J. Fawcett and R. Shaughnessy, "The Suicidal Patient," in *Psychiatric Diagnosis and Therapy* '88/'89, J. Flaherty, R. Channon, and J. Davis, eds. (Appleton and Lange, Norwalk, CN, San Mateo, CA: 1988), 50–51) Since there is clearly a duty to take protective measures when suicide is a foreseeable risk (*Vistica v. Presbyterian Hospital,* 432 P.2d 193 (1967)), it seems that the standard of care requires communication with the family when that is clinically indicated.

Q. 6:33 What is iatrogenic suicide?

Iatrogenic (caused by treatment) suicide can occur from misdiagnosis or improper treatment. A client may regress and become suicidal as a result of therapy for which he or she was improperly diagnosed or selected. Vulnerable clients are at risk in wild or regressive therapies, and at the hands of unskilled or unscrupulous therapists. Sexual exploitation and other mishandling of the transference and countertransference phenomena are not uncommon causes for suicide attempts by clients. Inexperienced and untrained therapists may be prone to clumsy interventions with, or abandonment of, anxiety-provoking, high-risk clients. Administrative discharge of difficult clients by reason of their disruption of the program, drain on resources, or third-party payment restrictions may lead to a charge of iatrogenic suicide. (R. Simon, *Clinical Psychiatry and the Law* (Washington, D.C., 1987) 272–272; see also

A. Stone, "Suicide Precipitated by Psychotherapy: a clinical contribution," *Am. J. Psychotherapy* 25 (1971): 18–26)

Q. 6:34 What are the factors in assessing liability for suicide?

If a client's actions or statements are such that a reasonably prudent therapist would have anticipated suicidal behavior, a duty of due care and treatment is owed. (*Lange v. United States,* 179 F. Supp. 777 (N.D. N.Y. 1960)) A mere mistake in assessing suicidal tendencies will not result in liability; there must be a showing that the diagnosis did not meet the standard of care. (*Dimitrijevic v. Chicago Wesley Memorial Hospital,* 236 N.E.2d 309 (1968)) The reasonableness of the clinician's actions will be judged relative to the circumstances of the case, including the severity and foreseeability of the risk. (*Lichtenstein v. Montefiore Hospital and Medical Center,* 56 A.D.2d 281, 392 N.Y.S.2d 18 (1977))

Q. 6:35 If the suicide was not foreseeable, will there be liability?

In theory, there can be no liability for failing to prevent that which one cannot predict. If a reasonably prudent therapist would not have foreseen the risk of suicide, there is no liability. When a client is in treatment for a suicidal state, or has declared himself or herself to be suicidal, foreseeability is automatic. Liability arises from a failure to guard against the foreseeable risk and institute appropriate preventive measures. (*Meir v. Ross General Hospital,* 445 P.2d 519 (1968))

As a practical matter, however, when a suicide has occurred, a surviving family and a jury are likely to take the position that the risk should have been evident, or if the clinician was aware of it, that he or she was negligent in failing to prevent it. Some authorities suggest that this attitude may result in the application of a strict liability standard to mental health providers. (R. Simon, *Clinical Psychiatry and the Law* (Washington, D.C., 1987), 270; T. Gutheil, "Medicolegal Pitfalls in the Treatment of Borderline Patients," *Am. J. Psychiatry* 142 (1985): 9–14)

Q. 6:36 What is "strict liability," and how does it apply to EAPs?

Strict liability is a concept applied by courts to product liability cases in which a seller is liable for any and all defective or hazardous products that unduly threaten a consumer's personal safety. Every participant in the manufacturing and selling of any facet of the product can be joined as a defendant. The seller of a product that is in a defective condition, or unreasonably dangerous to a user or consumer or his or her property, will be held strictly liable to an ultimate consumer or user for harm caused to him or her if the seller is in the business of selling such product, and the product is expected to and does reach the user or consumer without substantial change in the condition in which it is sold. This rule applies even if the seller has exercised all possible care in the preparation and sale of his or her product, and the user or consumer has not bought the product from or entered into any relation with the seller. (*Restatement (Second) of Torts* §402A)

Some people have argued that a therapist or counselor who undertakes to manage the care of a person who is inherently dangerous to the community, such as a substance abuser who drives or runs machinery, or a psychotic or severely character-disordered person bent on self-destruction or murder, should be strictly liable for failure to control him or her. Courts have generally declined to impose this standard in suicide cases. (*Stepakoff v. Kantar,* 473 N.E.2d 1131 (1985))

Q. 6:37 What should the EAP's policy be for handling suicidal clients?

An EAP should have a policy requiring referral for psychiatric evaluation for any client who indicates suicidal ideation. Although other mental health professionals may be well able to assess a suicidal state (indeed, in many states, other professionals with advanced degrees are qualified to certify clients for involuntary hospitalization), the client's family and its lawyer would raise issues of competence and negligence in a situation in which a nonpsychiatrist was managing a client known to be at risk for suicide.

Q. 6:38 Should clients who talk about suicide automatically be hospitalized?

It would not be practical, possible, or appropriate to hospitalize every client who talks about suicide. A skillful evaluation must be made in every case, however, to determine whether the client is (1) in an acute suicidal state or (2) chronically suicidal, that is, using fantasies and threats of suicide as a misadaptational life style. In both cases the client is at risk, but the underlying factors differ and determine the appropriate clinical response. From a clinical care point of view, and to demonstrate due care in diagnosis and treatment, detailed recording is important in establishing the accuracy of the differential diagnosis and the reasoning behind the treatment choice.

Dangerousness

Q. 6:39 Does an EAP have a duty to control the behavior of its clients to prevent them from harming others?

As a general rule, there is no legal duty to control the conduct of another so as to prevent him or her from causing physical harm to a third person unless (1) a special relationship exists between the actor (for example, the EAP professional) and the other (for example, the client) that imposes a duty upon the actor to control the other's conduct; or (2) a special relationship exists between the actor and a third person (the victim) that gives the third person a right to protection. (*Restatement (Second) of Torts*)

In *Tarasoff v. Regents of the University of California*, 551 P.2d 334 (1976), California took the position that the "special relationship" requirement is met by the therapist-client relationship, which also creates a duty to the community to protect it from the client. Since EAPs serve not only individual clients, but the employer and the workforce as a whole, it may well be argued that the EAP owes them all a duty of protection. Not all states will agree. In the case of *Estate of Johnson v. Condell Memorial Hospital*, 520 N.E.2d 37 (1988), the Illinois Supreme Court held that unless one has custody of a client (as a hospital does of a committed patient), one has no right to exercise control over him or her, and thus bears no liability to third persons for failure to do so. (See *Anthony v. United States*, 616 F. Supp. 156 (S.D. Iowa, 1985); but see *Burroughs v. Board of Trustees of Alachua Gen. Hosp.*, 328 So.2d 538 (1976) *contra.*)

> **Example.** The client becomes very upset at being confronted for coming to an aftercare group in an intoxicated condition. She runs out, jumps into her car, and speeds away. The counselor is concerned for the safety of the client and others and calls the police. The police give chase, and the police car strikes another vehicle, killing the driver. The estate of the decedent sues the EAP, charging that the counselor

should have restrained the client and should not have called the police. The court finds no liability, on the basis that the counselor had no right or duty to restrain the client, even if she could have done so, and so had no duty to the decedent.

Q. 6:40 If the EAP professional takes responsibility for a client who is acting dangerously, is he or she then responsible if that client causes harm?

If the circumstances are such that the EAP professional has "taken charge" of a client, he or she may have a duty to control the client's behavior. "One who voluntarily takes charge of a third person whom he knows or should know is likely to cause bodily harm to others if not controlled is under a duty so to exercise his control as to prevent the third person from doing such harm." (*Restatement (Second) of Torts* §319)

Example. The client is brought to the EAP office in an intoxicated state by a supervisor who found him passed out in a closet. The client insists that the supervisor is a member of a Satanic cult that is poisoning him by spraying arsenic through the heating duct near his lathe. The therapist determines that the client is suffering from an acute alcohol psychosis and starts to drive him to the hospital in her car. While the car is stopped for a red light, the client jumps out and runs back to the worksite, where he strangles the supervisor. The therapist is liable, and the EAP is thus vicariously liable, for failure to control the client of whom she had taken charge. Driving him in her car, rather than calling an ambulance, was negligent.

Q. 6:41 What are the general features of dangerousness?

Courts have not defined dangerousness with sufficient specificity that therapists can know for certain what kinds of behavior will give rise to a duty to warn or protect. *Black's Law Dictionary* (5th Ed. 1979) defines dangerous as "attended with risk; perilous; hazardous; unsafe," and danger as "jeopardy; exposure to loss or injury; peril." It is clear that a "serious risk of violence to another" (*Tarasoff v. Regents of the University of California*, 551 P.2d 334, 340 (1976)) is within the scope of these definitions. In assessing dangerous behavior to determine what intervention, if any, is indicated, five components must be considered: its nature, extent, probability, imminence, and frequency. (R. Simon, *Clinical Psy-*

chiatry and the Law (Washington, D.C., 1987), 314) The three major clinical features of violence are suddenness, aggressiveness, and destructiveness. (T. Jobe and J. Winer, "The Violent Patient," in *Psychiatry Diagnosis & Therapy/'88/'89*, J. Flaherty, R. Channon, and J. Davis, eds. (Appleton and Lange, Norwalk, CN, San Mateo, CA: 1988) One of the best predictors of violence is a history of violence.

Q. 6:42 What are the clinical features of dangerousness?

The clinical features of dangerousness include:

- *Violent ideation:* The client reports thoughts, fantasies, and dreams of killing, torturing, or maiming others. This may be accompanied by delusions or hallucinations commanding violent behavior.
- *Affect:* The client manifests intense, overwhelming rage, destructive impulses, drivenness, or fear of inability to control violent impulses.
- *Behavior:* The client may exhibit physical agitation accompanying psychosis, intoxication, or delirium; explosive rage; or domestic violence.

Q. 6:43 Are there signs of an immediate clinical emergency for which a therapist should be alert?

Violent clients have been known to attack therapists and others who happen to be present in the clinical setting. Aside from the very real need for self-protection, a therapist is responsible for taking reasonable precautions to protect other clients and staff from violent clients. (*Kelly v. Board of Trustees of Hillcrest Hospital*, 529 P.2d 1233 (1974)) Every mental health and social service provider must be aware of the following known danger signs of imminent violence:

- *Motor activity:* Irritable motor activity with an inability to be calmed is the most important sign of impending violence. A client who cannot sit still, paces about, acts out his or her story (rather than telling it), and exhibits a rising level of agitation is particularly dangerous.
- *Verbal indicators:* Any threats should be taken seriously. Loud, strident shouting and pejorative, defamatory, or sexually aggressive muttering can both be signs of impending violence.

- *Nonverbal indicators:* These include glaring eyes, demanding demeanor, tense, forward-leaning posture, and a hyperalert state.

(T. Jobe, and J. Winer, "The Violent Patient," in *Psychiatry Diagnosis & Therapy/'88/'89* (Appleton and Lange, Norwalk, CN, San Mateo, CA: 1988), 225)

Q. 6:44 Is there a "psychological profile" of dangerousness?

Many violent people manifest low self-esteem, coupled with an inability to delay gratification. They have a history of violence, often accompanied by a profound sense of entitlement. When they perceive themselves to have been wronged or injured, they are compelled to seek vengeance. These people are often diagnosed as having borderline, paranoid, or antisocial personality disorders. Borderlines tend to be self-destructive rather than dangerous to others, but they can become homicidal or assaultive if intoxicated or fragmented after a perceived rejection by the therapist or other significant person. Paranoids are subject to intense, psychotic-like transferences that may result in violent ideation or behavior. Hypomanic affect and an expression of outrage are signs of imminent danger. (T. Jobe and J. Winer, "The Violent Patient," in *Psychiatry Diagnosis & Therapy/'88/'89* (Appleton and Lange, Norwalk, CN, San Mateo, CA: 1988), 225)

Q. 6:45 Are there biological components of dangerousness?

Violence often accompanies drug or alcohol intoxication or withdrawal, delirium due to metabolic encephalopathy, minimal brain dysfunction, and certain psychomotor seizures secondary to temporal lobe epilepsy. (See G. Bach-Y-Rita, "Episodic dyscontrol: A study of 130 Violent Patients," *Am. J. of Psychiatry* 127 (1971):1473.) Many people who are prone to episodic rages have undiagnosed psychotic or neurological conditions that can be treated with medication. A careful history taken of the client and his or her mother may reveal head trauma or illness accompanied by high fever and convulsions long before, perhaps in childhood. Other clients who have never been diagnosed as psychotic, when questioned closely about the precipitants of their violent episodes, will admit to having "heard" some jeering remark or a command to strike out (auditory hallucinations).

Often, these clients have severe psychosocial problems that appear to explain their dangerous behavior, so it is easy to miss any biological component that may exist. It is a great tragedy, when treatment may be available for some of these people, that they are allowed to continue in their misery, abusing others because they cannot control themselves, and being abused in return. For this reason, the standard of care requires that any client with whom episodic violence is an issue must be referred for psychiatric and neurological evaluation.

Q. 6:46 What are the sociocultural features of violence?

In assessing for dangerousness, the clinician must be aware that the chances of violence are high for a client with a combination of several of the following features: male, 14–24 years of age (some authorities narrow it to 15–20 years), poor, low level of education, history of substance abuse and violence (including family violence), job and residential instability, and a history of arrests for violence.

Q. 6:47 What is the developmental profile of a dangerous client?

It is a truism that violence begets violence. Clients who are violent are likely to have a history of childhood violence, delinquency, repeated reckless driving offenses, child abuse and neglect, and parents with severe psychiatric disturbances. These factors, coupled with the other features and predictors set forth in this chapter, are diagnostically significant in predicting violence.

Q. 6:48 What is a protocol for dealing with a volatile client?

There is no one clinical protocol for dealing with all volatile clients. In an emergency, some steps include:

- Try not to be alone with a violent person; call for help.
- Do not let the client get between the therapist and the door.
- If the client seems to view the therapist as helpful and benevolent, induce ideas and emotions independent of the client's thinking; suggest that he or she can calm down and feel better now that they are working on the problem together. (However, this can also have an agitating effect.)
- Employ "active listening"; allow the client to ventilate while let-

ting him or her know that the therapist understands and empathizes (but be careful to avoid patronizing).

- Express concern for the client's feelings and well-being.
- Direct the client in exploring alternatives to violence.
- Check for the here-and-now transference: "You said everyone loathes a drunk. Do you think I loathe drunks?"
- Directly, but sensitively, inquire about the client's symptoms and violent thoughts or impulses.
- Perform a mental status exam.
- Take a careful history, including previous treatment records, and information from family, supervisor, security, or others. (If making an immediate referral for treatment, obtain the previous records and collateral history. In an emergency situation, get as much history as needed to support a working diagnosis.)
- Inform the client about legal realities; try to enlist him or her in voluntarily formulating a joint plan for protecting himself or herself and the object of the rage.
- Make a diagnosis or assessment.
- Consider the impact of the emergency intervention on long-term treatment goals.
- Refer for psychiatric consultation; if the client has actually committed violent acts, refer for neurological examination as well.
- Set up a treatment plan: for example, hospitalization (voluntary or involuntary); referral for outpatient treatment (set up an immediate appointment and coordinate transfer, preferably accompanying the client to see the outpatient therapist); other community referrals. Consider a conjoint session with the object of the client's rage for purposes of tension reduction and education about the client's condition. Determine what acts are necessary to warn or protect foreseeable victims.
- Implement the treatment plan, including required warnings or notifications and commitment, if necessary.
- Notify the EAP administration of the situation; consult with others; record the encounter in detail.

(*Tarasoff v. Regents of the University of California,* 551 P.2d 334 (1976); *Jablonski v. United States,* 712 F.2d 391 (9th Cir. 1983))

Q. 6:49 Does an EAP have a duty to warn a potential victim of a client's threat to do harm?

The case of *Tarasoff v. Regents of the University of California,* 551 P.2d 334 (1976), clearly established a duty to an identified potential victim to *act* to protect him or her from harm. Warning is one possible precautionary act. New Jersey expanded that concept, stating that a therapist has a duty to protect all parties reasonably identifiable and foreseen to be at risk. (*McIntosh v. Milano,* 403 A.2d 500 (1979)) However, Pennsylvania rejected the broader *McIntosh* view in *Leedy v. Hartnett,* 510 F. Supp. 1125 (M.D. Pa. 1981). The so-called "duty to warn" is probably really part of a broader duty to protect. Other states have created a duty to warn or protect. Every EAP provider should be aware of the position of his or her state on this issue and keep abreast of changes in the law.

Q. 6:50 If therapists have a duty to protect third parties from the violence of their clients, to whom does that duty extend?

The law is developing in many states defining the limits of the duty to protect. As would be expected, states vary in their approaches to the issue, largely, it seems, based on the facts of the first case that happens to be presented in that jurisdiction. The legal adage, "hard cases make bad law" may be amply demonstrated as the trend toward broadening liability progresses. In California, *Tarasoff v. Regents of the University of California,* 551 P.2d 334 (1976), imposed a duty to protect *identified potential victims.* However, California declined to extend the duty to protect to *unidentified persons* in the community. In *Thompson v. County of Alameda,* 614 P.2d 728 (1980), a juvenile delinquent was released from a county facility, where he had stated that he would kill an unnamed neighborhood child when he got out. The next day, he killed a little boy who lived next door. The court rejected the argument that the juvenile authorities had a duty to warn the police, the victim's mother, and parents of small children in the vicinity.

In a New Jersey case, the patient had identified a girl neighbor as the object of his obsession and violent fantasies, but he never actually threatened to act on his fantasies. Nonetheless, the New Jersey court found a duty to protect a person to whom a client "may present a probability of danger." (*McIntosh v. Milano,* 403 A.2d 500 (1979)). The federal district court in Nebraska defined an even broader duty to protect against *any reasonable likelihood of harm or injury to any foreseeable victim*. The key here is foreseeability. In *Lipari v. Sears, Roebuck & Co.*, 497 F. Supp. 185 (D. Neb. 1980), an outpatient at a Veterans' Administration hospital mental health clinic terminated treatment after less than a month. A month later, he shot up a nightclub with a gun purchased from Sears, wounding several people and killing the plaintiff's husband. The court found liability for failing to treat him properly or to commit him, holding that his violence was foreseeable and gave rise to a duty to act to prevent the behavior.

Q. 6:51 What must a therapist do to discharge the duty to protect?

A therapist who knows, or should know, that a client is at risk for imminently harming another must take whatever precautions are reasonably necessary to protect third parties. (*Lipari v. Sears, Roebuck & Co.*, 497 F. Supp. 185 (D. Neb. 1980) 185, 193) These steps may include warning the potential victim; notifying the proper authorities (for an EAP, this may include the employer and security); and hospitalizing the client voluntarily, if he or she is willing, or instituting commitment proceedings, if necessary.

In *Jablonski v. United States*, 712 F.2d 391 (9th Cir. 1983), the federal district court in California found two Veterans' Administration psychiatrists guilty of malpractice for failing to discharge the following duties: record and transmit information from the police, obtain past medical records, and adequately warn the patient's common-law wife that he was dangerous to her.

Q. 6:52 Is there strict liability for failure to prevent harmful acts?

At least in theory, a therapist is liable for failure to prevent a client from harming a third person only if he or she is negligent in diagnosing dangerousness or in failing to act reasonably to prevent it. The trend across the country, however, is an expansion of liability. Although the courts couch their judgments in terms of negligence, the fact patterns in the cases give rise to a concern that a strict liability standard will be applied when a therapy client or psychiatric patient kills or seriously injures another. Even if a duty to warn or protect has not yet been articulated in a given state, EAP professionals are well advised to practice as if it existed. In every state that has already imposed the duty, there was a first case. (See *Davis v. Lhim*, 335 N.W.2d 481 (1983) (Michigan); *Peter-*

son v. State, 671 P.2d 230 (1983) (Washington); *Hedlund v. Superior Court of Orange County,* 669 P.2d 41 (1983) (California).)

Q. 6:53 Does the duty to protect against a client's dangerousness extend to property?

The cases to date have largely concerned themselves with dangerousness to persons. In *Bellah v. Greenson,* 81 Cal. App.3d 614, 622 (1978), a California court specifically declined to extend the principle of *Tarasoff v. Regents of the University of California,* 551 P.2d 334 (1976) (see Q. 6:31) to property damage. Vermont took the opposite view, holding an outpatient counseling service liable for failing to prevent a client from burning down his father's barn because he was angry at his father. The agency was faulted for failing to obtain the client's recent medical records and having no formal written policy on interstaff consultation procedures for violent clients. (*Peck v. The Counseling Service of Addison County,* Vt. Sup. Ct. Docket No. 83-062 (June 14, 1985)) A Michigan case that indicates a likelihood of imposition of liability for property damage is *Duvall v. Goldin,* 362 N.W.2d 275 (1984), in which a patient suffering from epilepsy had a seizure while driving his car. The victim successfully sued the patient's physician for failing to warn his patient not to drive.

It stands to reason that if liability can be imposed for personal injury or wrongful death arising out of a breach of duty, it can likewise be imposed for property damage.

Q. 6:54 If a therapist warns of a client's dangerousness, is there possible liability for breach of confidentiality?

One of the major objections to the concepts of duty to warn or protect is the exposure of the disclosing therapist to a lawsuit by the client for breach of confidentiality or for defamation. In states in which an affirmative duty to warn exists, there will be no state law liability for reasonably doing what the law requires. In states in which no affirmative duty to warn or protect exists, and where no statute or case law authorizes disclosure to protect against dangerousness, a therapist might, theoretically, apply to a court for a declaratory judgment. Of course, the flaw in this suggestion is the reality that in most cases in which a warning is indicated, there will not be time for preparing and presenting a petition to a court. Most therapists agree that when the chips are down, they prefer to risk a suit for breach of confidentiality, rather than responsibility for failing to prevent a tragedy.

Q. 6:55 If an EAP is federally assisted, what procedures must be followed in disclosing client information for purposes of attempting to prevent harm?

Federally assisted providers of alcoholism and drug abuse treatment services must abide by 42 U.S.C. §§290dd-3 and 290ee-3 (statutes governing confidentiality of alcohol and drug abuse patient records) and 42 C.F.R. 200 et. seq. (regulations implementing the statutes). These statutes and regulations impose a strict duty of confidentiality and require application to a court for leave to disclose based on "good cause."

To protect client confidentiality and privacy to the extent possible, the proceedings are brought without naming the client; hence they are called "John Doe" petitions. The client is to be given notice of the proceedings unless notice would exacerbate the danger sought to be avoided. The court will hold a closed-door examination of the therapist and the records sought to be disclosed and will rule either to permit or to forbid disclosure.

Keeping in mind that the role of a therapist is to facilitate growth and healing, if the law must invade a clinical case, sometimes the law can be used as a clinical intervention. If the EAP counselor lacks the clinical skills or experience to bring this about, a consultant—perhaps a group or family therapist—can be hired to assist. (See C-1: Sample John Doe Petition to Allow Disclosure of Confidential Information.)

Q. 6:56 Should violence always be considered a symptom of a mental disorder?

Violence is not always a result or a symptom of a mental or emotional disorder. In fact, although not sanctioned by general community mores or the law, it is clearly a socially acceptable response to provocation in some subcultures. (J. Monahan, *The Clinical Prediction of Violent Behavior* (Rockville, Md.: NIMH (1981)) Outside of a subculture in which it is acceptable, and certainly in the workplace, violence is a maladaptive stress response and obviously cannot be tolerated.

Q. 6:57 Does the duty to warn or protect apply when the dangerous client is malicious, but not mentally disturbed?

Psychiatrists take the position that the management of violence is within their purview only when it is the product of mental illness. EAPs, however, are concerned with the general social functioning of their clients and often become involved in helping clients consider and develop alternative coping strategies for handling stress and provocation. Whether or not the violent propensities of a specific client are the result of mental illness, they constitute a management problem for EAPs. If there is a duty to warn or protect, it will apply regardless of the cause of the dangerousness. Differential diagnosis is obviously essential in determining the proper intervention with a dangerous client. Negligence in diagnosing and treating dangerousness will give rise to liability if it can be shown to be the proximate cause of injury to a third party. (*Peck v. The Counseling Service of Addison, Inc.*, Vt. Sup. Ct. Docket No. 83-062 (June 14, 1985))

Chapter 7

Ethics and Professional Liability

Ethics and law interface and overlap in clinical service delivery. EAP staff members with disparate professional backgrounds practice in widely varied settings. Although mental health and social service professionals are presumed to have been trained in ethical principles governing practice, this frequently proves not to be the case. Additionally, human resources professionals and others in sponsor organizations may be unfamiliar with the culture of the counseling professions. This chapter presents an overview of ethical principles and their legal implications, which is intended to both provide guidelines for behavior and enhance understanding between EAP professionals and their nonclinical counterparts in organizations.

Q. 7:1 What ethical principles apply in EAP practice?

The code of ethics of the profession of which the EAP practitioner is a member will apply to his or her practice in the EAP setting, as in any other setting. In addition to the various professional codes, there are industrywide codes, including those promulgated by such organizations as ALMACA and EASNA, which are applicable. If the EAP sponsor or employer promulgates a code to which employees are expected to adhere, that code also applies.

Codes of Ethics

Q. 7:2 What is a code of ethics?

A code of ethics is a statement of principles by which members of a professional or business group are expected to conduct their practices or businesses. It is a guide to behavior and everyday conduct and is also the basis for adjudication of issues in ethics when the conduct of an individual is alleged to deviate from the standards explicitly or implicitly set forth in the code. Some businesses, universities, and religious, social, or recreational groups also adopt codes of ethics for their employees, adherents, or members.

Q. 7:3 What types of behavior are the subject of a code of ethics?

As a rule, an ethics code will articulate standards of behavior in professional relationships with: those served; colleagues; employers and other individuals and members of other professions; and the community and society as a whole. It also embodies standards of ethical behavior associated with one's individual conduct to the extent that such conduct is associated with one's status and identity as a member of the covered group.

Q. 7:4 On what is a code of ethics based?

A group promulgating a code of ethics will develop it as a statement of the group's fundamental values, culture, and philosophy, and base it on the nature of the professional work and the conditions that promote these values.

Q. 7:5 Who is bound by a code of ethics?

Ordinarily, membership in the society or group or employment by the business is conditional upon (1) acceptance of the code of ethics promulgated by the organization and (2) an agreement to be bound thereby.

Q. 7:6 How is a code of ethics used as a guide in professional conduct?

Dilemmas and conflicts of interest often arise in human services delivery. Articulated principles of professional conduct offer a matrix within which to consider specific situations and decisional alternatives, as well as a guide to professional decision making. A code will also be helpful in evaluating professional behavior when its correctness or appropriateness is questioned.

Q. 7:7 Is one who is not a member of a professional society still bound by its code?

This is a somewhat complex issue. As a practical matter, the code of conduct of a recognized professional organization will be used to measure the conduct of any member of the profession, whether or not he or she is a member of the association. For example, a social worker cannot claim not to be bound by the ethical principle prohibiting sexual contact with clients merely because he or she is not a member of the National Association of Social Workers. The community and the courts, in inquiring about the standards of practice for professionals, will look to the recognized professional associations and their codes of conduct. One who is not a member of an association cannot, however, be tried or disciplined by the association. The most an association can do about professional misconduct of a nonmember is refer the complainant to the local licensing authorities for discipline, or to an attorney for consideration of an action for damages.

Q. 7:8 Is breach of ethics per se malpractice?

Often, a breach of ethics is also a breach of professional duty, but it may not always be malpractice per se. If the conduct complained of is negligent deviation from the standard of care and can be shown to be the proximate cause of injury to a client, the issue is not one of ethics, but of breach of the duty of due care. Proof of a breach of ethics will not relieve a plaintiff from the requirement of expert testimony to establish deviation from the standard of care, damages, and proximate cause. On the other hand, if it is established that the behavior that is the basis of a malpractice suit is also a breach of ethics, that will be persuasive evidence of a deviation from the standard of care.

Q. 7:9 Are all codes of ethics the same?

Many of the codes of conduct of the professions active in EAPs are similar and have many common features, but there are some significant differences. Conduct that is a direct breach of ethics of one profession may not be so considered by another profession. For example, the Code of Professional Conduct of the American Psychological Association prohibits dual relationships of any nature; the other helping professions do not specifically articulate such a general prohibition, but look to the circumstances of a given situation to determine whether a breach has occurred.

Q. 7:10 If there is more than one code of ethics that might apply in a situation, which code will govern?

Sometimes, a profession may boast of more than one primary association, each of which has its own code of conduct (for example, the National Association of Social Workers (NASW) and the National Federation of Societies for Clinical Social Work (a federation of state societies, each of which may have its own code)). Also, there may be overlapping codes applicable if a provider belongs to more than one professional organization (for example, the American Psychological Association and ALMACA). The differences among codes of the same profession are often more formal than substantive, and often are more evident in the adjudication process than in the principles of conduct. None of the codes is expected to be blindly followed in a vacuum.

Q. 7:11 If there appears to be an ethical dilemma and/or a conflict between two applicable codes of conduct, what can a professional do to resolve it?

In a word, consult. Every organization that promulgates a code of conduct has an ethics committee, or the equivalent, which will provide a consultant—usually free of charge—to assist in solving the problem.

In a sensitive situation, it is a good idea to confirm the result of the consultation in a letter. If one code specifically proscribes certain conduct and the other does not, it is recommended that the stricter code be followed. The fact that some other code does not forbid a behavior will not be a defense if the organization that does forbid it chooses to take action against its professional member.

Q. 7:12 What are the general principles of conduct for EAP professionals?

- *Propriety:* A professional is expected to maintain high standards of personal conduct in his or her professional capacity and identity.
- *Competence and professional development:* There is a duty to attain and maintain proficiency in professional practice and performance.
- *Service:* The service obligation of the profession is primary to the professional.
- *Integrity:* The highest standards of professional integrity are required.
- *Scholarship and research:* These functions should be conducted in accordance with the conventions of scholarly inquiry.

Q. 7:13 What are the basic principles of ethical responsibility to clients?

- *Fiduciary duty to clients:* The client's needs and best interests are primary.
- *Rights and prerogatives of clients:* Self-determination of clients should be respected and fostered.
- *Confidentiality and privacy:* A client's information obtained in the course of service delivery should be held in confidence, except as required by law or otherwise provided for in the client's contract with the provider.
- *Fees:* Fees should be fair, reasonable, and commensurate with the service provided and with due regard for the client's ability to pay.

Q. 7:14 If statutes or regulations conflict with ethical standards, what steps does the EAP professional take?

Ordinarily, EAP professionals adhere to the relevant laws, regulations, and practices. They are obliged to make known their commitment to professional standards and guidelines and, wherever possible, work toward a resolution of the conflict. Legal representation is mandatory in these situations. EAP providers can be extremely effective as agents for change when they participate in professional society legislative development activities, give testimony before legislatures and administrative bodies, and otherwise seek to educate and influence lawmakers.

Extratherapeutic Relationships

Q. 7:15 What is the ethical prohibition against exploitation of clinical relationships?

In one way or another, all codes of ethics prohibit exploitation of clients for the undue personal advantage, profit, or interest of the counselor. This rule of conduct precludes any behavior or ancillary activity or relationships that may impair clinical judgment or otherwise increase the risk of sacrificing the client for the benefit of the care provider.

Q. 7:16 Is every form of extratherapeutic relationship between counselor and client considered exploitative?

Only psychology specifically prohibits any dual relationship between client and therapist. Many authorities take the position that any extratherapeutic relationship between counselor and client must, by definition, exploit the client and/or the therapeutic situation to meet the needs of the counselor. Because a personal or business relationship is bound to interfere with professional therapeutic judgment, it is recommended that the boundaries of the therapy relationship be strictly enforced.

> **Example.** A female client became very interested in premenstrual syndrome (PMS) and did a lot of study and investigation on the subject. She developed a series of workshops to train counseling professionals and a plan for a business to provide training, consultation, and treatment for PMS. Because she was not a trained clinician and lacked general business skills, she required assistance in implementing her

ideas. She invited her EAP counselor to work with her. The two met outside of counseling sessions and worked on the workshop and clinic projects.

After some weeks, the anxiety and depression for which the client had sought help had vanished, and the counselor suggested termination of the clinical relationship. Within a week following termination, the client experienced a panic attack, called the counselor, and demanded to resume treatment. The counselor demurred, saying that their relationship had become too complicated, and it would be in the best interests of the client to see another therapist. The client became enraged and told the counselor that she no longer wanted to be involved in business with anyone who would treat her in such a shameful fashion. The counselor proceeded to run a series of workshops on her own and began organizing a PMS clinic.

The client's new therapist advised her to bring an ethics complaint against the counselor. The counselor was found guilty of having deviated from the code of professional conduct by exploiting the clinical relationship for her personal gain.

Q. 7:17 Is engaging in a dual relationship a basis for a malpractice claim?

In the example in Q. 7:16, the breach of ethics would support a cause of action for malpractice. For one thing, the therapist failed to recognize and properly deal with "transference cure" or "flight into health." This phenomenon often occurs when the client's symptoms clear up "miraculously" in the context of the transference. That is, the symptoms are not eliminated by a working through of the issues that cause them, but rather are temporarily masked or avoided as the client unrealistically feels his or her needs and longings fulfilled by a fantasy distortion of the therapy relationship. It is negligent for a therapist to behave in a manner that encourages these fantasies.

Q. 7:18 Is engaging in an extratherapeutic relationship abandonment of the client?

By engaging in the extratherapeutic relationship, the counselor in the example in Q. 7:16 effectively abandoned her client at the point at which she became interested in pursuing her own self-interest rather than her client's clinical needs. As a result, she was no longer available as a therapist when the client suffered a relapse that should have been predictable. The counselor certainly had a duty to be aware of the nature and extent of the client's character pathology before considering any extratherapeutic relationship with her.

Q. 7:19 Is an extratherapeutic relationship a basis for a breach-of-contract action?

Again, in the example in Q. 7:16, the breach of ethics is also a breach of the counselor's fiduciary duty under the clinical care contract. (See Ch. 3, "The Clinical Care Contract," Qs. 3:3–3:5.) Any exploitation of the client is a breach of contract. Sometimes exploitation is alleged, but the client cannot prove damages proximately caused thereby, and so a malpractice suit may not be successful. A client need not allege or establish injury or damages in bringing an ethics complaint to a professional association or licensing authority. Injury to the client may be an aggravating factor in imposing a penalty for a breach of ethics, but it is not an essential element. All that must be established is the unethical conduct. On that basis alone, the organization can sanction the member.

Q. 7:20 Is sexual activity with a client always a breach of ethics?

Yes—without exception. There is no defense to a charge of sexual activity with a client except a denial of the event. (See also Ch. 5, "Professional Liability," Qs. 5:74, 5:77, and 5:78.) Consent, assumption of risk, seduction by the client, or use of a technique of therapy are not defenses. A defense of personal impairment will not be successful either, because codes of ethics require professionals to be aware of their personal conditions and to take necessary steps to protect clients.

If serious psychological impairment is pleaded as a defense, the professional association will be obliged to take steps to suspend the impaired member and possibly refer him or her to an impaired professionals' committee or members' assistance program; however, it will also be obliged to notify state licensing authorities, which will take immediate steps to suspend or revoke the professional's license.

Fee Splitting

Q. 7:21 What is fee splitting?

Fee splitting is the dividing or sharing of a fee or giving something of value for receiving or making a referral.

> **Example 1.** An EAP counselor refers clients to a private practitioner in the community for long-term therapy. The practitioner pays the EAP counselor as a "consultation fee" a sum equal to 40% of the client fee being paid by the employer's insurance company. In fact, the EAP counselor does consult on a monthly basis to monitor the clients' progress, but that is part of the job for which he is paid by the EAP.
>
> **Example 2.** An inpatient alcoholism facility invites EAP professionals and their wives to a weekend at an elegant resort near the facility each time an inpatient is referred to and completes a 90-day program. An EAP counselor invariably refers clients to the 90-day program, even though it is considerably more expensive than a shorter program that is also available.

Q. 7:22 Is it unethical to give or receive a fee or other emolument for a client referral?

Fee splitting or kickbacks of any kind are not only unethical, but also illegal. The EAP professional is legally and ethically obliged to make all decisions and take all actions in the interests of the client and the employer. When a counselor receives compensation—directly or indirectly—for a referral, his or her objectivity and loyalty are, by definition, compromised. This is a direct breach of fiduciary duty. If a client-paid fee is being split, the fiduciary duty to the client requires that the receiver of the payment turn that money over to the client. If it is an employer-paid fee (whether paid directly by the employer or through an employer-financed benefit plan), the counselor's duty of loyalty to the employer requires that the payment be returned to the employer.

Q. 7:23 What are some legal ramifications of fee splitting?

If a fee has been split, or a kickback paid, and the client sues for malpractice or some other alleged wrong, the facts of the payment are certain to be disclosed in the discovery phase of the litigation, to the clinician's considerable disadvantage. Further, many professional licensing statutes expressly forbid fee splitting, so that a professional found guilty of the practice will have his or her license disciplined. Fee splitting is also a sound basis for termination of employment on the basis of "gross misconduct," which would render the discharged counselor ineligible for unemployment compensation.

Q. 7:24 Can an external EAP or private practitioner pay counselor-contractors on the basis of a percentage of fees received?

Although this practice is not uncommon, it is fee splitting, and thus unethical (and often illegal under licensing laws). The proper method of payment is a flat fee per hour or session irrespective of how much the EAP is paid. The hourly rate to be paid a counselor may take into account such factors as the income to the EAP from client fees and costs of doing business—such as rent, secretarial and billing services, utilities, and advertising—but payment to the counselor should not be tied directly to the payment by the client.

This issue often comes up in the context of a disagreement between the EAP and the contractor-counselor over fees or payments. When the counselor seeks to enforce his or her contract to receive payment promised and not delivered, the matter of fee splitting emerges. An illegal contract is unenforceable, so courts have been known to "leave the parties where they have placed themselves." The EAP will not be able to raise such defenses as not having been paid by the client, but the contractor will not be assisted in enforcing the fee-splitting arrangement. In such a case, the court may or may not require the EAP to pay the contractor the *quantum meruit*, the reasonable value of services performed by the contractor for the EAP. The contractor must prove by evidence not only what services were performed, but also the reasonable value thereof. An expert witness may be required for the latter purpose.

Ethics Among Professionals

Q. 7:25 Can a dispute among professionals, not involving a client, be the basis for an ethics complaint?

Codes of ethics set standards of behavior in all contexts of professional activity, not only activity directly related to clients. Professionals owe a duty of ethical responsibility to their profession and to colleagues and employers.

Example. The owner of an external EAP contracted with a number of counselors to provide services to employees referred following inpatient substance abuse treatment. The owner embarked on a series of sexual liaisons with various counselors (each woman believed that he would leave his wife and marry her). When one of the women confided in another, they all discovered the truth. They complained as a group to the ethics committee of the owner's professional association. He defended himself on the basis that he was a sex addict who required treatment, not punishment; he had not harmed any clients; and the women were as responsible as he for their respective relationships.

The ethics committee found that the owner's behavior compromised the fulfillment of his professional responsibilities to clients, was of a nature to reduce trust and confidence in the profession, deviated from accepted community standards in a manner that reduced the quality of his performance as a professional, and exploited his professional relationships with his employees. The owner was expelled from membership in the association, and a report was made to the state licensing authorities, which—after a hearing—found him to be impaired, suspended his license, and required him to have treatment for two years before they would consider reinstatement.

Q. 7:26 What are the basic principles of ethical responsibility to colleagues and employers?

- *Respect, fairness, and courtesy:* Professionals are obliged to treat each other with respect, courtesy, fairness, and good faith.
- *Other professionals' clients:* Other professionals should be given full consideration in relating to their clients.

- *Commitments to employers:* Commitments to sponsors and employers should be fulfilled.

Q. 7:27 What is the ethical obligation of a professional when he or she is contacted by the client of another professional?

A human services professional is charged with knowing and taking into account the traditions and practices of other professional groups working in the field and cooperating with such groups. It is unethical to offer one's own services directly to or solicit another professional's client. Clients do have an absolute right to change therapists, but the therapist who is contacted by another professional's client is obliged to carefully consider that professional's relationship with the client and proceed with caution and sensitivity to the therapeutic issues and the client's welfare. These issues must be thoroughly discussed with the potential client to avoid confusion and conflict.

The ethical responsibility not to steal another professional's client is only one component of such a situation. The clinical issues must also be explored. A necessary question to any potential transfer must be, "What makes you think you'll like me any better?" Accepting a client-initiated transfer without doing a complete clinical evaluation, including a consultation with the client's present therapist, exposes the new therapist to all kinds of clinical and legal risks. When the potential transferor forbids contact with the present or previous therapist because he or she was "not helpful" or "did not understand," or a similarly vague complaint, *beware!*

Q. 7:28 What is the ethical obligation of an EAP provider to allied or "competing" professions?

In the EAP field, there are strong feelings about who can and cannot treat substance abuse and what treatment modalities are appropriate. It is unfortunately not unusual to hear EAP providers decrying the knowledge, competence, or technical skills of allied professions. This is probably more likely to occur among paraprofessionals and others whose clinical training is narrow in scope and confined to substance abuse. Providers with broader training and education have ordinarily been exposed to other professions and have learned to respect and work with them to secure the best possible service for their clients. No one profession or professional can do everything; it is the ethical and legal responsibility of a provider to obtain complementary or alternative services for clients when indicated. Disparagement of allied or competing professions is unethical. A professional association confronted with a complaint from an allied association or its members takes a dim view of such behavior because it puts the association in an embarrassing and untenable situation in the professional arena.

Q. 7:29 What are the ethical obligations of an EAP professional in supervising other professionals or trainees?

Supervision of staff and trainees is an integral part of many counseling or therapy programs. Because of the powerful influence of a supervisor or trainer over the practice and future careers of supervisees, supervisors are held to high ethical standards in their supervisory relationships. A supervisor is ethically obliged to facilitate the professional development of supervisees and trainees. This obligation includes providing fair, objective, timely, and constructive evaluations and consultations, and (to the extent that he or she has any control over the situation) appropriate working conditions. Exploitation of professional relationships, including sexual harassment, is unethical. (See also Ch. 8, "Legal Issues in EAP Operations," Qs. 8:28, 8:30, and 8:31.)

Q. 7:30 What is sexual harassment?

Sexual harassment is deliberate or repeated comments, gestures, or physical contacts of a sexual nature that are unwanted by the recipient. Because a supervisee or trainee is dependent upon the goodwill of his or her supervisor for evaluations and advancement, many authorities take the position that any sexual overture toward a supervisee or trainee is harassment and must be presumed unwanted. This, in a way, parallels the concept that a client cannot give informed consent to sexual contact because of his or her dependency on the therapist. Sexual harassment of an employee, supervisee, or trainee is not only unethical, but is a violation of employment laws.

Reporting Unethical Behavior

Q. 7:31 Is there an ethical duty to take action when a professional becomes aware of unethical or unprofessional conduct on the part of another professional?

This is always a sensitive subject. Various codes of ethics explicitly or implicitly require action when a helping professional becomes aware of unethical conduct on the part of a colleague, but this may be easier said than done. For example, the Ethical Principles of Psychologists provides:

> When psychologists know of an ethical violation by another psychologist, and it seems appropriate, they informally attempt to resolve the issue by bringing the behavior to the attention of the psychologist. If the misconduct is of a minor nature and/or appears to be due to lack of sensitivity, knowledge, or experience, such an informal solution is usually appropriate. If the violation does not seem amenable to an informal solution, or is of a more serious nature, psychologists bring it to the attention of the appropriate local, state, and/or national committee on professional ethics and conduct.

The Code of Ethics of NASW states:

> The social worker should take action through appropriate channels against unethical conduct by any other member of the profession.

It is not always easy to know what "minor" or "serious" or "proper channels" are, or what "seems amenable" to informal solution.

Q. 7:32 What are the problems in taking action against another professional for unethical conduct?

Confronting a colleague with behavior is very difficult, especially for individuals who are not by nature aggressive. "Whistleblowing" is not always appreciated by employers and may result in unpleasant repercussions. Reporting unethical conduct to an employer, professional association, or legal authorities may subject the reporter to a charge of defamation per se. A fair, good-faith, honest report is privileged and should not subject the reporter to lawsuit, but privilege may not prevent a suit from being filed by a professional who perceives offense to be his or her only or best defense. Privilege is raised as a defense after the lawsuit is filed, and defending such a suit is a traumatic experience, even if the reporter wins. Truth and fair comment are also defenses to a defamation action.

Q. 7:33 If a counselor is told by a client of the unprofessional conduct of the client's previous therapist, but the client refuses to permit disclosure, what is the counselor's ethical course of action?

It is not unusual for a client to disclose to a counselor that he or she has been sexually abused or otherwise victimized by a previous therapist. Often, the client adamantly refuses permission to disclose this information to anyone, including the previous therapist. In such a case, there may be little the counselor can do. Attempting to convince the client to consent to action may be a breach of duty to the client. On the other hand, the counselor may be put in an untenable situation if he or she is aware of continuing referrals to the alleged abuser, or local state law requires reporting.

Q. 7:34 Is reporting the alleged abuse, but withholding the client's name, a viable solution?

To disclose to appropriate personnel that a complaint has been made, but not to back it up with the client's name and the circumstances, may subject the reporter to retaliation from the accused, if the latter finds out about it. A sudden falling off of referrals is bound, after all, to result in an inquiry as to why. Further, the client may fear even a disclosure without his or her name being used on the basis that the therapist will know or surmise the information came from the client. Some abused clients are deeply in need of therapeutic assistance to help deal with the abuse, but are also deeply ambivalent about denouncing the therapist because of love or guilt feelings toward the therapist, fear of retaliation (often these therapists are perceived by their victims as omnipotent), or fear of negative impact on a marriage or other relationship or reputation. Such a client will perceive himself or herself to be betrayed again if the current counselor insists on action.

Q. 7:35 If the alleged abuser is a member of the staff or a contractor of the same EAP, what are the counselor's obligations?

Notwithstanding the client's wishes or clinical issues, if the alleged abuser is an employee or contractor of the same EAP, the counselor must disclose the charge to the clinical director or supervisor. Such information cannot be withheld from the agency's administration, irrespective of the client's wishes. The client must be informed of the obligation to disclose, and protection and support provided. It must be explained to the client that he or she is a client of the EAP, not the counselor individually, and the counselor cannot hold a secret with the client against the EAP. This position is clinically viable, as well as legally and ethically appropriate. To do otherwise would be confusing and anxiety-provoking for the client and result in transference and countertransference issues detrimental to the client's welfare. Further, withholding this type of information would be a breach of duty to all other clients of the EAP, as well as a breach of loyalty to the organization.

Q. 7:36 What steps should an EAP take when the client's wishes are inconsistent with the legal and ethical obligations of the counselor and program?

Clinical, legal, and ethical consultation are required in such a case. Certainly, even if a counselor or program does not report the allegation, it must not make any further referrals to a professional whose ethical conduct or clinical competence is questionable. An outstanding source of consultation and guidance in therapist sexual abuse cases is Gary Schoener, director of the Walk-In Counseling Center, 2421 Chicago Avenue South, Minneapolis, Minn. 55404—(612) 870-0566. A few states are beginning to require reporting of sexual abuse under certain circumstances. Inquiry should be made into local law and documented.

Advertising Services

Q. 7:37 What are the ethical principles involved in advertising an EAP?

Advertising and publicity about an EAP may be targeted to potential sponsors or potential clients. In either case, it must be consistent with the professional advertising standards of the various professions providing EAP services. Most significantly, advertising should be scrupulously honest in representing the scope and nature of services to be delivered, and the limitations on service. Specifically, advertising and publicity should not contain:

- False, misleading, deceptive, or unfair statements;
- Any misinterpretation of fact or statement likely to mislead or deceive because in context it makes only a partial disclosure of relevant facts;
- A statement intended or likely to create false or unjustified expectations of favorable results;
- Any statement implying unusual, unique, or one-of-a-kind abilities;
- Any statement intended or likely to appeal to a person's fears, anxieties, or emotions concerning the possible results of failure to obtain the offered services;
- A statement concerning the comparative desirability of offered services; or
- A guarantee of privacy or confidentiality without a statement of the exceptions thereto.

Q. 7:38 May an EAP or individual professional hire a public relations firm to secure publicity in the media?

Hiring a public relations representative is not, in and of itself, unethical. However, there is an ethical prohibition against paying a representative of the press, radio, television, or other communication medium in anticipation of or in return for professional publicity in a news item.

Professional Ethics Committees and Ethics Complaints

Q. 7:39 How do professional associations process ethics complaints?

Every professional association has its own set of procedures for adjudicating ethics complaints. These procedures should be in writing and furnished to every complainant and member-respondent. The procedures must be uniformly followed, so that every member is treated fairly and by the same standards. Usually, associations require that complaints be in writing. Sometimes, the ethics committee will review complaints and assign the facts to the appropriate sections of the code of ethics. Other associations may send a copy of the code to the complainant and require him or her to locate the specific section alleged to be violated. The accused member is entitled to a clear statement of the conduct he or she is alleged to have committed and the ethical principle alleged to have been breached thereby. The member is also entitled to respond to the allegations. Some societies conduct their ethics proceedings completely in writing by an exchange of correspondence. Others hold hearings at which the complainant, respondent, and any witnesses may be heard.

Q. 7:40 Is a member entitled to be represented by an attorney in an ethics proceeding?

One always has a right to consult an attorney with respect to any matter having legal ramifications, but most professional associations do not permit a member to be formally represented by an attorney during a hearing. Usually, a lawyer may accompany the member and advise him or her, but may not speak or examine or cross-examine witnesses on the member's behalf.

Q. 7:41 Does a member have a right to due process in an ethics proceeding?

An ethics proceeding must be conducted in accordance with the bylaws and procedures adopted by the professional society. Usually, these do not provide for due process as it exists in the legal system. Due process requires the right to be present before the tribunal that pronounces judgment upon the question of life, liberty, or property (the right to practice one's profession is a liberty and property right protected under the Constitution); the right to be heard, by testimony or otherwise, and to controvert every material fact bearing on the matter involved; the right to confront one's accusers and cross-examine witnesses; and the right to an orderly proceeding with notice.

Private professional associations are not constrained by constitutional principles, so courts usually take the position that a member charged with an ethics violation is entitled only to a fair hearing. A fair hearing has many of the features of due process, but will not include the right of confrontation and cross-examination unless these are provided for by the rules of the association.

In recent years, in response to concerns of malpractice insurers that have a strong economic interest in putting poor risks out of business, many states have enacted legislation requiring professional associations to notify licensing authorities when a professional in health or a related field has been found guilty of unethical or unprofessional conduct. This will usually result in immediate action against the professional's license. As ethics proceedings begin to more directly and dramatically affect the right of a professional to practice his or her profession, it would seem logical that courts will require more due process protections in those arenas.

Q. 7:42 Can professionals who sit on ethics committees be sued by professional colleagues who are dissatisfied with the proceedings?

Some states have statutes immunizing health care providers who sit on ethics or peer review committees from lawsuits by dissatisfied respondents. These statutes vary in scope, so it behooves any professional who is invited to sit on such a committee to investigate the liability ramifications. Even when there is immunity, it will be qualified; any showing of malice will nullify the immunity. Further, if a respondent can establish that members of the ethics committee had an economic interest in putting him or her out of business, those members are open to an antitrust suit. Actions instigated or conducted maliciously can also give rise to suit for defamation and interference with advantageous economic relationships.

Q. 7:43 Does professional liability insurance protect ethics committee members against suits by respondents?

Usually, a professional liability insurance policy covers all aspects of one's professional activities, including service on boards and committees. The protection will ordinarily not extend to malicious, willful, wrongful behavior or antitrust or unfair competition claims. Organizations should have directors' and officers' liability insurance, but this usually does not cover members of committees. Ethics committee members should check their insurance policies, including the possibility of an all-risk umbrella that will protect against most claims not covered by other policies. If there is any possibility that a respondent can reasonably accuse a committee member of unfair competition or antitrust violations, legal consultation should take place before and during the ethics proceedings.

Ethical Duty to Maintain Confidentiality

Q. 7:44 What is the ethical duty of confidentiality in an EAP setting?

The ethical duty of confidentiality is substantially the same as the legal duty. (See Ch. 4, "Confidentiality Requirements.") There are loopholes in the legal duty, however, that may not apply in the ethical context. The legal duty to maintain client confidentiality is prescribed and attenuated by statutory, contractual, and common-law exceptions. If a counselor makes disclosures of confidential information in accordance with legal limits, the client will have no basis for a lawsuit. However, a counselor has an additional ethical duty to be sure that a client is not seduced or entrapped unknowingly into a situation in which his or her confidentiality or privacy can be invaded. Informed consent comes into play here, but the client's dependency and transference issues must be taken into account in assessing the ethicality of the counselor's behavior. It is exploitive and unethical for a professional to use a client's information for the professional's gain or interests, even with client consent, unless the client or his or her treatment cannot in any manner be adversely affected.

Q. 7:45 If an employer, union, or client demands unethical behavior, what is the EAP professional's duty?

Occasionally, a litigant employer or union (often through its legal department) demands that the EAP turn over client information or otherwise cooperate in a legal dispute involving, for example, an accusation of unfair labor practices, or the like. Sometimes, a client litigant demands information from the EAP about other clients—usually in the context of a claim of discrimination. The EAP is ethically obliged to resist any such demands by entering into litigation, if necessary, to protect client confidentiality and the integrity of the EAP and the individual EAP professional. If worse comes to worst, an EAP provider may be ethically required to resign from employment or give up a contract. In such event, a complaint to the ethics board of ALMACA, EASNA, or the professional association of the individual staff member may bring sufficient pressure to bear on the employer or union to protect the EAP from unfair retaliation for insisting on maintaining ethical standards.

Example. A client is embroiled in a lawsuit with his employer over his job termination as a result of a urine screening that was positive for cocaine use. The employer is requiring the client to agree to ongoing treatment, random drug tests, and a contract to attend five AA or NA meetings a week as a condition of reinstatement. The client raises constitutional issues, including the right to freedom of association, freedom of religion, and privacy, and avers that the employer has discriminated against him in implementing the EAP's recommendations for a last-chance contract. The client's lawyer subpoenas the EAP's records for a list of all client names, and all documents and memoranda dealing with the EAP, its policies and procedures, and its relationship with the employer.

The employer's attorney is disinclined to press the matter of confidentiality and refuses to take any steps to protect the record. The EAP is a small external EAP, just starting out in business, and the contract was deliberately bid very low in an effort to get established with the employer. It cannot afford the costs of fighting this battle. Legal consultation reveals that failure to protect the privacy and confidentiality of the other clients might result in lawsuits from them. Ethics consultation results in a decision that the EAP has an ethical and legal obligation to clients and the field to act, even at its own expense.

The EAP's attorney files a motion to quash the subpoena on the grounds that it is over-broad, seeks irrelevant and immaterial information, and violates the confidentiality and privacy of other clients. The court rules that certain of the memoranda are relevant and must be provided, but that clients' names and records are not to be produced. Instead, the court requires production of aggregate data about the program and its clients, including demographic data and information about race, job classification, referral recommendations, and so forth. The court states that if the plaintiff is unable to get the information he requires from these productions, he must pay to have the individual records edited to remove identifying information before it will order them produced.

Ethics and the EAP-Sponsor Relationship

Q. 7:46 What are the ethical components of informed consent in an EAP?

The EAP setting is rife with conflicts of interest among employer, sponsor, client, and the program. The EAP professional is ethically obliged to clarify the nature and direction of his or her loyalties and responsibilities and keep all parties informed of his or her commitments. Clients must be fully informed of the consequences of accepting or refusing EAP services, as well as their freedom of choice with regard to participation.

Q. 7:47 Is there an ethical duty to terminate EAP services?

There is an ethical duty to terminate clinical services or a consulting relationship when it is reasonably clear that the client is not benefiting from them. Termination of treatment must be implemented in a clinically appropriate fashion, and an offer of help in locating alternative services must be made.

Q. 7:48 Does an EAP professional have an ethical duty to intervene in unauthorized and unqualified practice?

Yes. Many EAPs use volunteers as peer counselors. A good program sets clear guidelines and limits for the activities of volunteers and peer counselors and provides appropriate training and supervision for their activities. Historically, some EAPs have been staffed entirely by volunteers and peers, often recovering substance abusers whose training and experience consist of their own treatment and self-help experiences. These individuals can be invaluable as case finders, referrers, and peer counselors, as long as they understand the limitations of their knowledge and do not exceed their competence in their work with other employees.

Sometimes volunteers have unrealistic views about their competence and make unsupervised assessments and referrals, even for inpatient treatment. If a client decides later that a mistake was made, the EAP is a target for a lawsuit. This is a serious political problem when an EAP, which is expected to provide a professional program, is perceived (accurately!) as displacing the "old-boy" networks of peer counseling, which were the origins of today's EAP programs and which are still a factor in many EAP programs today. Organizational development is often a component of an EAP, and the political situation in which it operates must be addressed here. At bottom, a professional has an ethical duty to act to prevent unauthorized and unqualified practice.

Q. 7:49 What is the ethical duty of the EAP provider in case finding and client recruitment?

Case finding and client recruitment are typically important components of EAP services to employers and sponsors. It is in the employer's economic and legal interests that workers use the EAP and follow its recommendations. Although the EAP professional may perceive the employer's and employee's best interests to be congruent in this situation, if the employee does not wish to participate in the EAP or receive services, an ethical dilemma exists. To what extent does the code of professional conduct permit convincing, manipulating, or threatening the client into accepting treatment?

The EAP provider has an ethical as well as legal duty to inform the client or potential client of the extent and nature of the services available. In addition, the client should be informed of the associated limits, rights, opportunities, obligations, consequences, and risks of accepting or refusing services, which might affect the client's decision about entering into or continuing treatment. This ethical duty arises directly from the professional's fiduciary duty and is in line with the duty to obtain informed consent. Thus, breach of this ethical duty would also be malpractice and breach of contract.

Q. 7:50 What is the ethical duty of a provider when service is limited or termination or interruption of service is anticipated?

EAP service availability is strictly determined by the program. A client or potential client must be fully informed at the outset about the program's inherent limitations. Usually, EAP availability ends with the termination of employment, with the result that the most needy clients may find themselves suddenly without service if their symptomatic behavior results in suspension or firing. As a general rule, services may not be withdrawn precipitously because of program limitations. Ethically and legally, an EAP is bound to continue service until an orderly, clinically appropriate referral and transfer can be made. This ethical duty is related to the contractual duty not to abandon.

Chapter 8

Legal Issues in EAP Operations

Good management, hiring, and supervision practices go a long way toward minimizing liability in an EAP setting. Issues explored in this chapter include negligent hiring and supervision and how an EAP can minimize liability through sound applicant screening and supervisory practices; what EAPs should do if they discover a client has been abused; recordkeeping requirements; the EAP's role in drug screening; and the EAP's legal responsibility to adequately monitor contractors and clerical and volunteer staff.

Q. 8:1 Are there liability ramifications in hiring and supervision practices?

EAPs are under a duty to their clients to use due care in hiring and supervising employees. If a client is harmed as a proximate result of negligence in hiring or supervision, the EAP will be directly liable.

Q. 8:2 How does liability for negligent hiring or supervision differ from vicarious liability?

An employer is vicariously liable for the wrongful acts of an employee performed in the course and scope of employment. If a client is harmed by a counselor whose actions are not within the scope of employment, vicarious liability cannot be held against the employer. Thus, for example, an employer will not be vicariously liable to a client who is assaulted and battered by an employee, because assault and battery is not part of the employee's job. Some courts have held that sexual abuse of a client by an employee therapist is not within the scope of employment, so the employer will not be held vicariously liable. (*Andrews v. United States,* 732 F.2d 366 (4th Cir. 1984)) Other courts have refused to relieve employers from liability, holding that until the facts are heard in the case, the court cannot determine what behaviors were within the scope of employment. (*Marston v. Minneapolis Clinic of Psychiatry and Neurology,* 329 N.W.2d 306 (Minn. 1982))

Whether or not the behavior complained of is held to be within the scope and course of employment, if an EAP is negligent in hiring and knew or should have known that the employee was a risk to clients, the EAP can be held directly liable to the client for negligent hiring. Some examples might be a person hired as a therapist who had no training to do the job or a counselor with a history of sexual abuse of clients. Similarly, if a program negligently fails to supervise an employee whose wrongful conduct is harmful to a client, the employer will be directly liable for negligent failure to supervise.

Q. 8:3 What is negligent hiring?

Negligent hiring occurs when an employer fails to adequately screen a job applicant prior to employment, with the result that a client is exposed to an incompetent or dangerous practitioner who causes harm to him or her.

Q. 8:4 What constitutes due care in hiring?

An EAP is obliged to perform a reasonable investigation of an applicant before hiring. All representations in a resumé should be verified in writing, including the applicant's explanation of any anomalies or gaps in his or her history. Educational claims should be verified by letter to the institutions and training programs that the applicant claims to have attended. Licensure and membership in professional associations should be verified. Licensing authorities and professional associations should be queried about whether any complaints have been received about the applicant and, if so, their disposition. References should be checked by both letter and phone call. Because of fear of lawsuits by former employees for whom negative references are given, many employers have adopted the practice of verifying only dates of employment. Sometimes, a telephone call to the former supervisor will result in more information, but often this is not the case. A record of the investigation and its results should be maintained in the applicant's file. (See D-1: Model Screening Instrument: EAP Clinician Applicants for Employment.)

Screening Applicants and Providing References

Q. 8:5 What are some methods by which an EAP can adequately screen applicants?

Given the sensitive nature of EAP work, it is reasonable for a potential employer to require that an applicant execute a written request and authorization to previous employers and trainers to disclose all information about the applicant, including copies of evaluations and history of any job discipline. The request and authorization should include a release of liability and an agreement to hold the previous employer harmless by reason of the disclosure. (See D-2: Model Screening Instrument: Verification of Information Provided by Prospective EAP Clinician and D-3: Model Indemnification for Reference Providers of Prospective EAP Clinicians.) An applicant who refuses such an authorization is not a good candidate for hiring.

Some employers do a routine credit check of applicants. This can reveal a great deal about an applicant's management of his or her life (for example, fiscal responsibility and general character). There are organizations that specialize in investigating the backgrounds of job applicants for a fee. An EAP may wish to consider employing such a service if screening of applicants proves too time-consuming or difficult. Applicants should be asked to execute signed authorizations to the credit bureau or investigator. As with the authorization to former employers, an applicant who refuses a credit or background check should not be considered for hiring.

Q. 8:6 Is an EAP liable to a subsequent employer if it fails to disclose dangerous propensities or other risk factors of a former employee when asked for a reference?

An EAP is at risk if it misleads another employer in giving a reference for a former employee. It is not recommended that an EAP give a false or incomplete report calculated to lull a potential employer into a false sense of security in hiring. On the other hand, no EAP wants the burden of a lawsuit from a former employee who cannot get a job because of a bad reference. Many employers remove themselves from this dilemma by simply confirming the fact and dates of employment and providing no other information. This makes it difficult to police the profession and protect clients from incompetent or unscrupulous providers.

An EAP may choose to respond to a reference inquiry by confirming employment and enclosing an authorization with a release of liability and hold harmless agreement, stating that it will give further information upon receipt of an executed copy thereof. The responsibility for following up falls to the potential employer and protects the EAP; the potential employer is put on notice that further inquiry is in its best interest; the employee has the option of withdrawing the application if he or she does not wish the information to be shared. Of course, any reference policy should be applied across the board to all reference checks to avoid charges of unfair treatment.

Q. 8:7 What steps can an EAP take to protect itself from lawsuits by former employees arising out of unflattering references?

In giving references, the EAP must be scrupulously accurate in stating only facts and occurrences. If there are two sides to a story being disclosed, the employee's side should be fairly stated. It is good practice to give or send to the employee upon termination of employment a copy of his or her record and the reference material that would be sent out pursuant to request. Some employers ask employees to sign off on their records at termination. An employee is then on notice and has the opportunity to take whatever steps he or she sees fit prior to seeking disclosure or a reference from the employer.

Q. 8:8 If an EAP has given a positive reference and later discovers serious wrongdoing on the part of a current or former employee, is there an obligation to notify the recipient of the reference?

Although there probably is no duty to correct a previously given positive reference if new information arises following its dissemination, to cover itself against such eventuality, an EAP should state in the reference that it is based on information known to it at the time. There may be situations, however, that are so egregious that the EAP may feel itself morally obligated to withdraw a reference. In such event, courtesy and ethical responsibility to colleagues and employees mandate notification to the employee. It is recommended that the EAP send a short letter stating that information has recently come to its attention that requires the rescission of the reference previously supplied, and that the writer will be willing to give further details in a personal meeting with the employee and the reference recipient.

Example. An EAP has sent a glowing reference for an employee to a graduate clinical psychology program that has accepted him for training. Then a client discloses to the EAP that she is pregnant by the counselor, she was his client five years ago when he was employed at another agency, she has been sexually involved with him sporadically since, and in fact he paid for an abortion of a previous pregnancy. The only reason she is reporting the present situation is because she thinks he is also involved with another EAP client who is pregnant, and she wants that client transferred to another counselor! The counselor reluctantly confirms the client's story. Concurrent with other steps, the EAP writes to the graduate program and rescinds its reference, offering to meet with the counselor and the program, if desired.

Q. 8:9 May an EAP refuse to hire a professional on the ground that he or she is not a recovering substance abuser?

Some programs take the position that only substance abusers can successfully treat other substance abusers. That this is patently not the case is evidenced by the hundreds of nonabusing professionals who do an excellent job in substance abuse treatment and EAPs in general. Other programs state that since recovering substance abusers are handicapped persons under the Rehabilitation Act of 1973, they are complying with the affirmative action requirements of Section 503 of the Act by hiring only such persons. It appears that this may be a form of reverse discrimination that is as unlawful as direct discrimination against the handicapped. Before implementing such a hiring policy, an EAP should seek the advice of competent counsel and consult with state and federal human rights authorities.

Q. 8:10 May an EAP require participation in Alcoholics Anonymous (AA) or Narcotics Anonymous (NA) as a condition of employment on its staff?

An EAP employee has the same constitutional rights to freedom of association and privacy as any other citizen. As a general rule, it is no more reasonable for an EAP to require attendance at NA or AA than to require membership in a specific club or church. If, however, an EAP staff member is a recovering substance abuser who has lapsed, violated work rules, been disciplined, and offered a last chance contract, participation in NA or AA is a reasonable requirement for reinstatement.

Policies and Procedures

Q. 8:11 Are there liability ramifications in EAP personnel and client care policies?

Every EAP should have definite policies prohibiting staff members from engaging in extratherapy social or business relationships with clients or their families. This may be difficult, particularly for staff members who attend the same AA meetings as clients (a practice that should be discouraged). The rule against fraternization should be extended to all EAP personnel, not just clinicians, because complications that arise from social or business contacts directly expose the EAP to considerable liability. The obvious risks are charges of undue influence, fraud, deceit, breach of confidentiality, breach of privacy, conflict of interest, and mishandling of transference. If an EAP employee breaches policy and a client claims damages as a result of the breaching behavior, the EAP is likely to be charged with negligent supervision.

Q. 8:12 What EAP personnel policies can help to minimize risk of liability for negligent supervision?

Policies and procedures for supervision, monitoring of staff behavior, EAP work rules, and disciplinary policies and procedures are primary tools for avoiding negligent supervision and its liability risks. Progressive discipline may be philosophically attractive and consistent with the humanistic ideals of the EAP, but any infraction of rules, policies, or procedures that constitutes a menace to clients should be cause for immediate removal from the field of risk.

Staffing

Q. 8:13 What are the issues for EAPs in staffing and case assignment?

The scope of the program and nature of the services will determine staffing. Some internal EAPs are staffed by employees of human resources or medical departments or by persons selected from the employment force for their perceived talent at leadership and human relations. Occasionally, EAP services are provided by a clerical employee assigned to the task along with his or her other work. It is probably fair to say that these arrangements are not really employee assistance programs; rather, the employer is providing certain help to employees on an ad hoc basis. Unless a person trained and skilled in mental health care or social service delivery is providing the services, EAP functions should be strictly confined to information and referral to trained providers.

As with any clinical care program, EAP staff members should be allowed to perform only those functions for which they have competence. Each program must, therefore, determine what services it will provide and then credential its staff to provide them. In choosing an external EAP, a sponsor is well advised to require that it hire trained clinical personnel. Permitting an incompetent person to provide services is negligent. Local state licensing and confidentiality law may indicate a basis for hiring and credentialing certain professionals rather than others. In assessing cases, if it is evident that a client has legal problems, it makes sense to assign him or her to a staff member whose professional credentials and licensure provide confidentiality and communications privilege protection. Permitting an incompetent person to provide services is negligent.

Q. 8:14 What insurance protection is necessary when the EAP contracts with an independent professional to provide services to EAP clients?

When an employer with an internal or external EAP contracts for services with an independent EAP provider, the contract should specify who is carrying what insurance. Usually, an independent contractor is required to carry its own insurance, and the EAP or sponsor should be named as an additional insured under the contractor's policy. Proof of insurance from time to time, and a letter of instruction by the contractor to its carrier directing that the EAP and/or sponsor be notified in the event of cancellation or lapse, should be a condition of the contract.

Handling Client Abuse

Q. 8:15 What should an EAP do if it discovers that a counselor has abused a client?

Upon reasonable suspicion that a counselor has engaged in behavior that is abusive or dangerous to a client, the EAP must immediately suspend the counselor from all clinical responsibilities and begin an investigation. Ordinarily, this suspension will be with pay while the investigation is being carried out. A clinical consultant, the EAP's lawyer, and the insurance carrier should be brought in immediately to institute "damage control." The investigation must be conducted with due care for the subject client's clinical issues and general well-being, as well as the reputation of the clinician. Interviews with those persons likely to have the facts should be tape recorded or else conducted with someone taking close notes. Whether to interview other clients of the counselor is an issue to be decided on a case-by-case basis with the advice of the consultants.

If the investigation results in a finding of misconduct, all clients of the counselor must be immediately transferred to other therapists. What to tell the clients and how to handle the abrupt disappearance of the therapist are extremely complicated clinical questions that should be answered in conjunction with the clinical consultant.

The EAP's disciplinary procedures should be followed scrupulously. A court reporter's transcript should be made of any hearing. It is not recommended that the miscreant be permitted to resign in exchange for a clear record or silence agreement, although that may seem the easiest course in the short run. Such an agreement might compromise the EAP at a later time as events unfold. Some state statutes require reporting of sexually abusing therapists to licensing authorities. If sexual abuse of a child has occurred, it must be reported under most child abuse reporting statutes. In some states sexual abuse of a psychotherapy client is a crime. Legal counsel should be consulted with respect to reporting.

Q. 8:16 What are the EAP's responsibilities to a client who has been abused by an EAP staff member?

The EAP owes an abused client the highest level of service to attempt to ameliorate the injury done to him or her. Some authorities suggest that the EAP has a conflict of interest in such a situation, and the client must be referred to an outside treater, rather than being transferred in-house. Others feel that this may be perceived by the client as a punishment or abandonment by the program. The importance of excellent clinical consultation in deciding on a course of action cannot be overestimated. Often, a frank discussion with the client to ascertain his or her wishes will point to the correct direction. Under no circumstances should a cover-up be attempted, nor any admission of liability made. The client should be told that what has occurred is unacceptable, that it is not the client's fault or responsibility, and that the EAP is taking all steps to correct the situation.

Q. 8:17 Should an EAP make an ethics complaint to the abuser's professional association?

Although the EAP would probably rather avoid any more involvement in an abuse situation than is absolutely necessary, an ethics complaint is recommended when it is warranted. Most codes of ethics require action by professionals who are aware of unethical conduct, so failure to report might in itself be a breach of ethics. Further, in the event of action by the client or the abuser against the EAP, the fact of the ethics action will inure to the EAP's credit.

EAP-Sponsor Relationship

Q. 8:18 Are there liability risks when the EAP staff acts as a consultant to the sponsor?

Most EAPs have a consultation component that is extremely valuable to sponsors. Consultation may be to the human resources department, management at all levels, and supervisors. It may involve advising on policies, benefits, or handling of individual cases. The risk of liability for consulting to the system is probably not great, except when it involves individual employees who are or may become clients. The EAP must carefully avoid conflicts of interest and breaches of confidentiality in these situations. If the EAP is being accessed to assist in managing an employer personnel problem, the subject employee should probably be referred for outside service rather than being served by the EAP.

Q. 8:19 Should EAPs be involved in fitness-for-duty evaluations, last chance agreements, or drug screening?

Some EAP professionals feel that it is outside the scope of employee assistance to be the agent of the employer in conducting fitness-for-duty evaluations, structuring or mandating last chance agreements, or, except possibly as part of monitoring clients' compliance with treatment program requirements, administering drug screening. Fitness for duty is a human resources issue and may be best handled through the employer's personnel and medical departments. Once fitness or unfitness for duty has been established, the EAP can be called in to render assistance to the employee consistent with the findings.

Most EAP professionals feel that it is not within the scope of employee assistance to determine whether discipline should be carried out or suspended, or an employee should be allowed a last chance. It is appropriate, however, for management to seek consultation of the EAP on an employee's prognosis and clinical needs, and management may then choose to incorporate the EAP's recommendations into its disciplinary or reinstatement determinations. The precise role of the EAP should be clearly articulated in written policies and procedures. This will prove particularly important if an employee perceives himself or herself to be the object of discrimination and attempts to link the EAP with the employer in an employment law dispute.

EAPs are sometimes asked by employers to implement drug screening programs. At first glance, the EAP may seem the logical entity to carry out this task, but more careful consideration may suggest otherwise. Drug screening is used as a prevention device in the context of employer policies and work rules prohibiting employee drug use. A positive drug test will result in corrective or punitive measures, particularly if the test is done for cause. If the EAP administers the testing program, it is clearly operating as a social control officer for the employer, not an assistance program for the employee. The credibility of the EAP and, therefore, its effectiveness in achieving its stated goal are compromised.

Q. 8:20 What are the liability risks for an EAP in fitness-for-duty evaluations, last chance agreements, and drug testing?

So long as the EAP is scrupulously careful in conducting these activities, the risk is probably no greater than in other EAP functions. An important factor in minimizing legal risk is speed. Clinical staff may then make determinations about immediacy of treatment needs.

Recordkeeping

Q. 8:21 What records should an EAP keep?

An EAP is obliged to keep those records required in its contract with the sponsor (for example, statistics to establish the quantity, types, and demographics of service, and such other data as are necessary for fiscal accountability). In addition, clinical care standards require records of each client's clinical experience with the EAP sufficient to assure continuity of care, quality control, and utilization review.

Q. 8:22 Who owns the records?

If the EAP is internal, the sponsor owns the EAP and therefore will own the EAP records. Nonetheless, the records must be kept separate from other sponsor personnel records and must be kept confidential for all but EAP purposes. An external EAP owns its own records; any attempt by a sponsor to contract otherwise should be firmly resisted. Although the program owns the records, clients have rights to the information contained therein. These rights may be established by statute or court decisions, so every EAP must check into local law on the subject.

Q. 8:23 If a program is terminated, what should be done with its records?

Some EAPs will be governed by statutes or regulations directing the disposition of records when a program terminates. This should be ascertained by consultation with local counsel. If the program is being replaced by another program or provider, the records may be transferred to the successor after notification to clients and an opportunity to object. Records of current clients who are being transferred should be provided to the successor providers. The regular client consent is required. For closed cases, if there is no requirement that records be retained, many EAPs notify their former clients that they will send the records to them for their own use or disposal or, upon receipt of a properly executed consent, send the records to a provider designated by the client, and, if not otherwise instructed within a reasonable period of time, will destroy them.

Q. 8:24 What clinical records should an EAP keep?

The standard of care requires that sufficient recording be done to establish that the care given the client was competent and nonnegligent. (*Cohen v. New York*, 51 A.D.2d 494 (1976), *aff'd*, 364 N.E.2d 1134 (1977)) Most clinicians agree that the following constitutes the minimum adequate record:

- Face sheet, including demographic data and personal statistics;
- Statement of problem as perceived by referral source, client, and counselor;
- Precipitating factors and family and environmental factors;
- Relevant clinical history, including substance abuse history;
- Description of assessment procedures;
- Formulation and diagnosis (or the equivalent, if these "medical model" terms are not attractive);
- Treatment plan;
- Disposition;
- Progress notes for each client or collateral contact;

- Discharge or termination summary; and
- Follow-up.

Q. 8:25 Should clients have access to their records?

Modern clinical theory holds that clients must be partners in their clinical care. Clients' rights activists believe that everyone has an absolute right to access to and a copy of any record kept about himself or herself. Some states have laws requiring client access; others do not, but even those states that do not mandate access permit it and usually have some mechanism by which a client can require clinical records to be disclosed to a clinician of his or her choice if the treater does not wish to disclose them to the client. The federal regulations on drug and alcohol records do not mandate client access but do not forbid it. The EAP and the client will both be best served by total client access to records from both a clinical and a legal perspective. In the event of legal action in connection with EAP services, the records will be discoverable. There is no advantage in withholding a record, and openness is consistent with EAP treatment philosophy.

Q. 8:26 How long should an EAP retain client records?

Records should be kept as long as they are needed to ensure continuity of care, to facilitate audit and accountability, and to protect the EAP in the event of a lawsuit arising out of the clinical care relationship. Every state has a statute of limitations barring lawsuits that are not brought within a prescribed period of time after the acts complained of occur. From a professional liability perspective, an EAP should ascertain the statute of limitations for breach of contract and malpractice in its jurisdiction and maintain records for at least that period of time. At least one major company's EAP, however, takes the position that it is not very likely to be sued, and that there is a danger that records might be accessed and used against clients. Therefore, this company shreds everything but the face sheet and a log of client contacts six months after closing a case. Legal consultation is recommended to arrive at a record maintenance policy.

Q. 8:27 What are some rules for records security?

Records should be kept in locked cabinets on the EAP premises. Any waste paper containing client names or information should be shredded before disposal. Under no circumstances should client records be taken from the EAP office except for consultation purposes. If records are transported for consultation, they should be kept in a locked briefcase in the possession of the carrier, never left in the trunk of a car. Client records and information should not be faxed. If client information is sent through the mail, it should go via certified, registered, or express mail or private mail service, with a signature required by recipient. Students or trainees should not be permitted to take copies of client records, make recordings of sessions, or use client information for class presentations unless the supervisor and client have given informed consent. If client names and information are kept on computer, either the computer should not be on-line or a very tight computer security system should be used.

Monitoring EAP Employees

Q. 8:28 Is there a duty to supervise EAP staff and their activities with clients?

There is a clear duty on an EAP to supervise staff in their care of and activities with clients. (*Andrews v. United States,* 732 F.2d 366 (4th Cir. 1984)) Negligent supervision will result in liability if a client is harmed by the wrongful act of a staff member, whether or not in the course and scope of employment.

Example. An EAP secretary was having an extramarital affair with a union official. The official was embroiled in a bitter union election contest with a man whom the secretary knew to be an EAP client. In an effort to be "helpful" to her lover, she gave him a copy of the opponent's EAP record. Among other facts reported therein, the record revealed that the opponent had tested positive for the HIV virus, which he had contracted as the result of a blood transfusion he had received following a serious accident four years previously. The official spread the story that the opponent was "a faggot with AIDS." It took very little effort to trace the source of the story. The secretary was sued for breach of privacy and confidentiality, and defamation. The official was sued for breach of privacy and defamation. Both were held individually liable. The EAP was sued for breach of confidentiality and privacy on the theory of *respondeat superior,* but was found not guilty on the basis that the secretary's actions were not within the scope of her employment. The EAP was found guilty, however, of negligent supervision.

Q. 8:29 What is the EAP's duty with respect to training the nonclinical staff?

EAP administrators have a duty to train and monitor the clerical staff, with particular attention being paid to client contacts and confidentiality. The support staff is a major point of interface between the EAP and the rest of the world and is, therefore, a source of risk or protection to the program and its clients. Professionals are expected to be aware of confidentiality and privacy laws and their ethical responsibilities to clients. The support staff must be specifically trained in these areas. Not only the principles, but also specific rules and techniques for protecting client confidentiality should be taught, including stock phrases for answering inquiries. For example, secretaries should be cautioned about not leaving client information at the photocopy center or on desks or in typewriters where passers-by can view them. They should be instructed to shred sensitive material that goes into the trash, lock files at night, and take care not to be overheard when talking on the telephone.

Secretaries who handle intake calls must be particularly cautioned against behavior that could be interpreted as commencing clinical services and thereby accepting immediate EAP responsibility for client well-being. The more information a program has at intake, the more liability will attach at that point for any failure of due care in not seeing a client quickly enough in an emergency. A secretary should be trained to inquire about an emergency and to access a clinical staff person immediately if there is any chance that some danger to a client may exist.

Q. 8:30 What is supervision?

Supervision, consultation, and monitoring are terms for similar activities that are often confused and used interchangeably. These activities have varying legal consequences, however, so an EAP should be able to distinguish among them and use them appropriately.

Supervision involves directing and overseeing the practice and activities of an employee who is subject to the control of the supervisor. The supervisor is responsible for client care and for guidance of the therapist. Ordinarily, the supervisor does not personally interview the client, but supervises through interview sessions with the therapist, who presents case material for review and instruction and reviews statistical, program, and clinical case records. Sometimes audiotapes or videotapes of client sessions or observation via two-way mirror are used for supervision. Supervision, or preceptorship, is a primary method of educating and training psychotherapists and counselors.

Q. 8:31 What is monitoring?

Monitoring is the ongoing inspection, scrutiny, audit, and review of the activities of a therapist or program over which one has no professional control but for which there is responsibility of oversight. This may involve review of individual cases; the program, modalities, techniques, and behaviors of the direct service providers; and the outcomes.

Q. 8:32 What is consultation?

Consultation involves no treatment relationship between the consultant and the client and no responsibility for client care. The consultant's relationship is with the consulting professional, not the client, and the consultant relies on information provided by the treating clinician as a basis for giving the treater an opinion and advice. The treater is not under the control of the consultant and is not obliged to follow his or her advice. (Whether failure to follow the consultant's advice may be malpractice is another issue.)

Q. 8:33 What are the legal ramifications of negligent supervision?

A supervisor is in control of the treatment and is responsible for the client's care. Accordingly, if the supervisor is negligent in overseeing and directing the care and the client suffers harm, the supervisor will be liable. If the client is actually the client of the supervisor who has assigned the case to a therapist as his or her employee or agent, the supervisor will also be vicariously liable for the supervisee's negligence.

Q. 8:34 What is the EAP's duty with respect to continuing education and in-service training of its clinical staff?

The implied warranty of competence requires that clinical care providers be current in their knowledge and techniques. Because an EAP will be vicariously liable for damages resulting from the incompetence of its employees, or directly liable for failing to adequately supervise them, the EAP has a duty to screen and monitor continuing professional education of staff and provide such in-service training as is reasonably necessary to assure proper service. Continuing education may be mandated as a condition for continued employment, but programs are under no obligation to finance it.

Use of Consultants

Q. 8:35 Can a consultant be liable for negligence?

If a consultant sees a client directly for diagnosis as a basis for opinion and recommendation, he or she could be held directly liable for negligence in performing the consultation. If the consultant relies entirely upon information presented by the consulting therapist, however, the risk of liability would arise only if the advice provided was negligently based on inadequate information. When a consultant sees the client, the client must be fully informed of the consultant's limited role, and that the consultant's relationship is not with the client, but with the therapist. Any subsequent contact with the consultant by the client should be met with a polite, but firm, referral back to the therapist.

Q. 8:36 Is an EAP responsible for monitoring the activities and behavior of nonemployee professionals with whom it contracts to provide services to its clients?

An EAP is duty-bound to monitor the activities and behavior of a nonemployee independent contractor who is providing service to clients under EAP aegis, even though the contractor's practice is not under the control of the EAP. Clients are entitled to assume and rely upon the fact that the EAP knows and approves of what its contractors are doing, and that whatever the contractor does is therefore appropriate. The EAP is responsible for the protection of its clients and, accordingly, must stand behind the behavior of its contractors.

Example. The counselor was an independent practitioner under contract with the EAP to provide group after care services to clients who had been discharged from inpatient treatment. She was beginning a private practice and wished to build up a client list, but she was concerned that the EAP would not approve of her plan to offer additional services on a private basis to the EAP clients and their families. She wanted EAP client intake information for use not only for the group, but also in the event that the clients came into individual treatment with her. So as not to draw attention to her plan, rather than copying the intake records at the EAP office, she took the originals to a copy shop. Later, she realized that in her anxiety she had neglected to pick up the copies. A search of the copy shop did not turn up the intake records, which included much sensitive information about the clients. On advice of her own attorney, she has confessed her actions to the EAP and the clients. Although the records have still not turned up, none of the clients have been contacted in any way about the information. However, all of the clients are distressed, anxious, and angry. The contractor's lawyer has advised her to notify her malpractice carrier, according to the terms of the policy. The EAP's attorney predicts a suit for breach of confidentiality and failure to monitor, and the EAP is nervously awaiting the outcome of these events.

Q. 8:37 What are the legal ramifications of failure to adequately monitor the practice of a contractor?

Liability will arise for an EAP when a client is harmed by acts or behavior of a therapist to which the client should not have been exposed or subjected, and that would have been avoided but for the failure of the EAP to adequately monitor its contractor.

Q. 8:38 When should consultation be used?

Consultation should be obtained whenever there is a question about a course of action with a client if the EAP provider feels uncertain and a supervisor is unable to settle the matter. Any time there is a question of dangerousness to self or others, or a conflict of interest between the client and the treater or program, a consultation is the best protective maneuver against liability risk. It is a clear indication that the clinician is not negligent. When the EAP provider is a senior clinician who is not being supervised, consultation from time to time is a good idea on general principles. Any time a client shows signs of physical illness or a need for input from another discipline, consultation is mandatory.

Q. 8:39 Must client consent be obtained before consulting?

No. Consultation is considered a routine part of clinical care, and disclosure of client information for consultation purposes is not considered a breach of confidentiality. However, if the client is to have access to the record, it may be desirable to inform him or her either about consultation in general terms, or about a specific consultation. Otherwise, if the client later reads the record, the consultation note will come as a surprise and may be upsetting. ("You mean you talked about me to someone else and never told me?") The treater decides whether or not to consult; the client does not have a right to prevent it. On the other hand, a client also has a right to demand a consultation if he or she is concerned about any aspect of care.

Q. 8:40 Can an EAP be held responsible for the negligence or wrongful acts of a consultant?

Unless the EAP was negligent in choosing or informing the consultant, it will not be liable for the consultant's behavior or negligence.

Monitoring Volunteers

Q. 8:41 What is the EAP's responsibility for screening in volunteer recruitment?

It is hard to turn away volunteers, but an EAP is responsible to clients for the competence and behavior of its personnel, whether paid or unpaid, so the program should use reasonable care in screening volunteers for suitability for the activities in which they will participate.

Q. 8:42 What volunteer program issues have legal implications?

The volunteer component of an EAP can be marvelously effective in engendering goodwill and maximizing utilization of the program. It does, however, add liability risk. Volunteers are, by definition, not professionals. They cannot have, or be expected to have, the knowledge base and discipline of trained professionals, and they have not been acculturated through supervised structured training experiences to approach psychosocial problems with clinical understanding and methodology. For those activities that require gross recognition of problem behavior and good common sense, volunteers can be invaluable. When volunteers perceive themselves to be "Dr. Freud," and are allowed to act as clinicians, tragedy and liability are foreseeable results.

Q. 8:43 What factors should be taken into consideration in setting up a volunteer program?

The scope and structure of a volunteer component should be thought out with extreme care, keeping the specter of client endangerment and concomitant program liability in mind. The following questions should be addressed:

- What is the role of volunteers in the program?
- What functions will a volunteer perform? What is the scope of a volunteer's duties and prerogatives?
- What methods will volunteers use? What records will they keep?
- What are the confidentiality issues? How can client confidentiality be assured? Do local confidentiality and privilege laws make a volunteer program untenable?
- What personal characteristics are required for volunteers?
- What competencies are required for the volunteer tasks?
- What training is required to develop competency? Who will provide training? Will training be done on company time? At company expense?
- What supervision is required?
- What method of recruitment is to be used?
- How will unsatisfactory volunteers be terminated?
- What liability insurance is required to cover the volunteers, the supervisor, and the program?

Q. 8:44 What factors should be considered in screening and recruiting volunteers?

The nature and scope of the volunteer program will be the basis for determining qualifications for volunteer participation and the type of screening required to assure individual suitability. Perhaps the best way to prescreen the pool of possible volunteers is to request nominations from supervisors and union shop stewards. Some programs want only volunteers who are recovering substance abusers with a substantial period of sobriety and a history of regular participation in AA or NA. Other programs are concerned that this will discriminate against other suitable individuals whose participation could be valuable, particularly for employees whose job or personal difficulties are not substance abuse related.

Employees who evince unresolved personal difficulties are probably not very good candidates for volunteer programs, although some authorities suggest that people with certain "life scripts" can manage their problems by choosing to be "cops" rather than "robbers," or "therapists" rather than "patients." (Berne, *Games People Play* (1978); Steiner, *Scripts People Live* (1975)) A history of drug dealing or sexual acting out suggests unsuitability for peer counseling activities.

Volunteers should be required to complete a written application form inquiring about present and past employment, arrests or convictions, health (including history of mental health and substance abuse problems that could affect ability to function as a case finder or peer counselor), and so forth. In addition to a written application, a personal interview to discuss the applicant's motivation and personal agenda is vital. A serious problem for recovering substance abusers is the "double hat" issue: Can the recovering person take care of his or her own needs while working with others? Is he or she at risk for transference or countertransference problems that can negatively affect himself or herself or a client?

Q. 8:45 Should volunteer participation be time limited or open ended?

This is as much a philosophical and political issue as a practical one. If there are many more potential volunteers than are required by an EAP, it would make a certain amount of sense to have rotating panels to give everyone a chance to participate. Additionally, if a volunteer is less than adequate, but not so unsatisfactory as to require removal from the program, a time limit on his or her participation may be a blessing. On the other hand, once a volunteer is trained and experienced, it is a pity to lose his or her expertise.

Q. 8:46 Are there situations that require terminating a volunteer from the program?

From a risk-avoidance perspective, grounds for termination from the volunteer program should be stated in the program policies and procedures. Causes for termination include insobriety, being disciplined for a work-rule infraction, conviction of a crime, violation of EAP policies and procedures, evidence of current mental instability, or serious physical illness of a nature to prevent the volunteer from safely participating in the program.

Q. 8:47 Are volunteer programs covered by rules protecting handicapped workers?

Volunteer programs are probably not covered by Sections 503 and 504 of the Rehabilitation Act of 1973, but the EAP should seek legal counsel before making any decisions if the issue arises.

Q. 8:48 What functions should volunteers be permitted to assume?

Volunteers are best used as case finders. Many programs use volunteers as peer counselors with great success. If an EAP sponsors peer counseling, training and supervision of the volunteer counselors are absolutely essential. The major points to be covered in training are the limited areas of the counselors' activities, the need for confidentiality, and the legal ramifications of what they do. On no account should an EAP countenance diagnosis or treatment by volunteers, or referral for inpatient or outpatient treatment. These are functions for professionals. Regular group or individual supervision and consultation with volunteers is a must.

Q. 8:49 What records should peer counselors keep?

Volunteers should keep records of every contact made in the name or under the aegis of the EAP. These records should be turned over to the EAP regularly, preferably at least weekly, and they should be reviewed by professional staff.

Chapter 9

Substance Abuse Laws

This chapter deals with state and federal substance abuse treatment laws that govern EAP activities and EAP sponsors under certain circumstances, including federal substance abuse treatment confidentiality law, the federal Drug-Free Workplace Act of 1988, and federally mandated drug testing. Since EAP professionals are frequently called upon to counsel clients in trouble with the criminal justice system, criminal law related to substance abuse is also explored.

Q. 9:1 What substance abuse laws govern EAPs?

Any local, state, or federal law applicable to any activity or employee of an EAP will apply to the EAP. Multistate EAPs must know the law in each state in which they operate, since each location will be governed by applicable state law.

Q. 9:2 When do federal laws or regulations generally apply to EAPs?

Federal law generally applies only to businesses or activities regulated by the federal government, involved in interstate commerce, federally assisted, or having contracts or otherwise doing business with the federal government. If an EAP meets any of these criteria, it will be covered by certain federal laws.

Q. 9:3 If there is an apparent conflict between federal and state law, which one prevails?

The general rule is that when the federal government has enacted laws or regulations related to a subject it has preempted the field, and the federal law will govern. Local law enforcement officials resent being told that federal law protects or prevents a treatment provider from answering questions about a client. They sometimes respond with threats of prosecution for obstructing justice, or the like. Under such circumstances, immediate legal consultation is required.

Q. 9:4 Do all states require licensure of substance abuse treatment providers?

State laws regulating the practice of health and allied health professionals vary widely. Some states have no certification or licensure requirements. Others have laws applying only to inpatient or licensed substance abuse treatment programs. The EAP must verify local legal requirements with a local attorney.

Q. 9:5 If an internal or external EAP does no inpatient or day treatment, is it an alcoholism or drug abuse treatment facility under state substance abuse law?

An EAP that does social service, mental health and substance abuse assessments, referrals and/or outpatient counseling, and aftercare but no inpatient or day treatment may or may not be considered a "treatment facility." This depends on the definition of treatment facility under applicable state law.

Q. 9:6 Is there anything a spouse and children can do to protect themselves from financial ruin at the hands of a substance abuser?

When, by reason of substance abuse, an individual's decision-making capacity is impaired so that he or she may waste his or her estate and expose the family to financial ruin, the substance abuser can be adjudicated incompetent and a personal representative (conservator or guardian) can be appointed to manage the financial affairs. The spouse of the impaired person would ordinarily be appointed the personal representative.

Insurance Coverage for Substance Abuse

Q. 9:7 Must substance abuse services be covered by health insurance policies?

Health insurance benefits are determined by the terms of the contract between the insurance company and the purchaser of the plan. Some states have legislation requiring that health insurance cover substance abuse and mental health benefits. Since the health insurance plan sponsor negotiates the coverage and has control over what services are eligible for reimbursement, if health insurance does not cover EAP services, it is due to a decision by the health plan sponsor.

Q. 9:8 Can an employee health plan place conditions on payment for substance abuse services?

The plan can place any conditions it deems feasible consistent with its contract and insurance laws, and any state law that may apply. It is very common for a plan to refuse to pay for uncompleted treatment. In such event, the employee-patient will be personally responsible for the costs of the portion of the treatment that was received.

Q. 9:9 Can an insurance plan require preadmission qualification for inpatient substance abuse services?

Yes.

Q. 9:10 May a hospital refuse to accept a person for medical or surgical treatment on the grounds that he or she is a substance abuser?

Federal law prohibits discrimination by federally assisted health care providers on the basis of alcoholism or drug addiction. (9 U.S.C. §794 (Section 504 of the Rehabilitation Act of 1973)) A federally assisted provider, for purposes of the Rehabilitation Act, includes any health care provider receiving federal money of any kind (e.g., Medicare, Medicaid) and any provider having tax-exempt status as a not-for-profit or religious organization.

Obligation to Report Drug Offenses

Q. 9:11 Does an EAP provider have a right or obligation to report drug offenses to law enforcement authorities?

The general rule is, no. A professional who is in the business of diagnosing and treating substance abuse is bound by applicable federal and local state confidentiality laws. These must be studied and a determination made by each EAP about the reporting obligations of its personnel.

All EAPs advertise themselves to employees as being confidential services, so EAP clients come for care under the assumption that they will not find themselves in court or prison because of information communicated to the EAP. However, under some state laws, it is a crime to fail to report a crime of which one has knowledge. This reporting requirement will be superseded by a statute imposing a duty of confidentiality on mental health and social service professionals, but the duty of confidentiality is prescribed differently by the various states.

For example, in some states, confidentiality is imposed by the licensing or registration statutes for certain professions (for example, social work, psychology). In other states, it may be imposed by a statute specific to the type of service being provided (for example, mental health care, substance abuse treatment). In some states, both licensed substance abuse programs and certain licensed professionals that provide substance abuse services are authorized and required to protect client confidentiality, but

EAPs are not licensed programs covered by the statute. The result in such a state could be that EAP substance abuse services are protected if provided by an employee who is a member of a profession designated by the statute, but are not protected if provided by a member of another profession. Further, some states exempt from confidentiality information concerning certain specified criminal acts (for example, homicide, or all felonies).

Example. In State A, psychologists and social workers are licensed and are prohibited from disclosing a client's confidential communications except in cases of homicide. Employees of licensed substance abuse treatment programs are similarly prohibited, irrespective of their discipline or licensure. There is no state statute imposing a duty of confidentiality on EAPs, guidance counselors, or certified alcoholism counselors. An EAP employs two counselors: a licensed social worker, and a person with an M.A. in guidance counseling who is also a certified alcoholism counselor.

The client being evaluated by the social worker discloses that he is a polydrug user who deals to support his habit. The social worker may not disclose the client's drug use or dealing, and so is not required—nor has he the right—to report the client's illegal activities to the police. However, if the client were assigned to the guidance counselor/alcoholism counselor, that person is not prohibited by statute from disclosing client confidences, and so risks criminal prosecution himself as an accessory after the fact if he does not report the criminal behavior.

Q. 9:12 If non-EAP personnel discover drug sale, possession, or use, is there an obligation to report to law enforcement authorities?

If it is not the EAP, but other company personnel who discover the illegal drug activities—whether or not on the employer's premises—there is no legal basis for withholding the information from law enforcement authorities, and those in possession of the information have a legal duty to report the criminal acts. A large employer should have a policy and procedures for orderly handling of such situations.

Liability for Alcohol-Related Injuries

Q. 9:13 If an employer serves alcohol at a company Christmas party or picnic, is the employer at risk if injury results?

Employers have been held liable for injuries to third persons resulting from alcohol served by the employer at employer functions. The dram shop laws of some states impose liability for injuries to the drinker or others, not only on purveyors of alcohol (which is an inherently dangerous substance, so that the strict liability law applies), but also on noncommercial "hosts." If there is a charge to the employees for the party, that will bring the situation even closer to the traditional dram shop concept. If alcohol is served to a minor (no one under 21 can drink legally in any state), the employer is criminally liable.

Searches of Employer Premises

Q. 9:14 Can law enforcement officials obtain a warrant to search an employer's premises for evidence of illegal activity on the part of an employee?

Yes. If law enforcement personnel have probable cause to suspect that evidence of an employee's criminal activity is to be found on the premises of a third party that is unconnected to the crime, a warrant permitting the search may be obtained.

Q. 9:15 If evidence is found of criminal activity other than that for which the search warrant was specifically issued, can that evidence be used to prosecute the alleged perpetrator of the unexpected activity?

Any evidence turned up in the course of a legal search can be used for prosecution of any criminal activity, whether or not it is an activity contemplated by the probable cause finding upon which the warrant was issued.

Q. 9:16 Is a warrant always needed before conducting a search?

Unless the search results from an arrest made for a crime in progress, immediately after a crime has been committed, or as a result of information discovered while in hot pursuit of a perpetrator, a warrant is required before a person or private property can be searched without consent. Of course, an employer may give consent to conduct a search of premises without a warrant.

Federal Substance Abuse Treatment Confidentiality Laws

Q. 9:17 What federal statutes and regulations govern confidentiality of substance abuse treatment?

Alcohol abuse treatment is governed by 42 U.S.C. §290dd-3, and drug abuse treatment is governed by 42 U.S.C. §290ee-3. The regulations implementing these statutes are found in 42 C.F.R. §2 et. seq (1989).

Q. 9:18 What is the definition of "program" for purposes of the federal substance abuse confidentiality laws?

A program is a "person" that in whole or in part holds himself/herself/itself out as providing alcohol or drug abuse diagnosis, treatment, or referral for treatment. Person, for these purposes, means an individual; partnership; corporation; federal, state, or local government agency; or any other legal entity. (42 C.F.R. 42 C.F.R. §2.11 (1989). §2.11)

Q. 9:19 If a company that engages in interstate commerce or has government contracts has an internal EAP, is the EAP governed by federal alcoholism or substance abuse statutes or regulations?

This is a complicated issue, which should be explored with the company's attorney. For most purposes, it may be assumed that the answer will be no. The federal substance abuse regulations apply only to programs that are conducted by or under contract with, licensed, authorized, or registered by the federal government; supported by federal funds or state or local governments that receive revenue sharing; or tax-exempt. Most internal EAPs in for-profit businesses will not meet these criteria. The fact that a company that has an internal EAP is doing business in interstate commerce is not relevant for purposes of the federal substance abuse legislation and regulations.

Q. 9:20 If a company is a federal contractor, is its internal EAP governed by the federal substance abuse legislation and regulations?

No, unless the contract is to provide EAP services.

Q. 9:21 Would an EAP that contracts with a federal agency to provide services to its federal employees be covered by federal substance abuse law?

Not always. An EAP that is part of a government agency will always be bound by federal substance abuse law. If, however, a government agency or federal court contracts with a private for-profit program that is not federally assisted under 42 C.F.R. §2.12(b) (because the *program* is not federally conducted, regulated, or supported in a manner that constitutes federal assistance), the client's records will not be covered by the federal regulations.

Q. 9:22 If a company contracts with a not-for-profit, tax-exempt entity for external EAP services, is the EAP covered by the federal substance abuse regulations?

Yes.

Q. 9:23 Under what circumstances can information be disclosed under the federal regulations?

Information may be disclosed with the prior written consent of the client—but only to such extent, under such circumstances, and for such purposes as may be allowed under the regulations—and without consent under specific circumstances.

Q. 9:24 What constitutes a valid written consent?

The consent *must* be in writing, and must contain the following elements:

- The specific name or general description of the program or person permitted to make the disclosure;
- The name or title of the individual, or the name of the organization to which disclosure is to be made;
- The name of the client;
- The purpose of the disclosure;
- How much and what kind of information is to be disclosed;
- The signature of the client and, when required for a minor client or deceased client, the signature of the person authorized by the regulations to give consent;
- The date on which the consent is signed;
- A statement that the consent is revocable at any time, except as to disclosures already made in reliance upon the consent;
- The date, event, or condition upon which the consent will expire if not previously revoked by the client; and
- A notice prohibiting redisclosure.

(42 C.F.R. §2.31 (1989))

Q. 9:25 Who has the power to consent to disclosure of a minor client's substance abuse treatment information?

This depends partly upon whether the law of the state in which the minor (person who has not attained the age of majority under state law) is receiving treatment requires parental consent.

If state law does not require parental consent to substance abuse treatment of a minor child, the minor client has the power to consent to disclosure of his or her treatment information.

If state law requires parental consent to substance abuse treatment of a minor child, both the minor client and his or her parent or guardian must give consent.

Q. 9:26 Under what circumstances may the EAP notify the parents of a minor that he or she is receiving substance abuse treatment?

If state law does not require parental consent to substance abuse treatment of a minor child, the program may not disclose the fact of treatment to the parents without the consent of the minor client. The prohibition against disclosure extends to disclosure for purposes of obtaining payment for the treatment. However, unless state law requires the program to deliver services irrespective of ability to pay, if the minor cannot pay for services, the program may refuse to provide services until he or she authorizes disclosures necessary to obtain payment.

If state law requires parental consent to substance abuse treatment of a minor child, an application of a minor for treatment may be disclosed to the person authorized by state law to consent to the treatment only if either (1) the minor has given a written consent or (2) the minor lacks the capacity to make a rational choice regarding consent. (42 C.F.R. §2.14(c) (1989))

Q. 9:27 Under what circumstances will a minor child be deemed to lack capacity to make a rational choice about notifying his or her parents about an application for substance abuse treatment?

If the minor is extremely young or, because of his or her mental or physical condition, cannot make a rational decision, and the situation poses a substantial threat to the minor's life or physical well-being or that of another person that might be reduced by notifying the minor's parent or guardian, the minor will be considered to lack capacity for rational choice.

Q. 9:28 If a minor lacks capacity for rational choice, what information may be conveyed to the parents?

The parents may be notified of the facts relevant to reducing a threat to the life or physical well-being of the minor client or other threatened individual.

Q. 9:29 Who makes the determination about a minor's capacity?

The determination of a minor's capacity is made by the program director, who is defined as: (1) in the case of an individual practitioner, that individual; (2) in the case of a program that is an organization, the person designated as director or managing director, or otherwise vested with authority to act as chief executive of the organization. (42 C.F.R. §2.11 (1989))

If an EAP is operated by a federal agency, is it the director of the agency or the director of the EAP who makes the decision? The regulations do not imply that it would be anyone other than the director of the federal agency, nor that the director may designate this function. If the EAP is operated by a large corporation, does the CEO of the corporation make the decision? Common sense indicates that it be the director of the EAP—or if the EAP is part of another department, the director of that department—but that is not what the regulations say. Is this significant? That depends upon how many minors are employed by federal agencies or large corporations that have internal EAPs. If the situation arises, absent advice of the general counsel of the agency or company to the contrary, the director of the federal agency or the CEO must be the one to make the decision!

Q. 9:30 Who has the right to consent to disclosure of substance abuse treatment records of a deceased client?

Client identifying information relating to the cause of death may be disclosed under laws requiring the collection of death or other vital statistics or permitting inquiry into the cause of death. Disclosure of any other information that identifies a deceased client as an alcohol or drug abuser is permitted only if a written consent to the disclosure is given by the personal representative of the decedent, if one has been appointed; if not, by the client's surviving spouse, if any; or if none, by any responsible member of the client's family. (42 C.F.R. §2.15 (1989))

Q. 9:31 Who has the right to consent to disclosure of substance abuse records when the client is incompetent?

If a client has been adjudicated as unable to manage his or her own affairs (for any reason other than insufficient age), any consent required by the regulations may be given by the client's guardian or other person authorized by state law to act on the client's behalf. If a client who has not been so adjudicated suffers from a medical condition that prevents the client from taking effective action on his or her own behalf, the program director may give consent only for purposes of obtaining payment for treatment. (42 C.F.R. §2.15 (1989))

Example. The client of an external EAP has a stroke before he is able to sign the consent forms necessary to enable the EAP to obtain payment from the company's insurance company for EAP services provided over the past month. The director of the program can sign the necessary forms, but only to disclose the facts of treatment relevant to payment for the services.

Q. 9:32 If a client has given consent to disclose, but it has expired or has been revoked, may the EAP complete a partially made disclosure?

The regulations provide that disclosure may not be made on the basis of a consent that has expired or has been revoked. This can prove extremely inconvenient when the client revokes his or her consent because of acting-out behavior, and the EAP has made partial disclosure that may cause a third person who is relying on the information to be severely damaged. Such an example would be a client being allowed to operate dangerous machinery on the basis that substance abuse treatment is proceeding successfully. If this is a possibility, it is best to have an agreement in which revocation of consent will result in notification of that revocation to relevant persons. Of course, even this agreement may be rescinded. A protection for the EAP may be to include in the agreement a clause by which the client agrees to hold the EAP and counselor harmless and promises to indemnify them against any damages sustained by reason of such notification.

Q. 9:33 If an EAP is providing services to a client whose treatment is a condition of the disposition of criminal proceedings, or of parole or other release from custody, what information may the program disclose and to whom?

The EAP may disclose to those persons within the criminal justice system who have a need for the information in connection with their duty to monitor the client's progress (for example, a prosecuting attorney who is withholding charges against a client, a court granting pretrial or posttrial release, probation or parole officers responsible for supervision of the client), as long as the client has signed a written consent. In this situation, the right to revoke the consent will *not* be included in the consent form, as would otherwise be required. The consent must state the duration of the consent, which may not be longer than the expected time of the treatment and the final disposition of the legal proceeding. It must also state the type of criminal proceedings involved, the program, and the person(s) to whom disclosures will be made. The consent must also state that it is revocable upon the passage of a specified amount of time or the occurrence of a specified event—not later than the final disposition of the conditional release or other action in connection with which the consent was given. (42 C.F.R. §2.35 (1989))

Q. 9:34 When may disclosure be made without client consent?

Disclosure may be made without client consent to medical personnel who need information for the purpose of treating a condition posing an immediate threat to the health of any person and requiring immediate medical intervention. If personnel of the Food and Drug Administration (FDA) have reason to believe that the health of a person may be threatened by an error in the manufacture, labeling, or sale of a product under FDA jurisdiction, and the information will be used for the sole purpose of notifying clients and their physicians of potential dangers, information identifying a client as a substance abuser may be given to the FDA. Any disclosures must be documented immediately in the client's record. (42 C.F.R. §2.51 (1989))

Q. 9:35 May an EAP disclose substance abuse treatment information for research purposes?

An EAP may disclose client identifying information if the program director is satisfied that the recipient of the information is a qualified researcher and is doing the research under a protocol under which the identifying information will be kept under strict security, will not be disclosed except back to the EAP, and will not be disclosed in any report of the research or otherwise. (42 C.F.R. §2.52 (1989))

Q. 9:36 Under what circumstances may an EAP disclose client information for audit and evaluation activities?

As long as client records are not removed from the EAP premises, they can be disclosed in identified form for audit purposes if the auditor agrees in writing not to redisclose them except back to the program or pursuant to court order, and the audit is being performed on behalf of:

- A government agency that provides support to the agency or is authorized to regulate it;
- A third-party payor covering the program's clients or a peer review organization performing utilization or quality control review; or
- Another qualified evaluator or auditor (as determined by the program director).

Records or copies of records may be removed from the program premises for auditing purposes if the auditing body agrees in writing to maintain the identified records in strict security, destroy all client identifying information upon completion of the audit, and limit disclosure to the program (unless pursuant to a court order for investigation or prosecution of criminal or other activities). (42 C.F.R. §2.53 (1989))

Q. 9:37 If an EAP professional believes it necessary to disclose client information without consent and under circumstances other than those specified by the federal regulations for nonconsensual disclosure, is there a mechanism for such disclosure?

Yes. Federal statutes and regulations require a court order for permission to make such disclosures. (42 U.S.C. §§290dd-3(b)(2)(C) and 290ee-3(a)(2)(C); 42 C.F.R. §2.5 (1989)) A court may authorize disclosure only under the following circumstances:

- The disclosure is necessary to protect against an existing threat to life or serious bodily injury, including circumstances that constitute suspected child abuse and neglect and verbal threats against third parties.
- The disclosure is necessary in connection with the investigation or prosecution of an extremely serious crime, such as one that directly threatens loss of life or serious bodily injury, including homicide, rape, kidnapping, armed robbery, assault with a deadly weapon, or child abuse and neglect.
- The disclosure is in connection with litigation or an administrative proceeding in which the client offers testimony or other evidence pertaining to the content of the confidential communications.

Example 1. The client tells the counselor that he has discovered that his wife is having an affair with his brother. He has set up a videotape camera through a hole in the bedroom wall, and he intends to kill his wife and brother when he has taped proof of their behavior. A court order may be obtained to permit warning the wife and brother.

Example 2. The client discloses to the EAP professional that he molested and then strangled a neighborhood child. The counselor believes that this client constitutes a clear and present danger to other children, but the client refuses hospitalization for evaluation or treatment. He is not subject to mental health treatment commitment. The court may be petitioned to permit disclosure to law enforcement authorities.

Example 3. The client has sued the EAP professional for malpractice and has testified about his treatment. The counselor's lawyer wishes to use the client's record to impeach his credibility. Application may be made to the court for leave to disclose pertinent information. (This is a form of the client-litigant exception to a communications privilege.)

Q. 9:38 How does an EAP go about obtaining a court order for disclosure for noncriminal law purposes?

Application is made to a court of competent jurisdiction (this varies from state to state) either separately, or in conjunction with a pending civil action in which it appears that client records are needed to provide evidence. The application is made by way of a petition to the court. Unless the client has given written consent to use his or her name in the petition, or the court has ordered the record of the proceeding impounded, the petitioner must use a fictitious name rather than identifying the client. The client must be given notice in a manner that will not disclose his or her identity to other persons, as well as an opportunity to respond in writing to the petition or appear in person for the limited purpose of providing evidence on the statutory and regulatory criteria for the issuance of the court order.

The court must conduct the entire proceeding in the judge's chambers unless the client requests an open hearing. The proceeding may include an inspection by the judge of the client's record, a review of other evidence—including examination of necessary witnesses—and oral arguments or written briefs on the law. (42 C.F.R. §§2.64(a)–2.64(c) (1989))

Q. 9:39 What are the criteria for entry of a court order permitting disclosure for noncriminal law purposes?

An order may be entered permitting disclosure only if the court finds that good cause exists. The criteria for good cause are:

- Other ways of obtaining the information are not available or would not be effective; and
- The public interest and need for the disclosure outweigh the potential injury to the client, the treatment relationship, and the treatment services.

Q. 9:40 What must the court order contain?

The court order must:

- Limit the disclosure to those parts of the client's record that are essential to fulfill the objective of the order;
- Limit disclosure to those persons whose need for the information is the basis for the order; and
- Include such other measures as are necessary to limit disclosure for the protection of the client, the treatment relationship, and the treatment services (for example, sealing the court record from public scrutiny).

(42 C.F.R. §2.64(d) (1989))

Q. 9:41 Do the regulations provide for a court procedure to authorize disclosure and use of substance abuse treatment records for criminal investigation or prosecution?

An order for disclosure and use of substance abuse treatment records in the investigation and prosecution of a crime can be obtained only if the court finds that *all* of the following criteria are met:

- The crime involved is extremely serious (including homicide, rape, kidnapping, armed robbery, assault with a deadly weapon, and child abuse and neglect);
- There is reasonable likelihood that the records will disclose information of substantial value in the investigation or prosecution;

- Other ways of obtaining the information are not available or would not be effective; and
- The potential injury to the client, the treatment relationship, and the ability of the program to provide treatment services to other clients is outweighed by the public interest and the need for disclosure.

Additionally, if the applicant is a law enforcement official, the person holding the records must have been given an opportunity to be represented by independent counsel; if the record holder is an entity within federal, state, or local government, it must in fact have been represented by counsel independent of the applicant. (42 C.F.R. §2.65 (1989))

Q. 9:42 Who may apply for an order permitting disclosure of substance abuse treatment records for criminal law purposes?

The record holder (for example, the EAP) or any person conducting investigative or prosecutorial activities in connection with law enforcement may apply for the order.

Q. 9:43 If the applicant for disclosure for criminal law purposes is other than the EAP, what procedure must be followed?

The petition must be brought without use of the client's name. Such a petition will use the pseudonym "John Doe" to identify the client; hence the proceeding is called a John Doe petition. (See C-1: Sample John Doe Petition to Allow Disclosure of Confidential Information.) It may be brought as a separate proceeding or as part of an application for a subpoena or other compulsory process. Unless the order is being sought for purposes of investigating the program, the program must be given notice, an opportunity to appear and be heard for the limited purpose of presenting evidence on the criteria for issuance of the order, and an opportunity to be represented by independent counsel. The proceedings must be conducted in the judge's chambers, and may include inspection of the record, examination of relevant witnesses, review of evidence, and oral arguments and written briefs on the law. (42 C.F.R. §2.65 (1989))

Q. 9:44 What are the procedures and criteria for court orders authorizing disclosure and use of client records to investigate or prosecute a program or a person holding the records?

Any administrative, regulatory, supervisory, investigative, law enforcement, or prosecutorial agency having jurisdiction over the activities of a program or person holding client records may apply for an order to criminally or administratively investigate the program or person (or employees or agents thereof).

The application may be filed separately or as part of a pending civil or criminal action against the program, person, employee, or agent, in which it appears that client records are needed to provide material evidence. The application must be filed using a fictitious name (John Doe), unless the court has ordered the court record sealed.

At the discretion of the court, the order may be issued without notice. However, if the order was granted without notice, the program or person holding the record and the client whose record is being disclosed must be given an opportunity to seek revocation or amendment of the order, limited to presentation of evidence on the legal criteria for issuance of the order.

Client identifying information must be removed from the records ordered disclosed. No information obtained as a result of such a court order may be used to investigate or prosecute a *client* or used as a basis for an application for a court order permitting its use for that purpose. (42 C.F.R. §2.66 (1989))

Q. 9:45 Under what circumstances can undercover agents and informants be placed in programs to criminally investigate employees or agents of a program?

If a law enforcement or prosecutorial agency has reason to believe that employees or agents of a program (*not clients*) are engaged in criminal misconduct, it may apply for a court order authorizing placement of an undercover agent or informant as an employee or client. The program director must be given adequate notice of the application and an opportunity to be heard (for the limited purpose of providing evidence on the criteria for issuance of the court order). Exceptions to this rule are if the application asserts a belief that the program director is involved in the criminal activities to be investigated, or that the director will intentionally or unintentionally disclose the proposed placement of the agent or informant to the employees or agents who are suspected of criminal activity.

Q. 9:46 What are the criteria for issuance of a court order authorizing placement of undercover agents or informants in a program?

The court must determine that good cause exists before authorizing the placement of undercover agents in a program. The court must find:

- There is reason to believe an employee or agent of the program is engaged in criminal activity;
- Other ways of obtaining evidence are not available or would not be effective; and
- The public interest and the need for placement of the undercover agent outweigh the potential injury to clients of the program, treatment relationships, and the treatment services.

Q. 9:47 What must the order contain?

An order authorizing placement of an undercover agent must:

- Be limited to no more than six months;
- Specifically authorize the placement;
- Prohibit the agent from disclosing any client identifying information except as required to criminally investigate or prosecute the program or its employees or agents; and
- Include other protective measures to avoid disruption of the treatment services and any real or apparent breach of client confidentiality.

No information obtained by an undercover agent may be used for criminal investigation or prosecution of a client, or as a basis for an application for a court order permitting disclosure for such purpose. (42 C.F.R. §2.67 (1989))

Q. 9:48 Under the federal regulations, what notice of prohibition against redisclosure must accompany any disclosure pursuant to client consent?

Every disclosure made pursuant to a client's written consent must be accompanied by the following written statement:

> This information has been disclosed to you from records protected by Federal confidentiality rules (42 CFR Part 2.) A general authorization for the release of medical or other information is NOT sufficient for this purpose. The Federal rules restrict any use of the information to criminally investigate or prosecute any alcohol or drug abuse patient.

Q. 9:49 Does federal law require or prohibit client access to substance abuse treatment records?

The federal regulations neither require nor prohibit a client's access to his or her substance abuse treatment records. (42 C.F.R. §2.23 (1989)) State law may govern client access and should be explored. If a client is given access, he or she may copy the records. The program can charge a reasonable fee for the copying. The client's written request to see records is not required to give him or her access or a copy. From a clinical perspective, it is foolish to say that a therapeutic relationship is based on trust and then restrict a client's access to his or her records. In those states that have required client access to mental health records for years, there has been no documented case of a client having been harmed by reason of access to his or her own clinical records. Furthermore, general privacy and individual rights principles require that a person be given access to anything written down about him or her. All EAPs should have policies and procedures governing client access.

Q. 9:50 Must a client be given notice of the federal confidentiality regulations?

A client of a program governed by the federal regulations must be given written notice at the time treatment commences, or as soon thereafter as his or her clinical condition permits, of the federal regulations on confidentiality of substance abuse treatment records and the contents thereof. (42 C.F.R. §2.22 (1989)) The notice must include:

- A general description of the limited conditions under which a program may acknowledge that an individual is present at a treatment facility or disclose outside the program that he or she is a chemical abuser;

- A statement that violation of the federal law and regulations by a program is a crime, and that suspected violations may be reported to appropriate authorities;
- A statement that information related to a client's commission of a crime on the premises of the program or against program personnel is not protected;
- A citation to the federal law and regulations; and
- A statement that reports of child abuse and neglect made under state law to appropriate state authorities are not protected.

The Drug-Free Workplace Act of 1988

Q. 9:51 What is the Drug-Free Workplace Act of 1988?

The Drug-Free Workplace Act of 1988 is part of the Anti-Drug Abuse Act, passed by Congress in November 1988. (Pub. L. No. 100-690, 41 U.S.C. §701 et seq.) Under the Act, any federal contractor with a contract of $25,000 or more, or any recipient of a federal grant in like amount, is required to certify to the contracting governmental agency that it will provide a drug-free workplace.

Q. 9:52 What is a "drug-free workplace" as defined in the Act?

A drug-free workplace is a site for the performance of work done in connection with a specific grant or contract with an agency of the federal government in the amount of $25,000 or more at which employees working on the grant or contract are prohibited from engaging in the unlawful manufacture, distribution, dispensation, possession, or use of a controlled substance in accordance with the requirements of the Drug-Free Workplace Act of 1988. (41 U.S.C. §706)

Q. 9:53 Who is an "employee" under the Act?

An employee is an employee of a contractor or grantee directly engaged in the performance of work pursuant to the government contract or grant.

Q. 9:54 What controlled substances are covered by the Act?

All substances listed in Schedules I through V of Section 202 of the Controlled Substances Act (21 U.S.C. §812) are covered:

- *Schedule I.* Substances with a high potential for abuse and dependence, for which there is no currently accepted medical use in the United States: heroin; psychedelics (LSD, mescaline, peyote, psilocybin, DMT, DED); amphetamine variants (MDA, MDMA, DMA, PMA, STP, DOM, DOB, PCE, TCP); methaqualone; marijuana (although there are medical studies indicating medicinal use for it and for THC, its active ingredient); hashish.
- *Schedule II.* Substances with a high potential for abuse, but that have currently accepted medical uses, often with severe restriction. These are usually available only by written prescription (oral order in an emergency; no refill permitted): opium; morphine; codeine; Dilaudid; Demerol; cocaine; Percodan; amphetamines; Ritalin; Preludin; Phencyclidine (an animal tranquilizer); barbiturates (amobarbital, pentobarbital, and secbarbital).
- *Schedule III.* Substances with lower potential for abuse than those in Schedules I and II, with currently accepted medical uses. These are available by written or oral prescription, refillable five times within six months with physician's authorization: derivatives of barbituric acid (except those listed in another schedule); Doriden; Noludar; nalorphine; chlorphentermine; phendimetrazine; paregoric; Tylenol #4 with codeine.
- *Schedule IV.* Substances with lower potential for abuse than those in Schedule III, with currently accepted medical uses. Available by written or oral prescription, refillable five times in six months with physician's authorization: barbiturates (barbital, phenobarbital); chloral hydrate; Placidyl; Valmid; Equanil; Miltown; Darvon; Talwin-NX; Benzodiazepine antianxiety drugs (Librium, Valium, Ativan, Serax, Dalmane, and Tranxene).
- *Schedule V.* Substances with lower potential for abuse than those in Schedule IV, with currently accepted medical uses. May be available without prescription (state laws vary): cough and antidiarrheal medicines (Actifed with codeine, Lomotil, Parepec-

tolin, Robitussin A-C cough syrup; Triaminic expectorant with codeine).

Q. 9:55 What is "conviction" for purposes of this Act?

Conviction means a finding of guilty (including a plea of nolo contendere) or imposition of a sentence, or both, by any judicial body charged with the responsibility to determine violations of federal or state criminal drug statutes.

Q. 9:56 What is a "criminal drug statute" for purposes of this Act?

A criminal drug statute means a criminal statute involving the manufacture, distribution, dispensation, or possession of any controlled substance.

Q. 9:57 Who is a "contractor" or "grantee" for purposes of this Act?

A contractor or grantee means the department, division, or other unit of an individual or entity responsible for performance under a federal contract or grant.

Q. 9:58 What actions are required to constitute "providing a drug-free workplace" under the Act?

The contractor or grantee (other than an individual) must:

- Publish a statement notifying employees that the unlawful manufacture, distribution, dispensation, possession, or use of a controlled substance is prohibited in the workplace, and specifying what actions will be taken in the event an employee violates the prohibitions.
- Establish a drug-free awareness program to inform employees about the dangers of drug abuse in the workplace; the employer's policy of maintaining a drug-free workplace; any available drug counseling, rehabilitation, and EAP; and the penalties for drug abuse violations.

- Require that every employee be given a copy of the drug-free workplace statement.
- Notify employees that as a condition of employment on the government contract, they must abide by the terms of the drug-free workplace statement and notify the employer of any criminal drug statute conviction for a violation occurring in the workplace, no later than five days after the conviction.
- Impose a sanction on, or require satisfactory participation in a drug abuse assistance or rehabilitation program by, any employee who is so convicted.
- Make a good-faith effort to continue to maintain a drug-free workplace through implementation of these requirements.

(41 U.S.C. §§701 and 703)

Q. 9:59 What are the requirements for a contractor who is an individual?

An individual who is a federal contractor or grantee must certify that he or she will not engage in the unlawful manufacture, sale, distribution, dispensation, possession, or use of a controlled substance in the performance of the contract. (41 U.S.C. §701(a)(2))

Q. 9:60 What must a grantee or contractor do when it is notified that an employee has been convicted of violation of a criminal drug statute for a violation occurring in the workplace?

The grantee or contractor must take appropriate personnel action against the employee, up to and including termination, or require the employee to satisfactorily participate in a drug abuse assistance or rehabilitation program approved for such purposes by a federal, state, or local health, law enforcement, or other appropriate agency. (41 U.S.C. §701(a)(1)(F))

Q. 9:61 What are the penalties for a federal contractor's or grantee's noncompliance with the Act?

If a contractor or grantee makes a false certification of compliance or violates the certification, or if enough employees of the contractor or grantee have been convicted of violation of criminal drug statutes for violations occurring in the workplace to indicate that the contractor has failed to make the good-faith effort to provide a drug-free workplace required by the Act, the contractor or grantee is subject to suspension of payments, termination of the contract, and debarment from any federal contract or grant for a period of five years. The sanctions will be imposed in accordance with the Federal Acquisition Regulation, Executive Order 12549, and procedures of the government agency that granted the contract. (41 U.S.C. §701(b))

Federally Mandated Drug Testing

Q. 9:62 Does federal law require employee drug testing?

Federal agencies and the military have been required for some time by statute and regulations to test their employees. As this book is being written, federal agencies with power to regulate certain private industries are promulgating regulations requiring that certain private employers test at least some of their employees for use of illegal drugs. The power of the federal government to direct the actions of private industry is limited by the Constitution. Wage-and-hour legislation, collective bargaining law, and occupational safety and health law are examples of federal intervention in employment. At present, the issue in the drug testing requirements is public safety, but it appears that the federal initiative in this direction is just beginning. It stands to reason that the regulation of interstate commerce and the protection of public health and safety and the public fisc could, when convenient to the government, be considered sufficient grounds for extension of the federal antidrug initiative into all areas of commerce currently subject to any federal regulation whatsoever.

Q. 9:63 What private industries are federally mandated to initiate employee drug testing at this time?

The Federal Highway Administration (49 C.F.R. §392 (1989)), the Federal Railroad Administration (49 C.F.R. §§217–219 (1988)), the Nuclear Regulatory Agency (10 C.F.R. §§2, 26 (1989)), the Federal Aviation Administration (14 C.F.R. Part 61), and the Department of Transportation Urban

Mass Transportation Administration (UMTA) (49 C.F.R. §653 (1988)) have promulgated regulations requiring testing of employees in safety-sensitive or security-sensitive jobs in private industries they regulate. The Federal Register should be consulted regularly for additional regulations of this type, which are proliferating.

Q. 9:64 What significance do these federal regulations have for other industries?

Since there is a clear trend toward employee drug testing, the federal regulations provide guidelines both for mandated employers and for employers that are not yet mandated but are developing testing programs. The law of employee drug testing is developing on a daily basis, and it is to be assumed that a program replicating one promulgated by the federal government will be more likely than others to pass muster in the event of a court challenge. By way of illustration, some provisions of the UMTA Rule are explored here.

Q. 9:65 What is the scope of the UMTA Rule?

The goal of the Department of Transportation is a drug-free transportation workforce. Recipients of federal financial assistance from UMTA, and operators of those recipients, are required to have antidrug programs for employees who perform safety-sensitive functions. The program includes testing (1) before employment; (2) after an accident, when there is reasonable cause (or suspicion) that illegal drug usage was a factor in the accident; (3) at random; and (4) before a return to duty involving performance of safety-sensitive functions, after a positive drug test.

Impairment by reason of drug use is not an issue; no employee, irrespective of impairment, is permitted to perform safety-sensitive functions while a prohibited drug, or the metabolites of a prohibited drug, are in his or her system. In addition to drug testing, an antidrug program must have an employee education and training program that provides information about the effects and detection of drug use. The UMTA Rule does not limit drug testing to the four situations specified above. An employer is not prohibited from testing in other situations, such as in accordance with a fitness-for-duty policy or as part of a routine physical examination.

Q. 9:66 Does the UMTA Rule require a rehabilitation component?

No, although UMTA encourages rehabilitation. The goal of the UMTA Rule is not job security for employees, but a safe transit system; it simply does not want drug users operating mass transit equipment. UMTA does not consider its role to include mandating rehabilitation or job security for employees who fail a test, use drugs on the job, or come forward voluntarily to request rehabilitation. Employers are free to develop their own policies with respect to those issues.

Q. 9:67 For what substances does the UMTA Rule require testing?

Obviously, a mass transit driver or dispatcher is not permitted to work with alcohol in his or her system, and there is nothing in the UMTA Rule to prohibit an employer from requiring a test for alcohol or any other controlled substance, but the Rule *mandates* testing only for certain *prohibited* drugs. This limitation on mandatory testing is strictly pragmatic: UMTA was concerned about overburdening both the mass transit operators and the drug testing laboratories by requiring tests for all controlled substances. It requires testing for five categories of substances—marijuana, cocaine, opiates, phencyclidine (PCP), and amphetamines—that are most likely to be abused by transportation industry workers. (49 C.F.R. §653.11 (1988))

Q. 9:68 If an employer wants to test for other drugs, may it do so?

Yes, but not on the same sample used for the mandated tests. A separate sample must be obtained to test for other substances.

Q. 9:69 If a state law prohibits drug testing, what can an employer who received UMTA assistance do?

Until December 1989, such employers were afforded waivers; thereafter, they are obliged to conform or lose their funding. It is intended that transportation operators in these states see to it that local legislation is amended to conform to the federal rule.

Q. 9:70 Does the UMTA Rule require an employer to test every applicant for a safety-sensitive job?

No. Only an individual selected to fill a position must be tested.

Q. 9:71 What must an employer disclose to applicants about the preemployment testing?

An employer must notify an applicant that the urine sample he or she is being asked to deposit will be used for a preemployment drug screening, but the UMTA Rule does not require employers to notify applicants about test results. Mass transit employers are encouraged by the Rule to set out their policies with regard to notifying applicants about test results.

Q. 9:72 What is the mandate for postaccident tests?

Except in cases in which it is determined that the performance of a safety-sensitive employee was not a contributing factor in the accident, postaccident drug testing is required if (1) there is a death or an injury requiring an individual to be taken to a medical facility; (2) there is more than $5,000 in property damage; or (3) the accident must be reported to the Federal Highway Administration, the Federal Railroad Administration, or the Coast Guard. (49 C.F.R. §653.5(a) (1988)) Testing is to be done as soon as possible, but not more than 32 hours after the accident. Contrary to the recommendation of the National Traffic Safety Board, only urine testing for certain illegal drugs, not blood testing for alcohol, is required. (There is no prohibition against a blood alcohol test, if it is the employer's policy to do so.) (49 C.F.R. §653.15 (1988))

Q. 9:73 What are the requirements for reasonable cause testing?

The UMTA Rule does not delineate what constitutes "reasonable cause," but it does require that the circumstances triggering the decision to test be substantiated by specific contemporaneous physical indicators of probable drug use, including observations of behavioral changes and/or performance indicators over a period of time in conjunction with contemporaneous physical evidence. Employers are free to create their own policies setting out specific circumstances or events that will trigger reasonable cause testing within this standard. Two supervisors are required to determine that an employee should be tested for reasonable cause, except in the case of small transit operators, which may use one supervisor. (49 C.F.R. §653.15 (1988))

Q. 9:74 What are the requirements for random testing?

UMTA believes that random testing is an effective deterrent to drug use in the workplace. Employers must phase in random testing over the first 12 months in which tests are to be conducted. After that time, 50% of employees must be tested each year. The choice of employees for testing must be truly random. (49 C.F.R. §653.17 (1988))

Q. 9:75 What is the mandate for return-to-duty testing?

Any employee who has failed a postaccident reasonable cause drug test or a random drug test must be tested before being allowed to return to safety-sensitive duties. This does not imply that an employer must allow such an employee to return to work, but only that if the employer decides to give an employee a second chance, the employee must first undergo additional testing. Further, such an employee may also be tested unannounced for a period of up to 60 months after returning to duty. In addition, an employee who failed a drug test or refused to take one would have to obtain a determination from the employer's medical review officer (MRO) that he or she could return to duty. (49 C.F.R. §653.17 (1988))

Q. 9:76 What education and training are required under the UMTA Rule?

Employers are allowed to devise their own education programs. Supervisors who will be responsible for making reasonable cause testing determinations must receive at least an hour of training. There is no time prescribed for education of other employees. Employers are encouraged to provide employees with substantive drug abuse information on an ongoing basis. UMTA contemplates that EAPs will play a major role in the education and training components. (49 C.F.R. §653.9(a)(2) (1988))

Q. 9:77 Under what guidelines is drug testing to take place?

UMTA has modified the Mandatory Guidelines for Federal Drug Testing Programs of the Department of Health and Human Services (DHHS). (53 Fed. Reg. 11,970, April 11, 1980) The Department of Transportation (DOT) has published its guidelines as 49 C.F.R. Part 40. A positive drug test must be confirmed. At present, both the screening test and the confirmation test must be by immunoassay and gas chromatography; as better technology is developed, that will probably change. Only laboratories certified by DHHS may do testing required by federal agencies.

Q. 9:78 When a specimen tests positive for illegal drugs, what is the next step?

An employee may seek a retest by written request within 60 days from receipt of test results. He or she may be required to advance the cost of the retest, but this will be refunded if the original test results are proved wrong. The employee will be interviewed by the MRO and given an opportunity to offer an acceptable medical explanation for the failed test. If he or she is able to do so, the MRO will report that the test was passed. If not, the MRO will report the results to the employer. An employee will be relieved of duty at least until the prohibited substance has left his or her body and the employee has passed a return-to-duty test. (49 C.F.R. §§653.29, 653.27, and 653.9(a) (1988))

Q. 9:79 What is an MRO?

Employers are required to have MROs. The companies need not hire full-time MROs, but may contract for the service. An MRO must be a licensed physician with training in substance abuse. The MRO receives, reviews, and interprets all positive test results and determines whether the results are valid. The MRO also determines whether a positive test result has a legitimate medical explanation. This determination is made only after reviewing information provided in confidence by the employee. If there is a legitimate medical explanation for the positive results, the MRO reports to the employer that the employee has passed the test. The MRO is also responsible for determining, from a medical standpoint, whether an employee who has failed the test may return to duty. (49 C.F.R. §653.27 (1988))

Q. 9:80 Who has access to an employee's test results, and for what purpose may they be used?

Results of an individual's test may be disclosed only with the written consent of the employee. (49 C.F.R. §653.33 (1988)) Employers may retain the results of preemployment tests for purposes of defending against legal or administrative actions by a job applicant arising out of the drug testing activities, but even then, the results can be released only with the testee's consent. Both employers and MROs must retain all records related to the collection process and reports of individuals not passing a mandated postemployment drug test for at least five years. Records of persons passing a test must be kept for at least one year. (49 C.F.R. §653.31 (1988))

Q. 9:81 Are all transit company employees subject to the testing mandate?

No. Only those employees who perform safety-sensitive functions must be tested, although an employer may develop a broader policy if it wishes. Mandated testees are employees whose duties are related to the safe operation of transportation services, or controlling the dispatch, movement, or maintenance of revenue service vehicles or equipment, and their supervisors. Security personnel are not included in the mandate, although UMTA encourages employers to include them in the antidrug program. Volunteers are also not mandated testees.

Q. 9:82 Why is alcohol not included in the UMTA mandated testing?

UMTA is concerned about impairment resulting from the abuse of substances other than those specified in the testing requirements (primarily, alcohol). It has decided, however, that its goal of a drug-free transportation industry will be best served by confining its mandate to illegal substances at this time. The decision was purely pragmatic. It differentiates between legal and illegal substances: Since alcohol is legal, penalizing an employee for its use would require establishing violation of existing legal prohibitions against its use (for example, actually driving while under the influence) or impairment due to use; illegal substances can be prohibited outright. The commentary to the UMTA Rule points out, by the way, that the Federal Highway Administration regulations prohibit driving with a blood alcohol level in excess of .04%.

Federally Sponsored Drug Treatment

Q. 9:83 Are there federally sponsored programs for treatment of substance abuse?

Yes. The United States Public Health Service is authorized to provide care for addicted persons who are civilly committed to treatment under the Narcotics Addict Rehabilitation Act of 1966, or for addicts and other persons with drug abuse and drug dependence problems who voluntarily submit themselves for treatment. (42 U.S.C. §257)

Q. 9:84 Who is eligible for treatment in a federal program?

Any addict or person with a drug problem may apply to the Surgeon General for admission to a Public Health Service hospital equipped for the accommodation of addicts or other persons with drug dependence problems.

Q. 9:85 Where is Public Health Service treatment provided?

The Public Health Service may provide treatment in its own hospitals, or it may contract with the Veterans' Administration and other federal agencies to use their treatment and rehabilitation facilities.

Q. 9:86 Is Public Health Service treatment an absolute right?

No. Admission is at the discretion of the Public Health Service. Voluntary applicants for admission are accepted only if there is space at a facility after the Service has accommodated all eligible addicts or other persons with drug abuse and dependence problems who have been convicted of federal crimes. (42 U.S.C. §259(b))

Q. 9:87 What are the criteria for voluntary admission to a Public Health Service drug treatment facility?

The Public Health Service screens applicants to determine whether they in fact are addicts or suffer from drug abuse problems; whether hospital treatment is likely to result in cure; and the estimated time of treatment. To be admitted, an applicant must agree to submit to treatment for the maximum time estimated by the Service to be necessary to effect a cure. (42 U.S.C. §259(b))

Q. 9:88 Is treatment free?

Not necessarily. A patient may be required to pay for his or her subsistence, care, and treatment at rates fixed by the Public Health Service. Indigent applicants will be transported to the hospital and treated at government expense.

Q. 9:89 If a person volunteers for treatment at a Public Health Service facility, does he or she lose any civil rights?

Admission for treatment does not result in the forfeiture or abridgement of any civil rights. (42 U.S.C. §259(d))

Q. 9:90 If a person volunteers for treatment at a Public Health Service facility, may that be used against him or her in a court proceeding?

Admission to a Public Health Service facility cannot be used against a patient in any court proceeding. The record of voluntary commitment is confidential and is not to be divulged. This protection is not absolute, however. In *Panella v. U.S.*, 139 F. Supp. 159 (D. N.Y. 1956), a patient in a federal Public Health Service hospital stabbed another patient, who sued the government under the Federal Tort Claims Act. The record of the stabber made at the time of his admission, as well as his treatment record thereafter—including observations of the staff—were held to be protected under the statute. However, any part of the stabber's record containing information from guards, inmates, or others about any assaultive tendencies of the stabber, as well as records pertaining to the stabbing, were ordered produced.

Q. 9:91 Under what circumstances can a person found guilty of a federal offense receive treatment rather than punishment?

Under federal law, an eligible offender found by the federal court to be a drug addict likely to be rehabilitated through treatment can be committed to the custody of the Attorney General for treatment, if there are adequate treatment facilities and personnel available. The commitment for treatment cannot be longer than a sentence for the crime of which the person was convicted. (18 U.S.C. §§4252–4253)

Q. 9:92 What is the definition of "addict" for purposes of this statute?

An addict is any person who habitually uses any narcotic drug, as defined by the Controlled Substances Act, so as to endanger the public morals, health, safety, or welfare, or who is or has been so far addicted to the use of such narcotic drugs as to have lost the power of self-control with reference to his or her addiction. (18 U.S.C. §4251(a))

Q. 9:93 Who is an "eligible offender"?

An eligible offender is anyone who is convicted of a federal crime except an offender who is:

- Convicted of a crime of violence;
- Convicted of a drug charge, unless the court determines that the purpose of the criminal behavior was to enable the offender to obtain a narcotic drug for his or her personal use because of an addiction;
- On probation following conviction of a felony, or against whom a felony charge is pending, unless the authority with jurisdiction over the offender consents;
- A person with a history of two prior felony convictions; or
- A person who has been committed on three or more occasions for treatment on account of narcotic addiction.

(18 U.S.C. §4251(f))

Q. 9:94 What treatment may an offender receive under the Narcotics Addict Rehabilitation Act?

Treatment consists of confinement and treatment in an institution, or treatment under supervised aftercare in the community, and includes but is not limited to: medical, educational, social, psychological, and vocational services; and services designed to protect the public and benefit the addict, by eliminating his or her dependence on addicting drugs or by controlling his or her dependence and susceptibility to addiction. (42 U.S.C. §4251(c))

Q. 9:95 Are there state law equivalents to the federal Narcotics Addict Rehabilitation Act and similar statutes?

Every state has its own laws with respect to treatment of addicted persons accused or convicted of crimes. The EAP should be familiar with applicable local laws, in order to counsel clients in trouble with the law who may be eligible for services, rather than punishment.

Q. 9:96 Can an alcoholic or narcotics addict be involuntarily committed for detoxification and treatment?

As a practical matter, if an alcoholic or narcotics addict is incarcerated under the criminal law, he or she will either be committed for detoxification and treatment or will be forced to detoxify "cold turkey." For this reason, clients who have criminal law problems should be counseled about treatment alternatives and their rights to treatment under various state and federal statutes.

As to civil commitment for alcoholism or addiction, many states take the position that treatment for these disorders must be voluntary to be effective, and the cost of involuntary treatment in public institutions would be prohibitive. These states do not provide for involuntary commitment for substance abuse treatment. If, however, the substance abuse is secondary to a mental illness, commitment may be possible for the mental illness. (See Ch. 11, "Mental Health Law," Qs. 11:13–11:26, for more on commitment.)

Federal Criminal Drug Laws

Q. 9:97 What is "drug trafficking"?

Drug trafficking is a federal offense. It is the unauthorized manufacture, distribution (delivery, whether by sale, gift, or otherwise), or possession with intent to distribute of any controlled substance.

Q. 9:98 What are the federal penalties for drug trafficking?

The penalties vary according to the severity of the offense. For example, a first-time violation of trafficking in 5 kilograms or more of a substance containing a detectable amount of cocaine will result in a sentence of 10 years to life in prison. If death or bodily injury occurs from the use of the substance, the minimum prison term is 20 years. A minimum term of 5 years of probation following imprisonment must also be imposed. In addition, there is a minimum fine of $4 million for an individual, or $10 million for other than an individual (e.g., a business). The sale of drugs within 1,000 feet of a school, or by a person over 21 years of age to a person under 18 years of age, will result in up to double the sentence. An additional 5-year sentence and an additional fine of up to $50,000 will be imposed if drugs are sold to a person under age 18, or if a child under the age of 14 is employed, hired, or used in the trafficking.

Q. 9:99 What is "simple possession"?

Simple possession is possession of a controlled substance in a small enough quantity to give rise to the presumption that it is intended for personal use, rather than distribution or sale.

Q. 9:100 What are the federal penalties for simple possession?

A first-time violator found guilty or pleading guilty to simple possession may be placed on probation for up to a year, with judgment and all further proceedings deferred. At the end of the probationary period, if the violator has stayed "clean," the case can be dismissed without adjudication. If the violator is under 21 years old, he or she may apply for expungement of the record.

Q. 9:101 Are drug trafficking, possession, cultivation, and use also state offenses?

Yes, and often the state penalties are more harsh than the federal penalties.

Chapter 10

EAPs and Employment and Labor Laws

When employees are referred by supervisors to the EAP, it is generally in connection with a discipline or performance problem. Therefore, it is important for internal EAP administrators to understand how labor and employment laws function to govern employee relations in the workplace. Additionally, the human resources professional who is responsible for referring employees to external programs will need to understand how employment laws relate to the functioning of the EAP. Among the legal issues discussed in this chapter are employment at will, discipline and workplace due process, employment discrimination (and especially handicap discrimination), drug testing, and AIDS workplace issues.

Q. 10:1 What employment or labor laws are relevant to EAPs?

EAPs are affected, directly or indirectly, by all laws relating to employment and labor. Federal statutes include the National Labor Relations Act (NLRA), the Railway Labor Act (governing unions in the railway and airline industries), the Fair Labor Standards Act (FLSA), the Civil Rights Act of 1964, the Rehabilitation Act of 1973 (Rehabilitation Act), the Immigration Reform and Control Act of 1986 (IRCA), and the Occupational Safety and Health Act of 1970 (OSHA). Every state also has laws relating to employment. EAP providers and human resources personnel should be familiar with federal and state laws, particularly as they affect EAP activities.

Employment at Will

Q. 10:2 What is "employment at will," and does it exist today?

Employment at will is an employment relationship in which (1) employers are free to hire and fire employees and (2) employees are free to accept employment or quit at will. The concept no longer exists in its pure form in the United States. Employers may not fire "for any reason or no reason." Statutes may proscribe firing for reasons of discrimination (e.g., race, religion, national origin, sex, non-job-related disability, union affiliation, or refusal to submit to sexual harassment). For example, it is against public policy to fire an employee in retaliation for: refusing to commit perjury (*Petermann v. International Brotherhood of Teamsters*, 344 P.2d 25 (1959)); filing a workers' compensation claim (*Frampton v. Central Indiana Gas Co.*, 297 N.E.2d 425 (1973)); engaging in union activity (*Glenn v. Clearman's Golden Cock Inn, Inc.*, 13 Cal. Rptr. 769 (1961)); performing jury duty (*Nees v. Hocks*, 536 P.2d 512 (1975)); or calling an employer's attention to the company's violations of law (*Sheets v. Teddy's Frosted Foods*, 427 A.2d 385 (1980)).

Q. 10:3 When the employment relationship forbids firing without "just and proper cause," how is just cause to be defined?

Since just cause is rarely defined in employment contracts, union arbitrators have developed something similar to a "common law" definition, which they apply in cases charging unjust discharge. It consists of a set of guidelines set forth in the following questions:

- Did the company give the employee forewarning or foreknowledge of the possible or probable disciplinary consequences of the employee's conduct?

- Was the company's rule or managerial order reasonably related to the orderly, efficient, and safe operation of the company's business?
- Did the company, before administering discipline to the employee, make an effort to discover whether the employee did, in fact, violate or disobey a work rule or management order?
- Was the company's investigation conducted fairly and objectively?
- At the investigation, did the "judge" obtain substantial evidence or proof that the employee was guilty as charged?
- Has the company applied its rules, orders, and penalties evenhandedly and without discrimination to all employees?
- Was the degree of discipline administered by the company in the case in question reasonably related to (1) the seriousness of the employee's proven offense and (2) the employee's record of service with the company?

A "no" answer to any one or more of these questions normally (but not always) signifies that just cause for discipline did not exist. (*Grief Bros. Cooperage Corp.*, 42 Lab. Arb. 555, 1964)

Q. 10:4 How may an employer give foreknowledge or forewarning?

The foreknowledge or forewarning may be given orally or in writing. The writing may consist of typed or printed sheets, handbooks, or books of shop rules. The rules and the penalties for their infraction must be clearly spelled out and must have been actually communicated to the employee.

Q. 10:5 How does an at-will arrangement affect an EAP?

The conditions under which an employee may be terminated are significant in establishing the policies and procedures of the EAP and their interface with the employer's disciplinary system. An at-will arrangement is not inconsistent with a fitness-for-duty policy, but it is obviously inconsistent with a progressive or punitive discipline plan that sets forth causes for termination.

Q. 10:6 How do statutes and regulations affect the employment contract?

Whether or not there is a collective bargaining agreement, statutes (such as OSHA and wage and hour legislation) and regulations (such as Section 504 (Rehabilitation Act) protection for handicapped workers) set the limits of the employment contract. These laws and regulations provide recourse to government administrative agencies and the courts for action against the employer beyond that authorized by the employee's contractual rights.

Q. 10:7 Does an employee handbook create implied contractual terms?

The courts are divided about whether a handbook is to be read as an employment contract. If the handbook clearly states that it is not to be so read, most courts seem willing to respect the employer's intention. If, however, the employer's intent in distributing the handbook has not been articulated, and the employee claims to have relied on its provisions (such as a stated policy to discharge only for just cause), a court may well interpret the handbook as setting forth contractual terms. (See *Toussaint v. Blue Cross and Blue Shield of Michigan*, 292 N.W.2d 880 (1980), for a discussion of the handbook question and the matter of employment contracts that are at will or terminable for cause.)

Q. 10:8 Will lack of actual communication of rules and penalties vitiate just cause for discipline in all cases?

No. Certain offenses, such as insubordination, intoxication, drinking or drug use on the job, and theft of company property or from fellow employees, are so serious that any employee is expected to know that such conduct is grossly offensive and heavily punishable.

Employer-Employee Relationships in a Unionized Setting

Q. 10:9 What is the NLRA, and how is it relevant to EAPs?

The NLRA is the federal statute that is the backbone of labor law.

It governs the rights of employers, and of labor unions and their employee members; the mandates and prohibitions that apply to labor organizations; and collective bargaining and employment practices. Especially in the area of employee discipline, EAPs and their activities will be affected by the collective bargaining agreement and its implementation.

Q. 10:10 What is a collective bargaining agreement?

A collective bargaining agreement is a labor contract between a union and the company, setting forth the terms and conditions of employment of unionized employees.

Q. 10:11 How does the collective bargaining agreement affect individual employee rights?

In an organized workplace, the collective bargaining agreement between the union and the employer establishes employment terms for the individual employee. An employee who has a complaint against the employer that is covered by the collective bargaining agreement is constrained by its terms in the manner of seeking redress, but also has a right to representation by the union in prosecuting the grievance. The union has the right, as well as the duty, to act on the employee's behalf.

Q. 10:12 What is the role of a union when one of its members is involved in disciplinary proceedings?

Whenever a union member is at risk of discipline, he or she has a right to be represented by a union official (usually an officer or steward) at every step of the proceedings, including any initial meeting or interview that could lead to discipline. The union has an obligation to investigate employee grievances and represent all members in grievances or disciplinary proceedings through arbitration.

Q. 10:13 What is the role of the labor arbitrator?

The labor arbitrator, as the protector of the bargain made by management and the union, must carry out the intent of the parties. The source of the arbitrator's authority is the collective bargaining agreement, and the agreement must be interpreted in accordance with the "industrial common law of the shop'' and the needs and desires of the parties. The arbitrator does *not* have authority to invoke public laws that conflict with the parties' bargain. (*United Steelworkers of America v. Enterprise Wheel & Car Corp.*, 363 U.S. 593 (1960))

Q. 10:14 Is arbitration always binding?

Arbitration pursuant to a collective bargaining agreement is generally final and binding on the aggrieved employee. (See *Collyer Insulated Wire,* 192 NLRB 837 (1971).) However, there are exceptions. Irrespective of the collective bargaining agreement's grievance-arbitration mechanism, an employee is entitled to a trial to resolve and enforce his or her rights under statutes designed to protect employee rights or safety. An example is the right to a trial in an equal employment opportunity situation under Title VII of the Civil Rights Act of 1964 (78 Stat. 253, 42 U.S.C. §2000e et seq.). (*Alexander v. Gardner-Denver Co.*, 415 U.S. 36 (1974)) Cases may also be brought under Section 1983 (post–Civil War antidiscrimination law). (*McDonald v. City of West Branch, Mich.*, 466 U.S. 284 (1984)) Another exception to the rule of finality of arbitration is a union's failure to represent the employee properly. (*Hines v. Anchor Motor Freight, Inc.*, 424 U.S. 554 (1976))

A court will not enforce a collective bargaining agreement or an arbitrator's award that is against public policy. (*W.R. Grace & Co., Inc. v. Rubber Workers,* 461 U.S. 757 (1983))

Q. 10:15 In an organized workplace, may the employer promulgate rules and give orders unilaterally, or must these always be negotiated with the union?

Unless the collective bargaining agreement prohibits or restricts it, the employer has a right to promulgate reasonable rules and give reasonable orders without negotiating them with the union. A material change in working conditions, however, must be negotiated.

Q. 10:16 In an organized workplace, must the union agree to an EAP?

An employer can implement an EAP without bargaining for it as long as the EAP is simply an additional employee benefit and does not change work conditions in any manner. It is unreasonable to expect that an EAP would have no impact on work rules or employee discipline, so as a practical matter, union agreement may be necessary. Further, without union support, it is highly unlikely that an EAP will get off the ground.

Q. 10:17 Can a union start its own EAP?

Many unions have their own EAPs. They feel that they can trust their own programs and may be concerned that an employer-sponsored program will be nothing more than a tool to persecute and control members. If the union intends to use its EAP to enhance job safety and employment security, and to have it work cooperatively with the employer's disciplinary scheme, the union will have to bargain for the EAP's position in the organization.

Q. 10:18 Is a joint union-management program practical?

There are a number of highly successful jointly sponsored EAPs. With labor and management cooperating in the organization and implementation of an EAP, the probability of program success is significantly enhanced.

Discipline, Due Process, and Employee Rights

Q. 10:19 What is a discipline program?

A discipline program is a system of rules and procedures for enforcing work rules and correcting or punishing their infraction.

Q. 10:20 What are the two types of discipline programs?

Depending upon the philosophy of the employer, a discipline program may be punitive or affirmative (positive). In practice, there will be little or no difference between these approaches in cases of very severe infractions that are cause for immediate termination.

Q. 10:21 How does a punitive disciplinary plan work?

With a punitive disciplinary program, an employee is terminated if he or she commits a major disciplinary offense, such as stealing, striking a supervisor, or being intoxicated on the job. If an employee commits a minor offense, a several-step progressive disciplinary plan will be implemented. The objective of a punitive disciplinary plan is to punish an employee for each offense he or she commits. Progressive discipline usually involves:

1. Oral reprimand;
2. Written reprimand;
3. Suspension for a period of time without pay; and
4. Termination.

Q. 10:22 How does a positive discipline plan work?

In a positive discipline plan, the employee will not be punished for an infraction, but will be asked to consider his or her motivation in behaving inappropriately. Rather than being suspended without pay, the employee may be given a "decision day" off with pay to consider whether or not he or she wishes to remain employed by this employer. If the answer is affirmative, the employee will be asked to enter into a written contract for modification of his or her behavior in a manner acceptable to the employer. Positive discipline is said to work better in white collar, nonunion environments, as contrasted to blue collar, organized workplaces.

Q. 10:23 Must an employee obey a rule that he or she considers unreasonable?

An employee must obey a rule, even if he or she thinks it is unreasonable, unless the employee sincerely believes that obedience will seriously and immediately jeopardize his or her personal safety and/or integrity. Given a firm finding to this effect, an employee would properly be said to have had justification for disobedience. Under any other circumstances, the disobedience would be punishable. The proper recourse for the employee in an organized workplace would be a grievance; in an unorganized workplace, the employee would have no recourse if discussion did not bring about a change.

Q. 10:24 May an employee refuse to perform an assigned task that he or she perceives to be very dangerous?

Under OSHA, an employee has a right to choose not to perform an assigned task because of a reasonable apprehension of death or serious injury, coupled with a reasonable belief that no less drastic alternative is available. OSHA and its regulations prohibit retaliatory discharge against an employee who exercises any right afforded by the Act. (29 U.S.C. §660(c)(1); 29 C.F.R. §1977.12 (1979))

Q. 10:25 Is an employee entitled to representation during the disciplinary process?

In a nonunion workplace, a private-sector employee has no legal right to representation by an attorney in the disciplinary process. Unionized employees have a right to be accompanied by a union official to any meeting or proceeding that could lead to disciplinary action. Public employees may have a right of representation under certain federal or state statutes. Some employers allow employees to choose supervisors or co-workers who are not involved in the dispute to accompany them in grievance proceedings, but most will not permit a lawyer.

Q. 10:26 Can an employee refuse to incriminate himself or herself during a disciplinary proceeding?

The Fifth Amendment constitutional right to remain silent and not have such silence held against one does not extend to the workplace. A worker may choose not to make admissions or otherwise participate in a proceeding, but the employer has a right to make reasonable assumptions from this behavior.

Q. 10:27 May an employer conduct a search of employees' desks or lockers?

Employers may conduct reasonable searches of their employees' desks or lockers to locate drugs or other contraband (or material stolen from the company). The desks or lockers are the property of the employer, which can enter them at will.

Q. 10:28 May an employer search the person or automobile of an employee for illegal drugs?

If the employer has a policy of personal or automobile searches to which employees have agreed by accepting or continuing employment after notification of the policy, an employee's refusal to permit a search may constitute insubordination. If an employee refuses to permit the search, the employer's disciplinary program may be invoked. If the employer reasonably believes that an employee is conducting criminal activity on the company's premises, the employer may report the suspicion to the police, who may seek a search warrant that will permit them to conduct the search.

Q. 10:29 Does an employee have any protection against an employer's conduct in investigations?

State common laws against defamation, invasion of privacy, and infliction of emotional distress offer some protection to employees from high-handed employers. Employers may not be outrageous is handling disciplinary investigations. (*McLain v. Boise Cascade Corp.*, 533 P.2d 343 (Or. 1975))

Q. 10:30 Can an employee sue an employer for defamation by reason of disciplinary proceedings?

Unless an employer maliciously lies about an employee during grievance procedures, the law will generally recognize a qualified privilege to make true statements about the employee. Malice is the voicing of untrue statements, in spite of either knowing them to be false or recklessly disregarding information that suggests that they are false. Two devices are available to help protect an employer against a defamation suit: (1) limit the information about a disciplinary proceeding and the underlying facts only to management personnel who need to know and (2) require the employee to waive defamation claims before permitting him or her to have access to a grievance committee or peer review board. Obviously, the latter device is not available in a collective bargaining situation and may be otherwise precluded by contract between the employer and employee.

Q. 10:31 May an employer discipline first and investigate later?

Normally, an investigation must be made *before* disciplinary action is taken. Failure to do so is not ordinarily excusable on the ground that the employee will later have an opportunity to be heard in a grievance proceeding, because too much hardening of positions is bound to occur under such circumstances. In situations in which the misbehavior is very serious, however, the employer may be constrained to react immediately. The employee may be suspended pending the investigation with the understanding that (1) the final disciplinary decision will not be made until after the investigation, and (2) if the employee is found innocent after the investigation, he or she will be restored to the job with full pay for time lost.

Q. 10:32 If the employer has not treated a particular accused employee in the same manner as other employees similarly accused, what effect will this have on the discipline?

If the company does not apply its rules, orders, and penalties evenhandedly, it is discriminating against some employees. An employee treated more harshly than others has been discriminated against, and this will require modification of the discipline.

Q. 10:33 What may a company do to avoid a charge of discrimination if it has been lax in enforcing its rules in the past and now wants to apply them rigorously?

Notice must be given to the employees that irrespective of the company's leniency or carelessness in the past, henceforth the rules will be rigorously applied. It is important to establish that each and every employee has received actual notice of the change of policy. This is best accomplished by having each employee sign a statement to that effect.

Q. 10:34 What effect may an employee's past record have in the administration of discipline?

An employee's record of previous offenses cannot be used to determine guilt in the immediate or latest offense. It can properly be used only to help determine the severity of discipline once the employee has been found guilty of a breach. The only legitimate basis for treating one employee more harshly than another for the same offense is the respective records of each: an employee whose record is significantly better can be given a lighter punishment than one whose record is significantly worse.

Q. 10:35 Must employers allow employees access to their personnel records?

This is a matter of state law. Some states give employees limited rights to access to and/or copies of their personnel records under certain circumstances. If there is no law requiring access, an employer may deny it. Of course, in the case of litigation between employer and employee, any relevant records will be subject to discovery in accordance with the relevant procedure laws.

Q. 10:36 How long should employee disciplinary records be kept?

The general rule for retention of any records is: Keep them as long as they may be needed for use in defense in the event of legal action. Three years following termination of employment is a recommended period.

Q. 10:37 What is "due process"?

The Fifth and Fourteenth Amendments to the United States Constitution require due process before governmental action can deprive a person of life, liberty, or property. Contractual or statutory entitlements to protection against discharge except for cause give public employees enough of a property right in their jobs to trigger the constitutional guarantee of due process. Due process in the context of the workplace requires a fair hearing before discipline takes place. Fair hearing means "the opportunity to be heard at a meaningful time and in a meaningful manner." (*Boddie v. Connecticut*, 401 U.S. 371 (1971)) In situations in which the government may intervene in the disciplinary process (for example, Section 405 of the Surface Transportation Assistance Act of 1982 protects transportation industry employees from retaliatory discharge for refusing to operate a motor vehicle that does not comply with applicable state and federal safety standards), the employer also has a right to due process. (*Brock v. Roadway Express, Inc.*, 107 S. Ct. 1740 (1987))

Q. 10:38 Do private employees have a right to workplace due process?

No. Constitutional protections apply to protect individuals against the government only and do not extend into the private workplace. Although the law does not require a private employer to adopt a workplace due process policy, collective bargaining agreements always require it, and many employers consider it good business. Due process policies are considered effective deterrents to union efforts to organize employees; and white collar workers, in particular, expect due process, even though it is not imposed by law. Courts and administrative agencies tend to look more favorably on employers that discharge employees only after giving them the chance to be heard, and employees given due process may be less likely to sue when disciplined.

Q. 10:39 What is "informal due process"?

The most common form of due process is the "open door" policy—an invitation to employees to come directly to management (often including the president) if they have problems or grievances. This policy is often written and promulgated to the employees.

Q. 10:40 What is a more formal due process program?

Companies adopting more formal due process programs often follow the grievance/arbitration procedures found in collective bargaining agreements. The arbitrator's role may be assigned to a corporate employee, such as the personnel manager or corporate president, or to a professional arbitrator, such as a member of the American Arbitration Association.

Hiring and Discrimination

Q. 10:41 What are the legal restrictions on how a company advertises for new employees?

Employers may not reflect an intention to discriminate on the basis of age, sex, religion, national origin, race, veteran status, or non-job-related disabilities. If the employer has government contracts, it is mandatory that the words "equal opportunity employer" be included in any job advertisements and on employment applications.

Q. 10:42 What subjects may an employer *not* inquire about in the hiring process?

Employers are forbidden to inquire about age, race, national origin, religion, marital status, non-job-related disabilities, military service, criminal records, and credit history. If the job requires foreign-language skills, it is permissible to ask what languages an applicant speaks; it is not permissible to ask the applicant's primary language. An exception to the prohibition against inquiring about religion exists for employers whose "business" is a religious mission requiring adherence to a particular faith.

Q. 10:43 What inquiries may be made about an employee's health?

An employer may inquire about any health condition that would interfere with job performance. An employer may not refuse to hire an applicant on the basis of a health problem or disability unless the problem or disability interferes with work performance, and no reasonable accommodation to it can be made.

Q. 10:44 Can a preemployment physical examination be required?

Yes. It may be difficult or impossible to later terminate an employee whose health would have disqualified him or her for the job in the first place. Therefore, the best practice is to make a job offer contingent on an employee's passing a preemployment physical.

Q. 10:45 May a preemployment physical include a drug test?

Employers may screen for drugs and alcohol using urine and blood tests. Under the Drug-Free Workplace Act of 1988 and other federal regulations, some employers are *required* to test applicants for certain illegal substances. (See Ch. 9, "Substance Abuse Laws," Qs. 9:51–9:61.)

Employment Discrimination

Q. 10:46 What categories of persons are protected against employment discrimination?

A protected group or suspect class is a substratum of the population that has historically been discriminated against in employment and is now protected against it. It is now illegal to discriminate against blacks, Hispanics, women, older persons, and handicapped persons. Reverse discrimination is also not allowed, except as it may be part of an affirmative action plan, so in some situations, white males may be a protected group.

Q. 10:47 What is an affirmative action plan?

An affirmative action plan is a detailed plan to increase the representation of minorities and women in the workforce of an employer. Hiring quotas, although generally illegal, may be required as part of the remedy to correct past discrimination. Private employers bidding for government contracts are required to adopt affirmative action plans as a contract requirement.

Q. 10:48 What are the various forms of discrimination?

Religious discrimination occurs when an employer makes employment decisions based on an employee's religion, or fails to reasonably accommodate an employee's religious beliefs. Reasonable accommodation includes such practices as allowing an employee to wear a certain costume, emblem, or headpiece peculiar to the religion (but not if it interferes with safety); or allowing an employee to schedule work to permit absence on religious holidays (but not if it results in requiring some workers to work every Saturday so that an Orthodox Jew or Seventh Day Adventist never has to work on Saturday).

National origin discrimination occurs when an employer makes employment decisions based on a person's ethnic background. IRCA prohibits discrimination against legal aliens with respect to most jobs. When clear communication in English is required to perform a job, however, it is not discrimination to decline to hire someone who cannot meet that requirement.

Sex discrimination includes basing employment decisions on gender, sexual harassment, and unequal pay for similar work. Sexual harassment occurs if advancement is conditioned on sexual favors, or a hostile and embarrassing atmosphere is created in the workplace because the employer permits employees' lewd remarks, obscene language, or unwelcome advances to co-workers. Once a complaint is made to management, the company must take prompt, effective action to eliminate the harassment, or else face liability.

Handicap discrimination generally refers to making employment decisions based on an employee's *non-job-related* disability. Section 504 of the Rehabilitation Act forbids any program or activity receiving federal assistance to refuse someone employment based on a physical deficiency that does not prevent the person from performing the job. Many states have parallel laws governing non-government-assisted private industry. An employer may not fire or refuse to hire an *otherwise qualified person* because of a non-job-related handicap.

Handicap Discrimination

Q. 10:49 Who is a "handicapped individual"?

A handicapped individual is any person who (1) has a physical or mental impairment substantially limiting one or more major life activities, (2) has a record of such an impairment, or (3) is regarded as having such an impairment. (29 U.S.C. §706(7)(B))

Physical impairment is defined as "any physiological disorder or condition, cosmetic disfigurement, or anatomical loss affecting one or more of the following body systems: neurological, musculoskeletal, special sense organs, skin, and endocrine, respiratory (including speech), cardiovascular, reproductive, digestive, genitourinary, and hemic and lymphatic; or any mental or psychological disorder, such as mental retardation, organic brain syndrome, emotional or mental illness, and specific learning disabilities." (45 C.F.R. §84.3(j)(2)(i) (1985))

Major life activities are "functions such as caring for one's self, performing manual tasks, walking, seeing, hearing, speaking, breathing, learning, and working." (45 C.F.R. §84.3(j)(2)(ii) (1985))

Q. 10:50 What is a non-job-related handicap?

A person may suffer from a condition that impairs his or her daily activities but does not prevent him or her from performing on the job.

Q. 10:51 What is "an otherwise qualified person"?

An otherwise qualified person is one who can perform "the essential functions" of the job in question. (45 C.F.R. §84.3(k)(1985))

Q. 10:52 What accommodation of a handicap does the law require of an employer?

When a handicapped person is not able to perform the essential functions of the job, the employer must make reasonable accommodation for the handicap that would enable the individual to perform those functions. Reasonable accommodation may include:

- Modification of facilities to make them readily accessible to and usable by the handicapped person;
- Job restructuring or part-time or modified work schedules;
- Acquisition or modification of equipment or devices;
- Provision of readers or interpreters; and
- Other similar actions.

(45 C.F.R. §84.12) (1985))

The employer is not required to suffer undue hardship to make accommodation, such as "a fundamental alteration of the program." In considering whether an accommodation is reasonable or creates an undue hardship, the size and nature of the employer's business and the type and cost of the requested accommodation are to be considered. (45 C.F.R. §§84.22–84.23 (1985)) If a person's handicap cannot be overcome by reasonable accommodation, or accommodation would cause undue hardship to the employer, employment decisions made on the basis of handicap will not be considered illegal discrimination. (*Southeastern Community College v. Davis,* 442 U.S. 397 (1979))

Q. 10:53 What remedies are available to an individual whose rights under Section 504 are violated?

An employer that violates Section 504 by discriminating against a handicapped person in making employment decisions may have its federal financial assistance or contract terminated. The wronged individual may obtain injunctive relief and compensatory damages either under Section 504 or in a private right of action by lawsuit. Attorneys' fees may be awarded to any party except the United States.

Q. 10:54 What employers are required by federal law to take affirmative action to employ handicapped individuals?

Under Section 503 of the Rehabilitation Act, all government contractors and subcontractors with contracts in excess of $2,500 (except contracts for personal services) are required to take affirmative action to employ and promote qualified handicapped individuals. (29 U.S.C. §793; *see also* 45 C.F.R. §§60.741.1–60.741.30 (1987).)

Q. 10:55 What remedies are available to a worker under Section 503?

Unlike the situation under Section 504, there is no private right of action under Section 503. An aggrieved individual must file a complaint within 180 days from the date of the alleged violation with the Department of Labor's Office of Federal Contract Compliance Program (OFCCP). Some state statutes provide for private rights of action for violation of a state affirmative action statute.

Q. 10:56 Is alcoholism or drug dependency or addiction a protected handicap under Section 504?

Alcoholics and drug addicts, including persons with a history of drug use or in a methadone maintenance program, are handicapped persons under Sections 503 and 504 (*Davis v. Bucher,* 451 F. Supp. 791 (E.D. Pa. 1978)), but the law provides an exclusion from protection in the case of an individual whose "current use of alcohol or drugs prevents [him or her] from performing the duties of the job in question or whose employment. . .would constitute a direct threat to the property or safety of others." (29 U.S.C. §706(7)(B)) (See *Burka v. New York City Transit Authority,* 680 F. Supp. 590 (1988)). The exclusion does not apply to the federal government, which, as a "model employer of handicapped persons," has a greater affirmative duty in hiring the handicapped than other employers.

In *Crewe v. United States Office of Personnel Management,* 834 F.2d 140 (8th Cir. 1987), the Eighth Circuit stated that alcoholism is a protected handicap, but the government could deny employment to the plaintiff because of her delinquency in prior employment, dishonest conduct, and excessive alcohol abuse. The court found that her history of failure in past treatment efforts was such that the government could not reasonably accommodate her alcoholism.

In *Traynor v. Turnage,* 108 S. Ct. 1372 (1988), a veteran attempted to obtain benefits from the Veterans' Administration under the G.I. Bill after the 10-year limitation period. He claimed that his disease of primary alcoholism created an exception to the 10-year rule. The court distinguished between primary alcoholism and alcoholism attributable to an underlying psychiatric disorder. Primary alcoholism, the court held, was willful; drinking attributable to a psychiatric disorder was not. The court noted that 20% to 30% of all alcoholism is caused by mental illness, and it is only in the case of mental illness that an extension of time would be granted by the VA to alcoholics.

Some courts have distinguished between alcoholism and drug addiction in looking at what accommodation an employer must provide. There have been holdings that since most addictive drugs are either illegal, or are legal drugs that are being used illegally, lawbreakers are not entitled to leaves of absence for detoxification and other treatment.

Q. 10:57 Is AIDS a job-related handicap?

AIDS is considered a non-job-related handicap, since AIDS cannot be transmitted in any typical work situation. The Centers for Disease Control (CDC) has stated that AIDS can be transmitted only by blood and semen. It appears that other body fluids, such as tears and saliva, and breath cannot transmit the disease. Casual contact does not pose a danger to healthy persons. Many state human relations agencies have held that AIDS patients who are otherwise capable of performing their jobs cannot be terminated on the basis of having the virus.

Q. 10:58 What position has the federal government taken on AIDS?

This is an example of the left hand not knowing what the right hand is doing—except that in this case, there are more than two hands. The CDC takes the position that AIDS is not an issue in any workplace except a hospital or laboratory in which blood or semen is handled. Even in those places, it recommends only "universal precautions." Yet the Justice Department during the Reagan administration stated that fear of contagion was a valid defense to a discrimination charge. The only case law guideline is *School Board of Nassau County v. Arline,* 107 S. Ct. 1123 (1987), which is not an AIDS case at all, but a case dealing with tuberculosis. In that case, the Supreme Court held that the presence of this communicable disease did not automatically disqualify a teacher from performing on the job, even in a classroom full of children. Having a contagious disease can thus be job-related or non-job-related, depending upon the facts in the case. If the sufferer is otherwise qualified, he or she will be protected. This case, reviewed under the Federal Rehabilitation Act, is viewed by many as the Supreme Court's *de facto* position on AIDS as a handicap, as well.

Q. 10:59 Is obesity a job-related handicap?

Obesity is a handicap because it impairs many daily activities, can lead to diseases and physical problems, and may shorten life expectancy. It can be a job-related handicap; if personal appearance is an important part of the job, an employer may be found not to have discriminated if it refuses to hire or fires an obese individual. This issue remains hotly contested at this time, since we have cases in various jurisdictions disagreeing.

Q. 10:60 Is job reassignment a reasonable accommodation?

An assignment to a different shift, or to another job—even at a lower salary—is an appropriate reasonable accommodation to an employee whose condition is such that he or she can no longer perform the essential duties of the job. Failure to so reassign an employee when jobs were available that fit his qualifications was considered discriminatory. (*Rhone v. United States Department of the Army*, 665 F. Supp. 734 (E.D. Mo. 1987))

Q. 10:61 What preemployment inquiries may an employer that is subject to the Rehabilitation Act conduct?

An employer may not inquire, during a preemployment physical examination or otherwise, about whether a job applicant is handicapped or about the nature or severity of a handicap. A blood or urine test may not be used to determine pregnancy or whether a person is being treated for a psychiatric condition, for example. An employer may make inquiry, however, about whether the applicant can perform job-related functions.

Once an applicant has been selected for hiring, there is nothing to prevent the employer from conditioning an offer of employment on the results of a medical examination conducted prior to the employee's commencement of service, as long as all entering employees, regardless of handicap, are subject to such an examination, and the results are kept confidential and used only as permitted by the Act. Supervisors may be informed of any restrictions on the employee's work or duties and necessary accommodations. First aid and safety personnel may be informed if the employee may require emergency treatment. Government officials monitoring compliance may also be provided relevant information on request. (45 C.F.R. §84.14)

Q. 10:62 How is preemployment testing consistent with the Rehabilitation Act's protection of alcoholism, drug addiction, and other handicaps?

At first glance, there may appear to be an inconsistency, but in fact, this is not the case. An employer may (and in some instances *must*) refuse to hire a person who is *currently* a user of illegal drugs. Such a person is not "otherwise qualified." The refusal to hire is based not on the individual's addiction, but on his or her current use of illegal substances. Addiction is not an excuse or exception to a rule against hiring illegal drug users.

Q. 10:63 When a handicapped employee can no longer perform the functions of the job, may the employer cancel health and other benefits?

Yes. The Rehabilitation Act was designed to prohibit discrimination within the context of the employment relationship in which the employee is potentially able to do the job in question. If the employee cannot perform the job functions, the employer is not obliged to continue benefits unless the employment contract provides to the contrary. (Of course, under federal law, employers are obligated to provide continuation of benefits, commonly known as "COBRA" coverage, for a period of 18–36 months. The employer must offer this coverage at no more than 2% above what it costs the employer to provide these benefits.) There is a possibility, in certain situations, of a lawsuit for breach of the employment contract if the employer's failure to provide fringe benefits constitutes a violation of the employment contract. (*Beauford v. Father Flanagan's Boys' Home,* 831 F.2d 768 (8th Cir. 1987))

Q. 10:64 How many chances at rehabilitation must an employer give to a substance-abusing employee in order to comply with the requirement of "reasonable accommodation"?

A private employer need give only one opportunity to a substance abuser to receive treatment and get his or her problem under control. If an employee is offered a second chance and then reverts to drinking or illegal drug use, the employee may be discharged. In the case of a valued or crucial employee, the employer may feel pressed to condone that employee's failings and make special arrangements for him or her because of the special role that employee plays in the company. The problem in such cases will be vulnerability to a claim of discrimination if the employer is inconsistent in allowing additional chances to some employees, but not others.

Drug Testing and Privacy

Q. 10:65 May an employer impose drug testing requirements in an organized workplace without first bargaining with the union?

Drug or alcohol testing for current employees and job applicants is a mandatory subject of collective bargaining. The implementation of a drug or alcohol testing program is a substantial change in working conditions. (Memorandum GC 87-5, General Counsel of the National Labor Relations Board, Sept. 8, 1987; see also *Amer. Train Dispatchers Assn. v. Metro-North Commuter Railroad Co.*, 698 F. Supp. 1102 (N.Y. 1988), for a discussion of the distinction between "major" and "minor" disputes and the requirement of bargaining.)

Q. 10:66 Is drug testing a "search" within the meaning of the Fourth Amendment of the U.S. Constitution?

This issue is still being decided, but most courts that have considered it have concluded that toxicological testing of employees is a search within the meaning of the Fourth Amendment prohibition against unreasonable searches and seizures. Even if testing is a search, it is not in itself prohibited. The fundamental command of the Fourth Amendment is that searches be reasonable. (*New Jersey v. T.L.O.*, 469 U.S. 325 (1985)) It must be noted that the constitutional issues in drug testing are relevant only in the context of public employers. The Constitution protects citizens against the excesses of government only; it does not apply to the relationship between an employee and a private-sector employer.

Q. 10:67 Is drug testing in the context of a preemployment or routine annual physical examination permissible?

Yes. (See *Amal. Transit Union, Div. 1279 v. Cambria County Transit Authority*, 691 F. Supp. 898 (W.D. Pa. 1988), and *Wrightsell v. City of Chicago*, 678 F. Supp. 727 (N.D. Ill. 1988).)

Q. 10:68 May an employer conduct a search, including a urine test, on its premises?

An employer is not precluded from searching on its own premises for evidence of drug or alcohol use or presence. One case has held that a public employer, specifically, is not required to obtain a search warrant before searching its employees' offices, desks, lockers, etc. for work-related purposes. (*O'Connor v. Ortega,* 107 S. Ct. 1492 (1987)) This principle applies also to drug testing. (*Amal. Transit Union Local 933 v. City of Oklahoma City, d/b/a The Central Oklahoma Transportation and Parking Authority,* 710 F. Supp. 1321 (W.D. Okla. 1988))

Q. 10:69 Under what circumstances have courts approved random testing or testing for cause?

Courts are concerned with the privacy rights of employees. As long as testing is done in a medical context, in which the expectation of privacy is attenuated by the realities of a medical examination, reasonable expectations of privacy are reduced to an extent, and the intrusion into privacy is considered acceptable. When urinalysis is only one of several inquiries into fitness for duty, the sense of intrusiveness of a testing program standing alone is lessened. (*Jones v. McKenzie,* 833 F.2d 335 (D.C. Cir. 1987); *Wrightsell v. City of Chicago,* 678 F. Supp. 727 (N.D. Ill. 1988)) When a company has established specific, readily identifiable events as the trigger for tests, employees are considered to be sufficiently protected from management discrimination. Typical triggering events are the passing of the employee's birth month, involvement in an accident, and evidence of impairment on the job.

Q. 10:70 Can an employee who is fired for refusing to take a drug test be refused unemployment benefits?

Yes. In *Fremont Hotel and Casino v. Esposito* (760 P.2d 122 (Nev. 1988)), refusal to submit to a drug test despite having received notice of the company testing policy was held to be employee misconduct, and the employee was not entitled to unemployment benefits.

Q. 10:71 What is a "last chance agreement"?

A last chance agreement is a rehabilitation agreement under which an employer voluntarily reinstates an employee who has violated work rules relating to drugs and alcohol in exchange for a promise to enter into treatment and improve job performance. The employee agrees that, should he or she violate the terms of the agreement by failure to complete treatment or by further misconduct on the job, termination will result.

Q. 10:72 What is the role of the EAP in a last chance agreement?

Often, the EAP monitors employee compliance with the last chance agreement. This may consist of monitoring sobriety and attendance at treatment and NA or AA meetings, and so forth. The EAP may also be involved in scheduling and monitoring random drug tests that are part of the last chance agreement.

Q. 10:73 If an employer wishes to institute drug testing, what procedures should be followed?

Notice should be given to all employees that drug testing will commence on some future date. Many people think that a 30-day notice is appropriate, because it gives employees an opportunity to avoid drug use long enough to assure a "clean" test. Marijuana, for example, can leave traces for as long as approximately 28 days. The conditions under which the testing will be done must be spelled out in detail—particularly the trigger events for the tests. If the workplace is organized, the employer cannot simply institute tests without first bargaining with the union.

A government-approved laboratory should be chosen, if possible. The laboratory must be able to assure the integrity of the process, including the chain of custody of the sample. Although a split sample procedure is much more expensive than a single sample, it is recommended to assure accuracy of the tests. An employer that follows the procedures established in government regulations for drug testing will be less likely to be successfully sued than one that does not. (See Ch. 9, "Substance Abuse Laws," Qs. 9:72–9:82.)

Q. 10:74 What is "chain of custody"?

Chain of custody refers to the procedure used to establish and prove that the specimen is the one given by an individual and that it is in the same condition as when given. The specimen is labeled, sealed, and signed for. Each person who has contact with it in the transportation, testing, and storage process signs off, as well. Any questions as to contamination or mix-up of a sample can then be addressed to each person in the chain.

Q. 10:75 What is a "split sample," and how does this method work?

When a urine sample is given, it is split into two containers. One is used for the employer's test. If the test is positive for controlled substances, the employee has the right to have the other container tested at a laboratory of his or her choice.

Q. 10:76 What methods of drug testing are commonly used?

The method by which most drug testing is done is urinalysis. Usually, the first test to be performed is a preliminary immunoassay or thin-layer chromatography test that detects general classes of drugs. If the specimen tests positive, a confirmatory test is performed. A mass spectrometer device is used to bombard the sample with electrons to break up the chemical components. Each drug leaves its own signature by the way it fragments.

A blood test is performed to determine the presence of alcohol in the blood at the time the test is performed.

Q. 10:77 What does a drug test reveal?

A blood alcohol test establishes the amount of alcohol present in the blood. If a urinary ethyl alcohol test is performed, it can be correlated with blood alcohol content to determine the degree of the person's impairment. Because alcohol is oxidized in a fairly short period of time after it is ingested, urinary alcohol tests are rarely performed; a chronic alcoholic could test clean after 12 hours. Most other drugs of abuse leave metabolites (breakdown products of the drug's active ingredient) for some days after use.

A urine drug test reveals only whether or not an individual has been exposed to the drugs for which he or she is being tested. It gives no information as to the pattern of drug use, whether the user is chemically dependent or abuses drugs, or whether he or she is physically impaired by the drug at the time the sample is taken. Marijuana metabolites can be detected in urine for up to ten days after a single smoking session; they can be detected in the body's fatty tissue for weeks after a heavy marijuana smoker has last smoked. Cocaine, codeine, and valium can be detected for up to three days. Heroin, amphetamines, and PCP can be detected for up to four days. Barbiturates can be detected for up to two weeks.

The reports on the accuracy of drug tests vary, but there is no doubt that a certain percentage of the tests will result in a false positive or a false negative. By using two methods of testing a sample, false results should theoretically be less likely. One of the problems is that certain nondrug substances (for example, poppy seeds) leave the same metabolite as a drug (for example, opiates). Also, there is the phenomenon of a contact high, wherein one who has not smoked marijuana himself or herself may absorb the drug from breathing in other people's smoke.

Hair analysis is being developed as a method of drug testing that will eliminate some of the objections to drug testing. Strands of hair can be tested by a radioimmunoassay process to detect cocaine, heroin, marijuana, methaqualone, and PCP. Hair gives a history of drug use and can reveal which drug was used, in what amount, and at what time. Brain scan equipment is also being perfected that can detect drug effects. Brain waves, called drug-evoked potentials, correlate specific brain-wave patterns with specific substances.

Q. 10:78 Under what circumstances have employers been permitted to randomly screen?

When safety or security is at stake, in so-called high-risk workplaces, employers have been permitted to randomly screen. Under the Drug-Free Workplace Act and its regulations, some employers are required to randomly screen. The issue in random testing is being sure it is truly random and will not be used to harass specific individuals.

Q. 10:79 What constitutes "cause" for drug testing?

An accident in which there has been bodily injury or property damage, or observable behaviors that lead to a reasonable suspicion of impairment, are cause for testing.

Q. 10:80 What policies and procedures are required for a drug testing program?

Clear and practical policies and procedures are absolutely necessary if a drug testing program is to succeed. The policy must state the employer's attitude toward drugs and alcohol, and what will or will not be tolerated. It must also state the consequences of detection of these substances. Many employers have a policy under which a self-reporter will be given access to EAP and treatment services at no risk to his or her job, but an employee who does not self-report and is found to have used substances in contravention of the policy will be disciplined.

The procedures must spell out the drugs to be tested for, whether the testing is to be random, periodic (for example, annually after the birth month), or for cause. The testing protocol and events that will trigger a test must be stated, along with employee rights for review and the steps the employer will take if a test is positive.

The drug testing policy must dovetail with company work rules and EAP policies and procedures. It is particularly important that the company and EAP policies and procedures clearly delineate who is responsible for what functions of decision making. Ambiguity is likely to result in trouble (for example, an employee sues because he or she is dissatisfied with what has occurred in connection with a drug test).

Q. 10:81 May an employer use a drug test to determine other facts about an employee?

Federal regulations that mandate drug testing specifically prohibit the use for any other purpose of a sample given to test for specific drugs of abuse. Urinalysis can reveal such other facts about a person as pregnancy and other medications being taken that would reveal certain illnesses or medical conditions. Laws protecting handicapped workers prohibit inquiry or examination for non-job-related handicaps. Thus, it is illegal in most instances for an employer to use the drug testing process to invade an employee's privacy for any other purpose.

Q. 10:82 Should the EAP be involved in drug testing?

Often, the only department of a company with any expertise in drugs and alcohol is the EAP. Thus, it may be tempting to involve the EAP in testing either at random or for cause. This is not recommended, however. The function of the EAP is to assist employees, not to be a social control agent for the employer. An EAP that administers a drug detection program will immediately lose all credibility and usefulness for its real purpose. When an employee is on a treatment or recovery regime, however, and especially in connection with a last chance agreement, it is logical for the EAP to be involved in setting up whatever testing is to be used as a component of the treatment and aftercare. The matter of confidentiality and reporting to the employer must be scrupulously spelled out, understood, and accepted by the employee.

Q. 10:83 Does an employer have the right to control an employee's off-duty behavior?

This question is not as simple as it may appear. As a general rule, an employer has no right to interfere with an employee's off-duty behavior, *unless that behavior directly affects the employer.* For example, a bank may take the position that its officers cannot gamble, because this behavior would cast a doubt on the credibility and safety of the bank. Employers do have a right to prohibit drinking or drug use during meal breaks. Mood-altering substances remain in the body for varying lengths of time after they are consumed. A work rule against being in possession of or using such substances will include having them in one's system. An employee's off-duty drinking may be viewed as a serious problem if he or she has been disciplined for alcohol-related activities in the past. Last chance agreements often prohibit any use of psychoactive substances at all—during work or otherwise. Drinking may also be barred during off-duty times when the employee is subject to call. This is particularly prevalent in the transportation industry.

AIDS Testing

Q. 10:84 May an employer compel employees to submit to blood testing for the AIDS virus?

It is too early to answer this question definitively, but at present, it appears that the answer is no. The Eastern Nebraska Community Office of Retardation was prohibited from requiring employees to take AIDS tests for the protection of developmentally disabled persons receiving services from the agency. The rationale of the court was that the risk of AIDS transmission in the work environment was "extremely low, approaching zero." (*Glover v. Eastern Nebraska Community Office of Retardation,* No. 88-1678 (8th Cir. Feb. 6, 1989))

Q. 10:85 May an insurance company require an AIDS test of applicants for health insurance?

Apparently, yes. In *Health Insurance Assn. of America v. Corcoran* (531 N.Y.S.2d 456 (Sup. 1988)), the court held that since AIDS is an expensive illness from the point of view of health care costs, and seropositivity is a distinct indicator of potential increased health expense risk, testing for seropositivity "produces a statistically valid basis for actuarial risk classification purposes," and is therefore permissible.

Chapter 11

Mental Health Law

EAPs are often faced with legal issues related to mental health care. Although mental health law is related to substance abuse law, it is not the same thing. This chapter addresses the nature of mental health law, clinical definitions of various types of illnesses, the rights of mentally ill patients, criteria for administering involuntary treatment, and the status of mental illness as a protected handicap.

Q. 11:1 What is mental health law?

Mental health law relates to that body of law that regulates the treatment of persons suffering from mental illness or other mental or emotional disturbances. It includes criteria for involuntary treatment of the mentally ill and patients' rights legislation.

Q. 11:2 Why is there a special body of law related to mental health care delivery?

Mentally ill persons have often been severely abused throughout history by health care, legal, and social systems that did not understand them. Psychiatric treatment has been used in some countries, such as the Soviet Union and Argentina, as a form of political oppression and social control. Americans are particularly sensitive to the constitutional guarantees of freedom of religion, ideas, and speech. Therefore, since the mental health care delivery system has the potential to oppress mental patients, it has become more strictly regulated, especially in recent years, in this country.

Q. 11:3 What is mental illness?

Mental illness is variously defined by statute. Some states do not define it statutorily at all, leaving it up to the judge in each case to decide whether or not a respondent can be so adjudicated, on the theory that "one knows it when one sees it." Each state has its own definition of mental illness. Examples of definitions are:

> "Mental illness" means a psychosis or other disease which substantially impairs the mental health of a person.

(D.C. Code Ann. sec. 21-501 (1981))

> "Mental illness" means an impairment of the emotional process, of the ability to exercise conscious control of one's actions, or of the ability to perceive reality or to understand, which impairment substantially interferes with a person's ability to meet the ordinary demands of living, regardless of etiology excluding developmental disabilities, simple alcoholism or conditions manifested only by antisocial behavior or drug addiction.

(Fla. Stat. Ann. sec. 394,4555(3) (1982))

Types of Mental Illnesses

Q. 11:4 Is a mood disorder a mental illness?

Major affective disorders are mental illnesses. "Simple" mood swings, between dysphoria (depressed, sad mood) and euphoria (elation), or grief and joy, are normal and experienced by everyone. Protracted extreme mood states that are inappropriate or unrelated to external stimuli are pathological and can be described as mental illnesses. It is not such states themselves that will bring a patient under court control, but behaviors indicating a need for intervention and meeting the criteria for commitment.

Q. 11:5 What are "affective disorders"?

Affective disorders are mood disorders. Everyone has mood swings; people respond to positive or negative events and may be normally joyful or sad. Moods are disordered when they are excessive or inappropriate to the stimuli that provoke them or are not otherwise a normal response to events. Affective disorders are categorized as manic episode, major depressive episode, bipolar disorder, major depression, and other specific affective disorders.

Q. 11:6 What are anxiety disorders?

In anxiety disorders, the patient suffers significant or severe episodes of anxiety symptoms for periods of time. The disorder may be generalized or specific, such as phobia, panic disorder, obsessive compulsive disorder, or posttraumatic stress disorder.

Q. 11:7 What is psychosis?

Psychosis refers to a mental condition in which the sufferer experiences delusions (fixed false beliefs unshared by others; for example, the television set is a tool of the Martians, who are sending messages understood only by the patient); hallucinations (seeing or smelling things that are not there, or hearing voices); incoherence (sometimes, but not always, caused by psychosis); loosening of associations (the person is "all over the place," with ideas floating around associated only loosely with each other); a marked poverty of content of thought; markedly illogical thinking (irrationality); or behavior that is grossly disorganized or catatonic.

Q. 11:8 What is schizophrenia?

Schizophrenia has at times been called a "garbage diagnosis" because it has been used as a catchall for a number of clinical entities. The American Psychiatric Association Diagnostic and Statistical Manual of Mental Disorders (DSM III-R) has attempted to eliminate this problem, at least to some extent, by clearly describing the set of symptoms that must occur in the context of specified time periods before one can label a patient schizophrenic. It is to be remembered that differential diagnosis is difficult with some psychotic patients, because various disease entities produce similar symptoms. This is particularly important, because research has demonstrated that patients who are labeled schizophrenic are less likely than others to receive aggressive or creative treatment, are hospitalized more frequently, and are not expected to improve.

Q. 11:9 What are the symptoms of a schizophrenic disorder?

A patient should not be diagnosed as schizophrenic unless he or she exhibits continuous signs of the illness for at least six months, including an active phase during which at least one of the following symptoms was manifested:

- Bizarre delusions (patently absurd, such as that people are controlling their thoughts);
- Somatic, grandiose, religious, nihilistic delusions other than paranoid;
- Jealous or persecutory delusions accompanied by hallucinations;
- Auditory hallucinations in which a voice keeps up a running commentary on the patient or two or more voices carry on a conversation;
- Auditory hallucinations on several occasions of more than one or two words, with no apparent connection to elation or depression; or
- Incoherence, marked loosening of associations; illogical thinking; poverty of content of speech and blunted, flat, or inappropriate affect; or delusions or hallucinations or catatonic or other grossly disorganized behavior.

Other criteria, including prodromal (before the active phase of the illness) and residual (following the active phase) symptoms are to be found in the DSM III-R.

Defining "Insanity"

Q. 11:10 What is "insanity"?

Insanity is not a medical term, but a legal and social term. It indicates a condition that renders a person unfit to be at liberty because of the unreliability of his or her behavior, which makes the person dangerous to self or others. The concept is used mostly in the context of criminal law as a defense to a crime. To be guilty of a crime, a person must have had an intent to commit a wrongful, illegal act. If one is mentally ill, it may be that he or she cannot form an intent, and so will be exculpated from criminal responsibility. There are several criteria for insanity. The Model Penal Code defines it as follows:

> A person is not responsible for criminal conduct if at the time of such conduct as a result of mental disease or defect he lacks substantial capacity either to appreciate the criminality (wrongfulness) of his conduct or to conform his conduct to the requirements of the law.

Q. 11:11 What is diminished capacity?

Diminished capacity is partial insanity. One who suffers from diminished capacity has an impairment of mental state such that he or she cannot be held fully responsible for his or her wrongful actions. Under this doctrine, although an accused is not so impaired as to be not guilty by reason of insanity, the court can take the disability into consideration in mitigation of the punishment or degree of the offense charged.

Q. 11:12 Are there other tests for insanity?

The various jurisdictions have adopted various definitions of insanity and various rules for determining lack of criminal responsibility by reason of mental state.

M'Naghten Rule: An accused is not criminally responsible if, at the time of committing an act, he or she was laboring under such a defect of reason from disease of the mind as not to know the nature and quality of the act, or did not know that it was wrong. (This rule was adopted by the majority of jurisdictions in the United States and dates back to 1843.)

Durham Rule: This is known as the irresistible impulse test of criminal responsibility. An accused is not criminally responsible for an act if he or she suffered from a mental illness or defect at the time the crime was committed and it is found beyond a reasonable doubt that the act was the result of the mental abnormality. Under this rule, even though the accused knew what he or she was doing and could distinguish right from wrong, if the accused was unable to refrain from committing the act, there will be no criminal responsibility. (*Durham v. United States*, 214 F.2d 862 (D.C. Cir.) (1954))

Involuntary Commitment and Treatment

Q. 11:13 Does a mentally ill person have a right to refuse treatment?

A mentally ill person has a right to refuse treatment (for example, hospitalization, psychotherapy, or medication), irrespective of how ill or disabled he or she may be. The only method for requiring a mentally ill person to enter a psychiatric hospital over that person's objection is by commitment. Even when committed, a patient may have the right to refuse medication or other therapy. (See Q. 11:22)

Q. 11:14 Under what circumstances may a mentally ill person be committed involuntarily for hospitalization or outpatient treatment?

The criteria for involuntary commitment are established by statute in each jurisdiction, so they will vary from state to state. Nearly every state requires that the person must first be found to suffer from mental disorder, disease, or defect; in addition, there must be a finding by a court that unless the person is committed, a specific adverse consequence will result. The adverse consequences upon which commitment may be based are generally abbreviated as "harmful to self or others" or "unable to care for self so as to guard self from harm." A few states have adopted a third criterion for commitment: gravely disabled.

Q. 11:15 What does "harmful" mean?

There are numerous interpretations of "harmful" in the context of mental health law. The Model State Law on Civil Commitment of the Mentally Ill, approved by the American Psychiatric Association, uses the following language: "likely to cause harm to others" and "as evidenced by recent behavior causing, attempting, or threatening such harm, a person is likely in the near future to cause physical injury or physical abuse to another person or substantial damage to another person's property." (*Issues in Forensic Psychiatry* (American Psychiatric Press, Washington, D.C., 1984))

Some jurisdictions (for example, Hawaii—see *Suzuki v. Alba,* 438 F. Supp. 1106 (D. Hawaii 1977), *modified,* 617 F.2d 173 (9th Cir. 1980)) require a recent overt act as evidence of dangerousness—that is, the patient must actually have done something dangerous. Of those jurisdictions, some accept a verbal threat as an overt act; some do not. Other jurisdictions (for example, Illinois—see *Mathew v. Nelson*, 461 F. Supp. 707 (N.D. Ill. 1978)) do not require an overt act, but will accept other evidence as a basis for finding a person "harmful." Although the Model State Law provides for commitment in the event of risk of harm to property, many state statutes do not.

Mere mental illness, no matter how serious, will not of itself be a sufficient basis for involuntary commitment. One of the other criteria must also be met. Mere dangerousness or "meanness" will not be a basis for commitment in the absence of mental illness.

Q. 11:16 What does "likely to harm oneself" mean?

Again, this phrase, or one similar to it, can be variously defined. Usually, it means that the person is likely in the near future to inflict substantial physical injury upon himself or herself. Mere unwise or irresponsible behavior is not usually sufficient. For example, compulsive overeating or smoking, or frequenting dangerous places, is not a basis for commitment, although the family of a person indulging in those behaviors may wish it were. Overt suicidality—a wish to die combined with a plan of execution, preoccupation with death, threats of suicide, or actual gestures—is the sort of behavior that will readily result in commitment on this ground.

Q. 11:17 What does "unable to care for oneself" mean?

Similar in some ways to "likely to harm oneself," unable to care for oneself indicates a person who, although not actively suicidal, is substantially unable to provide for his or her basic needs, such as shelter, food, clothing, health, and safety. With the rise in the number of homeless persons in the United States, there is considerable discussion about the part mental illness plays in the phenomenon. Mere lack of comprehension of one's mental illness and concomitant unwillingness to accept treatment will not ordinarily be sufficient to support a petition for involuntary treatment. When the patient's condition gets out of hand, however, a court may be persuaded to act.

Example 1. A psychotic patient who insists upon walking outdoors barefoot and clad in a sheet in subzero weather, carrying a sign proclaiming himself to be Jesus Christ and announcing the end of the world, will be committed on the grounds that he is mentally ill and unable to care for himself so as to guard himself from harm.

Example 2. The psychotic patient in Example 1 will probably not be committed if he indulges in the same behavior in midsummer, when he is in no danger of freezing to death.

Example 3. A diabetic and schizophrenic woman is unable to work, but refuses to retire or apply for disability. Because of her paranoia, she will allow no one into her apartment to clean it up (one of her symptoms is collecting *everything*). She rarely bathes, is incontinent, and may eat seven ice cream bars at a time. Her blood sugar level is dangerously high. A petition for commitment on grounds of "helplessness" is likely to be successful, but not because she is a "collector" or insists on violating her diet. It will be necessary to show that her self-destructive behavior, which will culminate in a serious illness or death, is the result of her mental illness.

Q. 11:18 What is "gravely disabled"?

"Gravely disabled" is a basis for commitment in some states, but not others. It seems to be another way of saying "unable to care for oneself." An example of one state's interpretation is:

> that as a result of mental or emotional impairment, [the person] is in danger of serious harm as a result of an inability or failure to provide for his or her own basic human needs such as essential food, clothing, shelter or safety and that hospital care is necessary and available and that such person is mentally incapable of determining whether or not to accept treatment because his judgment is impaired by his mental illness.

(Conn. Gen. Stat. Ann. §17-176 (1985))

In one way or another, whether or not a state specifies such a ground in so many words, there is usually a way to commit a patient who fits this description.

Q. 11:19 What is the procedure for commitment?

Commitment procedures are as varied as criteria for commitment. Most states have two methods of commitment. One is an emergency detention procedure, whereby the alleged mentally ill person can be picked up and taken to and detained in a facility for a brief time for examination. If he or she is found to be in need of involuntary treatment, certificates will be signed by the examining clinicians, and the person will be offered a judicial hearing. The second method is by petition to the court, asserting that the respondent (the alleged mentally ill person) is in need of immediate treatment and meets the statutory criteria of the jurisdiction. The petition may be accompanied by certificates attesting that an examiner believes the respondent meets the criteria for involuntary treatment.

Sometimes the initial hearing is held ex parte (without the other party being present). In any commitment, a judicial hearing is required at some point. Some jurisdictions provide for a jury trial. In all jurisdictions, the respondent is entitled to notice and sufficient time to prepare for trial, as well as representation by an attorney—at public expense, if necessary. The respondent is also entitled to an examination by a clinician of his or her choice.

Q. 11:20 What is the standard of proof in a commitment case?

The standard of proof to be met before a person can be deprived of his or her liberty through civil commitment must be no less than clear and convincing. (*Addington v. Texas,* 441 U.S. 418 (1978)) Many states (for example, California, Hawaii, Massachusetts, and New Hampshire) require a stricter standard of proof: beyond a reasonable doubt. The critics of the stricter approach argue that "given the lack of certainty and the fallibility of psychiatric diagnosis, there is a serious question as to whether a state could ever prove beyond a reasonable doubt that an individual is both mentally ill and likely to be dangerous." (*Addington,* 441 U.S. at 429)

Q. 11:21 Must it be established to the court that the person is treatable before he or she can be committed?

One of the arguments propounded by civil libertarian critics against civil commitment under any circumstances is that confinement for treatment is supportable only if the person can be treated, and that psychiatrically disturbed persons often are not treatable. Some states (for example,

Ohio and New Mexico) have moved to make treatability a criterion of commitment; most have not.

Q. 11:22 May a committed patient refuse medication or other treatment services?

Generally, yes. Commitment, per se, does not deprive a person of his or her constitutional privacy rights. In an emergency wherein a patient is at imminent risk for harming himself or herself or another, medication may be given over the patient's objection. To force medication on an unwilling patient in a nonemergency situation requires an additional adjudication of incompetence. A guardian will then have the right to refuse or consent to treatment on behalf of the patient. (*Rennie v. Klein,* 102 S. Ct. 3506 (1982) and its precedents)

Q. 11:23 Is informed consent to treatment required from a mentally ill person?

The general answer is yes, but this is a very complex and difficult matter. For one thing, many mentally ill people, even some psychotics, are able to give informed consent to or refusal of treatment. If a patient understands that he or she suffers from a condition that requires treatment and can comprehend the treatment alternatives (including no treatment at all) and their foreseeable risks and benefits, many authorities hold that the patient is capable of consenting to or refusing treatment. A patient who, because of a mental disorder, is unable to understand the nature and effects of mental hospitalization or treatment, even after these have been conscientiously explained, or cannot engage in a rational decision-making process regarding treatment, lacks capacity to make an informed decision with respect to treatment. (*Issues in Forensic Psychiatry* (Washington, D.C.: American Psychiatric Press, 1984), 85)

Q. 11:24 If it is clear that a patient lacks capacity to make an informed decision, but is acquiescent to the treatment suggestions proposed, can he or she be treated without a guardian's consent?

There is a presumption of competency unless a person has been adjudicated incompetent. When it is clear, however, that a patient lacks decision-making capacity, any treatment rendered is at the risk of the care provider. The patient, or someone on his or her behalf, will have a cause of action for failure to obtain informed consent—a form of malpractice—if the patient suffers an untoward effect from the treatment.

Q. 11:25 Is an organic brain syndrome or disease a mental illness?

The "mind-body dichotomy" has been argued for decades; to this date, there is not a satisfactorily clear distinction to enable a positive answer. The biological basis of mental illness is becoming more clear every day as research discloses brain chemistry phenomena, and pharmacological treatment supplements or replaces "talking therapies." Most states deal with this question by describing the criteria for commitment in terms of behavior, not disease entities. Thus, a person who suffers from Alzheimer's disease, acute alcohol psychosis, delirium tremens, or some other clearly organic condition that impairs his or her reason to the extent that dangerousness or helplessness results will, in most jurisdictions, be subject to involuntary commitment.

Q. 11:26 Is AIDS-related dementia a mental illness for purposes of involuntary hospitalization?

The approach to this question clearly lies in the manifestations of the illness in a given case. Again, it is not the etiology of the disease that determines eligibility for commitment, but the behavioral manifestations arising from it. As with other organic brain syndromes, the picture may be confused.

> **Example.** An AIDS patient is now hospitalized on a medical unit, but will soon be ready for discharge from acute care. Neuropsychological tests indicate that he is suffering from AIDS-related dementia. The patient is hostile and impulse ridden and acts out by, among other things, spitting into other patients' trays and the ward water fountain and spraying urine around the bathroom. He vents his outrage at being infected and tells anyone who will listen that he has every intention of taking as many people with him as he can when he dies. In fact, the spitting and urinating, although disgusting and unhygienic, are probably not very dangerous (The Center for Disease Control (CDC) says AIDS cannot be spread by urine or saliva); the threat of unprotected sexual activity with presumably unsuspecting victims is

dangerous. Although the patient is brain damaged and behaviorally disordered, there is evidence that he also suffers from a longstanding personality disorder. The medical staff wants to transfer him to a psychiatric unit, but he refuses.

Is the patient in this example committable? The answer may well depend upon the local judge's interpretation of "mental illness" or "disability." There is little legal precedent for guidance. Given the fact that AIDS is an invariably fatal disease, the risk to the community is clear and great. It is to be expected that a court would react in favor of protecting the public. However, is a high probability of spreading an infection, which may or may not make itself evident for years, behavior "likely in the near future to cause physical injury to another person"? Is the mere intent to cause injury, when in fact the threatened or actual behavior cannot actually cause the intended harm or any real harm, a sufficient basis for commitment? Very sophisticated expert testimony will be necessary in such cases, so that patients and potential victims are all protected—but also so that unfortunate legal precedents are not set.

Mental Illness and Substance Abuse

Q. 11:27 What are the legal complications when a client suffers from mental illness as well as a substance abuse problem?

The legal complications arise directly from the politics of the clinical world. The philosophical struggle (cynics will insist it is really a self-serving economic struggle) between psychiatry and substance abuse has polarized many care providers into totally rejecting the other group's role in treating these cases. This has encouraged or enabled legislatures to similarly dichotomize mental illness and substance abuse and limit the availability of legal intervention in substance abuse cases when, clearly, it may be the last chance for help.

Many states do not provide for involuntary commitment of substance abusers, even when dire health problems would appear to warrant it. However, if a substance abuser also suffers from a mental illness, the mental illness may be the basis for a commitment. It would be necessary to emphasize to the court that the substance abuse is secondary or ancillary to the mental illness, and that the court is being asked to address the mental illness plus dangerousness to self or others or helplessness. When a psychiatric entity, such as a psychosis or major affective disorder, clearly and obviously exists, the court may be convinced to act on that basis. It is not unusual, however, for a court to focus on the substance abuse and simply refuse to address the mental illness. Very good expert testimony is necessary to instruct the court in the clinical realities.

Q. 11:28 Might substance abusers also suffer from undiagnosed mental illness?

It is estimated by some authorities that as many as 25% of substance abusers also suffer from undiagnosed mental illness—often an affective disorder, and not infrequently, bipolar illness. This situation is exacerbated by the widespread use in substance abuse treatment of paraprofessionals whose training has been narrowly confined to recognition of substance abuse phenomena and a particular cognitive and behaviorally oriented treatment approach. On the other hand, critics of psychiatry insist that mental health providers are untrained in the diagnosis and treatment of substance abuse and tend to ignore the addiction, while concentrating on the psychological factors. Since the symptoms of substance abuse may appear similar or identical to those of other mental disorders, differential diagnosis may be impossible for a treater who is not trained to recognize both. A treater who ignores the possibility of a dual diagnosis, either because of ignorance or because of prejudice, may condemn a client and his or her family to a lifetime of misery and serious economic loss. If, in time, the mistake is corrected and the client or family becomes aware of what has happened, a malpractice suit is not unlikely.

Patient Rights Under Federal Law

Q. 11:29 Is there a federal mental health law?

Each state has its own mental health code that is interpreted by its courts. The reform of the mental health system, however, which was the basis for a major overhaul in mental health statutes across the country, arose in civil rights actions brought in the federal courts on the basis that the states were violating the constitutional rights of mental patients.

The first of these cases was *Wyatt v. Stickney* (344 F. Supp. 373 (M.D. Ala. 1972), *modified and remanded sub nom. Wyatt v. Aderholt,* 503 F.2d 1305 (5th Cir. 1974)).

The Mental Health Systems Act (42 U.S.C. §9501 et seq.) requires the states to review and revise, if necessary, their laws to ensure that mental patients receive the protection and services they require. The Act is sometimes called the Bill of Rights for Mental Health Patients. It establishes standards for state laws regulating mental health care providers and addresses the rights of mental patients.

Q. 11:30 What rights must be given mental patients in the planning and choice of their treatment?

The Mental Health Systems Act requires that an individual written treatment plan be developed for each institutionalized patient promptly after admission. The treatment plan is to be developed in cooperation with the patient, if possible, or persons named by him or her. The patient has a right to have his or her service needs periodically reviewed and reassessed, and to have the plan revised as his or her condition indicates. (42 U.S.C. 9501(B) and 9501(C) (Supp. V 1981))

Q. 11:31 What information must be given to a mental patient in connection with the plan?

Every patient has a right to be provided with a "reasonable explanation," in terms he or she can understand, of:

- The patient's general mental condition;
- His or her physical condition, if the facility has performed a physical examination;
- The objectives of the treatment being provided;
- The nature and significant possible adverse effects of recommended treatments;
- The reasons a particular treatment is considered inappropriate; and
- Any appropriate and available alternative treatment, services, and types of mental health services.

(42 U.S.C. §9501(1)(C))

Q. 11:32 Does the law provide for exceptions if the attending mental health professional concludes it is dangerous for the patient to have access to the information?

There is an exemption from disclosure to the patient in a case in which the psychiatrist believes that such disclosure would be harmful to the patient. (42 U.S.C. §9501(1)(I) (Supp. V 1981))

Q. 11:33 Is there a federal statutory right to refuse treatment?

A patient has a right to refuse an aspect of treatment in a treatment plan. The Mental Health Systems Act requires that the facility obtain the patient's informed, voluntary, written consent, except that during an emergency, treatment may be given without consent so long as it is pursuant to or documented at the same time by written order of a "responsible mental health professional," or as may be permitted by applicable law if the patient is committed. (42 U.S.C. §9501(1)(D))

Q. 11:34 Under what conditions does federal law permit a patient to be restrained or secluded?

A patient has a right not to be restrained or secluded except as a mode of treatment during an emergency situation. Restraint or seclusion may not be used unless it is pursuant to or documented at the same time by the written order of a responsible mental health professional. (42 U.S.C. §9501(1)(F))

Q. 11:35 What standards are applied to the treatment environment?

Under the Mental Health Systems Act, a mental patient has a right to be treated in a humane environment that gives reasonable protection from harm and appropriate privacy with regard to his or her personal needs. (42 U.S.C. §9501(1)(G))

Q. 11:36 What are the federal standards for confidentiality of mental patients?

The Mental Health Systems Act provides that patients' information is to be kept confidential, and that they have the right of access to their own records, except for information provided by a third party under assurances that the information would remain confidential.

The Act requires a state statute to provide that specific material in a patient's records may be withheld from the patient if the mental health professional responsible for the patient's care has made a determination in writing that access to it would be detrimental to the patient's health. Under that circumstance, the information is to be made available to a similarly licensed health professional selected by the patient who may, in his or her judgment, provide access to the material or otherwise disclose it to the patient. It is to be noted that some states (for example, Illinois) have not enacted such an exception, but require that a patient have total access.

Q. 11:37 What are the standards for patient communication?

A patient admitted to a residential or inpatient program must be given the right to have private conversation with others, to have reasonable access to a telephone and mail, and to receive visitors during regularly scheduled hours. (42 U.S.C. §9501(1)(J))

Q. 11:38 Are there circumstances in which a patient's right to freedom of communication can be curtailed?

If the care provider determines that denial of access to a particular visitor is necessary for treatment purposes, the access may be denied for a limited period of time. The denial must be by written order, stating the reasons for the restriction. (42 U.S.C. §9501(1)(J))

Q. 11:39 What recourse has the mental health professional if a patient insists upon a mode of treatment contrary to that considered to be appropriate by the professional?

If the patient persists in demanding treatment inconsistent with that determined by the professional to be appropriate, the Mental Health Systems Act does not require that the professional provide that treatment. (42 U.S.C. §9501(3)(B))

Q. 11:40 May a program discharge a patient who refuses treatment?

Yes. The Mental Health Systems Act specifically states that a program or facility is not prevented from discharging a patient for whom the provision of appropriate treatment, consistent with the clinical judgment of the mental health professional in charge of his or her treatment, is or has become impossible as a result of the patient's refusal to consent to treatment. Further, a program or facility may refuse to admit a patient who, while admitted on prior occasions to the program or facility, has repeatedly frustrated the purposes of admission by withholding consent to proposed treatment. (42 U.S.C. §9501(3)(B)) (State statutes may restrict these provider rights.)

Q. 11:41 Is there a federally sponsored agency to protect the patients' rights required by the Bill of Rights for Mental Health Patients?

In 1986, Congress passed the Protection and Advocacy for Mentally Ill Individuals Act of 1986. (Pub. L. No. 99-319) The Act provides for federal funding to states that establish protection and advocacy agencies to protect the rights of mentally ill patients against abuse and neglect and to assure enforcement of the Constitution and federal and state statutes. (42 U.S.C. §10801) Most states have established protection and advocacy agencies to ensure their eligibility for federal assistance to mental health and developmental disabilities programs.

Q. 11:42 If a client's rights appear to have been violated by a mental health program, what can an EAP do about it?

Mental health patients are vulnerable to abuse and neglect, particularly in state systems or if there are no family or friends to intervene. If there is concern about rights violations, whether in the public or private sector, the protection and advocacy agency should be contacted. Patients with their own resources may use private attorneys, but often these practitioners are unfamiliar with mental health law and will welcome direction from an agency.

Q. 11:43 What if the EAP and/or the patient's family believe that the protection and advocacy agency is not operating in the patient's best interest?

Because the protection and advocacy agencies are very skilled in mental health law and are adept at using the system, it is important that equally adept counteradvocacy be mobilized. Every EAP should have clinically knowledgeable legal counsel available for its own use. This lawyer will also be a good resource to clients or families. If court proceedings or other hearings are necessary, the EAP can help prepare the testimony, mobilize witnesses, provide witnesses, and otherwise participate in the interest of the client's welfare.

Q. 11:44 What rights does a hospitalized patient have with respect to obtaining treatment?

It is illegal to confine a person in a mental hospital against his or her will unless treatment is provided. (*O'Connor v. Donaldson,* 422 U.S. 563 (1975)) If a patient is committed and no treatment is taking place (assuming, of course, that this is because it has not been offered, not that the patient has refused it), legal steps should be taken. Efforts at intervention with the hospital authorities should be well documented, and the matter should be brought to the attention of the committing court by petition. In some jurisdictions, this may be accomplished by a petition for writ of habeas corpus.

Q. 11:45 What is a writ of habeas corpus, and how is it used in mental health cases?

Habeas corpus ("that you may have the body") is the name given to a variety of writs used to bring a person into court before a judge. The right to habeas corpus is the great constitutional guarantee of personal liberty, and every state has a habeas corpus statute. With a writ of habeas corpus, a person or institution holding another is commanded to bring the detainee into court to test the legality of the detention.

If a patient is being confined in a manner thought to be illegal or inappropriate, or under a state mental health code that allows detention for a period thought in the particular instance to be inordinate, a petition for a writ of habeas corpus may be presented to a court. If it appears to the court that it is possible that the person is being improperly held, the writ will be issued. When the writ is served on (delivered in accordance with local statute and rules) the person or institution holding the individual, within the period of time designated (ordinarily, a matter of hours), the individual must be produced in court. At that time, a hearing will be held and the legality of the detention will be determined.

If the detention is indeed inappropriate, the mere threat of a petition for habeas corpus, or the service of the writ itself, may result in the patient's release without a court hearing.

Chapter 12

Legal Problems of EAP Clients

Clients frequently have legal problems—often as an outgrowth of substance abuse or other psychosocial difficulties. Therefore, it is important for EAP professionals to have some understanding of how the law works so that they can advise clients within a broader range of knowledge and understand the legal difficulties clients may be up against. Moreover, human resources professionals also need a good understanding in this area, since they, too, may have to deal with employees' legal problems and possibly advise them in some capacity. This chapter covers such common areas of legal concern as child custody and visitation, divorce and parentage, juvenile delinquency, child abuse and neglect, and dependency. An overview of principles of criminal law is also presented.

Divorce and Child Custody

Q. 12:1 What is child custody?

Custody refers to the legal "possession," care, control, and education of children after a divorce.

Q. 12:2 What is sole custody?

With sole custody, the child is awarded to one parent alone, who lives with the child and has total power and control over his or her upbringing, education, religion, medical care, and other decisions, subject to whatever limitations statutes may allow and the court may order.

Q. 12:3 In a sole custody situation, what rights does the noncustodial parent have?

The noncustodial parent has relatively few, if any, rights of decision making. If, for example, the custodial parent refuses or insists upon elective health care (for example, braces, plastic surgery, psychological treatment) for the child, there may be little or nothing the noncustodial parent can do. He or she would have to apply to the court for a change in custody on the ground that the custodial parent was endangering the child, or that the best interests of the child otherwise required it. This is expensive, time-consuming, stressful, and not always likely to succeed.

The noncustodial parent has rights of access, that is, visitation, and reasonable contact with the child. Unless a court has decreed to the contrary on the basis of the child's best interests, he or she also has a right to be informed about the child's schooling and to participate in such events as parent conferences, and to be informed about the child's whereabouts and health. In some jurisdictions, these rights must be spelled out in the divorce decree. The noncustodial parent should inquire with great specificity about his or her rights and require that these be incorporated into the court orders as indicated by the local legal situation.

Q. 12:4 What is joint custody?

Joint custody refers to an arrangement in which the child is awarded by the court to both parents, each of whom has legal powers and rights as determined by the court decree. Specific provisions are made about the child's residence and access by the nonresidential parent. Joint custody does *not* mean that the child resides with each parent an equal amount of time.

Q. 12:5 Under what circumstances is joint custody awarded?

This varies widely, not only from one state to another, but from one judge to another within the same jurisdiction. Joint custody has been available for awhile, but it is still extremely controversial. Many people feel that if parents cannot get along while married, they will be unable to cooperate in coparenting. This is often, but not always, the case. Joint custody is sometimes awarded as a way to ease the disappointment and hurt of the parent with whom the child will not be living, and as a statement that both parents are fit custodians. It recognizes that both parents are to continue to have substantial roles in rearing the child.

Q. 12:6 In a joint custody arrangement, how are the powers of each parent defined?

The specific arrangements about access (sometimes called visitation) and decision making should be set out in a joint parenting agreement developed by the parents and their attorneys. This is then incorporated into the divorce decree or judgment.

Q. 12:7 What happens if the parents cannot agree?

The divorce court maintains jurisdiction over every divorce case after judgment for purposes of enforcing or modifying its decrees. Matters of custody, visitation, and child support are always subject to modification as the situations of the parties or children change. A parent who is aggrieved may apply to the court for enforcement or modification of the divorce decree. Because postdecree proceedings are expensive, some statutes require that the parties attempt to iron out their difficulties through mediation before coming into court. Even if a local statute does not require mediation, parties may insert a mediation clause into their marital settlement agreement.

Q. 12:8 What are the advantages of joint custody?

If it works, joint custody keeps both parents actively involved in the life of the child and enhances the child's connection with each. There is far less bitterness than when one parent is deprived of custody, and it is reported that there is much less difficulty with child support. Since both parents have responsibility for the child, theoretically neither is overwhelmed. In fact, the residential parent still bears the day-to-day burdens, as well as the satisfactions.

Q. 12:9 What are the disadvantages of joint custody?

Joint custody breaks down when the parents' residual anger, resentments, and disappointment with each other interfere with their ability to cooperate. If a parent is jealous of the other's relationship with the child, or the other's new significant other, or if there is animosity and acting out, joint custody results in confusion and unhappiness for both parents and child.

Q. 12:10 What is split custody?

In a split custody arrangement, the child lives with each parent part of the time. This may involve alternating part of each week or month, or it may be for more substantial periods of time (for example, six months with each parent). The parent with whom the child is residing at the time has the custodial power. The other parent has access or visitation rights.

Q. 12:11 What are the advantages and disadvantages of split custody?

Some authorities will say that the only advantage of split custody is the massaging of the ego that each parent receives. Shuttling a child back and forth between two homes is bound to create stress and confusion for him or her. Having to cope with two environments is complicated when the split custody requires a change of school, neighborhood, activities, and so forth. It may be argued, of course, that it builds flexibility and resilience. If the parents live in the same neighborhood, a split custody arrangement is likely to be more successful. The split custody may work far more to the advantage of the parents than of the child.

Q. 12:12 How does a court decide which parent should have custody?

The criterion for determination of child custody is the best interests of the child. Of course, the parents may profoundly disagree about what the child's best interests are, so a custody dispute generally involves a bitter trial, with accusations and recriminations on both sides. Relatives, neighbors, teachers, child development experts, psychiatrists, psychologists, and, of course, the parents give testimony. The child may be called as a witness, if he or she is old enough and the parents are selfish enough. Often, the judge will interview the child in chambers, either in the presence of the parents' lawyers, or not, as the local law requires.

Q. 12:13 Do mothers usually get custody?

Statistically, this is true, although both parents have equal constitutional rights to custody. Until recently, it was generally thought that the best interests of a "child of tender years" required being in the custody of the mother. To succeed in gaining custody, a father had to establish that the mother was unfit. During the last 20 years, however, fathers have rebelled and have succeeded in having this position struck down as unconstitutional. If a father really wants custody and can establish that it is in the best interests of the child that he be awarded it, he may very well prevail without the need to attack the fitness of the mother. He need only convince the court that the child will be better off with him than with her.

Q. 12:14 What rights have the children in determining with whom they will live?

This depends upon the jurisdiction. In some jurisdictions, when the children have reached a certain age, they are allowed to choose the parent with whom they will live, subject to the approval of the court. In other jurisdictions, they may be interviewed by the judge and asked their preferences, but the judge will make a determination based on his or her determination of the child's best interests.

Q. 12:15 What may happen when children are asked to choose?

Sometimes, children choose to go with the parent whom they perceive to need them the most, not the parent who will take best care of them. A type of role reversal occurs, in which the child becomes the caretaker of the parent to keep him or her from being lonely or having a breakdown. In other cases, a child may be so brainwashed by a parent that he or she will perceive the other parent as a monster and treat that parent as such. This is known as the parental alienation syndrome. (R. Gardner, *Parental Alienation Syndrome and the Differentiation Between Fabricated and Genuine Child Sex Abuse* (Creative Therapeutics Press, Cresskill, NJ, 1987)) Still other children may withdraw from the battle entirely, experiencing depression that may be manifested by severe behavioral disturbances, school problems, and so forth. In every divorce case, all but the very youngest children need and will benefit from counseling, and this should be strongly recommended.

Q. 12:16 Once child custody is awarded, can it be changed?

Courts try to stabilize the lives of children and so do not order custody changes lightly. Some state statutes specify that a petition for modification of child custody may not be filed within a certain period of time (for example, two years) after an order has been entered, unless the child has become endangered by the custodial conditions. In any event, a material change in circumstances as to the child's best interests must occur before a change of custody will be ordered. This is an area of divorce law in which possession *is* nine-tenths of the law! A parent who really wants custody should petition for it from the very beginning.

Q. 12:17 When postdecree divorce disputes seem unending, what theories should the EAP counselor consider in framing an approach to the problem?

From a psychodynamic perspective, postdecree divorce disputes "keep the pot boiling" between the couple, which obviously serves the psychological ends of one or both of them. When such behavior persists, it is clear that, irrespective of court decrees, the parties (or at least one of them) are not psychologically divorced. Family therapists refer to this situation as an "open-casket marriage." (The dead marital relationship lies unburied and moldering in a casket in the living room, infusing the atmosphere with noxious fumes that poison everyone involved.)

This relationship must be addressed, usually in the context of long-term intensive individual therapy, and if at all possible, with conjoint therapy of the divorced couple. Much resistance is likely to be encountered to any therapeutic intervention that might put an end to the situation, for the very reason that it is serving a pathological need for one party or both. Sometimes court intervention and a threat of removing the children who are being affected by the disturbed behavior of the parents may move the parents into therapy. This dramatic intervention may be suggested if nothing else seems to work.

Q. 12:18 What are the financial issues in a divorce?

The distribution of property (the marital estate), spousal support (called alimony in some jurisdictions, or maintenance in others), and child support are the three financial issues to be determined in any divorce. How these issues are determined will depend upon the law of the state in which the parties live (or are divorced).

Q. 12:19 What is property?

Property refers to real estate (land and buildings), as well as personalty (property that is not real estate). Personalty includes such items as cash, bank or money market accounts, pension rights, cash value of insurance policies, securities, jewelry, furniture, vehicles, and so forth.

Q. 12:20 How is property distributed in a divorce?

In some states (community property states), the marital estate is considered the property of the marriage and is divided equally between the parties. In other states (equitable distribution states), the law requires a fair, or equitable, division of the marital estate according to the laws of the state. Marital estate will be defined by state law. An example of one state's definition is: all property acquired during the marriage from any source except gift or inheritance. Thus, in that state, any property owned prior to the marriage remains the property of the person who owned it—unless that person converted it into marital property by placing it in joint tenancy.

Spousal and Child Support

Q. 12:21 How is a determination made on spousal support?

Years ago, a wife almost always received alimony or maintenance—

either for life or until she remarried. Today, this is far from the rule. Either spouse may be required to pay alimony or maintenance to the other, depending upon the relative earnings and needs of the parties. The property each spouse owns, as well as his and her earning capacity, will be factors in deciding spousal support. If both parties are earning or capable of earning, or a nonearning spouse has substantial income-producing property, it is possible that *no* spousal support will be awarded. If awarded, such maintenance may be for a limited period during which the maintainee is expected to "rehabilitate" himself or herself and become self-supporting. The longer the marriage, the more likely that spousal support will be awarded to equalize the financial positions of the spouses; it may be in the form of periodic payments or as a lump sum payable at one time or in installments.

Q. 12:22 Once spousal support is agreed upon or ordered by a court, can it be changed?

If the parties have entered into a marital settlement agreement, the matter of modification of spousal support must be addressed therein; spousal support may be made nonmodifiable by agreement. Unless there is an agreement to modify, spousal support may be modified by a post-decree petition to the court if there has been a "material change" in the circumstances of the parties.

Q. 12:23 What is child support?

Child support is the amount paid by the noncustodial parent to the custodial parent as a contribution to the support of the children. If there is joint custody, the nonresidential parent makes the payment to the residential parent. In a split custody arrangement, the parties will make support arrangements consistent therewith. Both parents are responsible for the support of the children. The parent receiving child support payments also contributes out of earnings, spousal support, or his or her estate, as well as by rendering services to the children. Child support payments contribute not only to the direct costs of the children (for example, food and clothing), but also to their housing and concomitant expenses.

Q. 12:24 On what basis is child support awarded?

Many states have statutory or court-developed guidelines for child support. In any event, the party seeking the support must be prepared to demonstrate the actual monthly costs of housing, utilities, food, clothing, medical bills, child care, education, recreation, and so forth. Often, a percentage of the earnings of the supporting parent is awarded, taking into consideration the earnings, if any, of the receiving parent.

Q. 12:25 Once child support is awarded, can it be changed?

Child support may be modified—up and down—when the circumstances, needs, and resources of either parent and/or the children have materially changed. If the supporting parent loses his or her job or otherwise experiences difficulties that make it impossible to pay part or all of the child support, that parent must immediately petition the court for a modification. Not paying or paying less than the ordered amount is a very poor solution. For one thing, until the court has modified its order, the support amount vests in the receiving parent, who may pursue it for years if he or she wishes. The delinquent spouse is at risk for severe penalties—even jail—for contempt of court.

Q. 12:26 If the supporting parent fails to pay child support, what can the custodial parent do?

Recently, states have been obliged by federal government pressure and back-breaking welfare caseloads to take a more aggressive position against nonsupporters. Child-support enforcement has become a state issue, whereas it was formerly the private problem of the custodial parent. A parental locator service is available through the Social Security office, and wage deduction orders are more the rule than the exception.

The reasons for failure to support are many, and some may even be legitimate. When there is a legitimate reason, court assistance should be sought immediately. Failure to do so should be explored as a clinical issue; it is probably the result of the psychological defense of denial, in which one avoids anxiety and sadness over a situation by seeming to pretend it does not exist. Denial is a maladaptive coping device that is usually found in certain personality types. Of course, the longer it goes on, the worse the situation becomes. Psychotherapy or counseling can be very helpful in assisting a client to find alternative, more suitable adaptive devices.

Not infrequently, failure of support is a response to outrage and resentment against the receiving parent. It must be pointed out to the supporting parent that no matter how justifiably angry one is at one's ex-spouse, depriving him or her of financial resources results in deprivation of the children, both financially and emotionally—a stressed-out, exhausted, impoverished custodian cannot give himself or herself optimally to children. The argument that child support goes to support the custodian must be placed in the context of providing the best possible environment for the children, even if the ex-spouse also benefits.

Q. 12:27 What are the tax aspects of spousal and child support?

Currently, spousal support is deductible from the earnings of the payor (the person who pays), and taxable to the payee (the person receiving payment). Child support is neither deductible nor taxable. Unallocated support, wherein both spousal and child support are paid in one sum and there is no specified allocation for each, is treated as spousal support for tax purposes. A rule of thumb for allocating exemptions is that the party providing more than half the support of a child takes the exemption for the child, but the parties may agree on another allocation if they wish (so long as no more than 100% of allowable exemptions is taken).

Q. 12:28 What is meant by a "contested" or "uncontested" divorce?

An uncontested divorce is one in which the parties arrive at a marital settlement agreement outside of court. The petitioners then appear in court briefly for the formalities of obtaining the court decree. A contested divorce is one in which the parties cannot arrive at an agreement; a trial is held with witnesses and evidence; and the judge decides custody, visitation, support, and property distribution. Most divorces are uncontested, but many require long, protracted and sometimes bitter pretrial court proceedings in the form of preliminary motions in which temporary custody and visitation, as well as temporary child and spousal support, are ordered during the pendency of the divorce. Often, numerous negotiating sessions take place, and not a few divorces are "settled on the courthouse steps" on the day of trial.

Q. 12:29 How do the lawyers ascertain the financial information on which to base a settlement?

After the divorce petition and an answer to it are filed, the discovery phase of the proceeding takes place. As in other trials, the parties formally request information from each other and may subpoena witnesses and documents for deposition. This ordinarily produces the information necessary to settle the case or, if settlement fails, to try it. If a party refuses to cooperate with discovery, court sanctions are available.

Q. 12:30 What if a party hides assets?

This is possible, but money usually leaves a trail. If a person is the sole owner of a business or professional practice with cash receipts, it is not too difficult to hide some part of them. A wage earner, on the other hand, is paid by someone else whose records will be available through discovery. If a party claims to have spent large sums of money that have disappeared since the divorce proceedings began, this will be considered waste of the marital estate, and the court will require restitution of the spouse's share. There is no question that a dishonest person can successfully cheat a spouse to a certain extent. If the amount in controversy is sufficiently great, accountants and detectives can be employed. However, care must be taken not to spend more money on discovery and the trial than the size of the estate warrants.

Q. 12:31 What role can the EAP play in facilitating a client's divorce and emotional recovery from it?

Divorce is one of the greatest stressors of modern life, for myriad reasons. This level of stress often triggers regression and invariably interferes with work to a greater or lesser extent. Depending upon the personality style of the client, the regressed behavior will be more or less maladaptive, but the pain is always intense. Individual counseling or psychotherapy is invaluable for anyone who is divorcing and is often helpful after divorce to help in the transition to single life and parenthood. EAP-sponsored support groups, usually time-limited (perhaps 10–20 weeks, with an option to extend), are an outstanding contribution. If such a program is impossible or impractical, the EAP must have referral resources available for its clients.

The EAP counselor can be individually helpful not only in counseling and referral, but also in locating instructional material for the client and in helping the client to deal with his or her attorney. Not infrequently, clients are unable to deal effectively with their lawyers. The counselor can assist by working with the client to develop a written list of questions to be put to the attorney. A "divorce notebook," in which the client keeps questions and notes, is an excellent tool. If necessary, the EAP counselor may go so far as to accompany the client to the lawyer's office for a consultation, facilitating understanding and mutual cooperation. Occasionally, a change of lawyer is the only solution.

Parentage

Q. 12:32 To what does the term "parentage" refer?

Parentage refers to a court proceeding in which a putative (alleged or reputed) parent of a child is named the legal parent, and the rights of access to and support of the child, as well as the inheritance rights of the child from the parent and the parent from the child, are established. In some states, these are called paternity actions or bastardy proceedings. With the advent of "fathers' rights" and the modern view against stigmatization of illegitimate children, the term "parentage" has come into vogue.

Q. 12:33 Under what circumstances would a parentage action arise?

The traditional circumstance is the filing of proceedings by an unwed mother to have the father's paternity established. The majority of parentage actions today follow this mold, but it is not infrequent for a putative father to file the proceeding so as to gain access to his child when the mother is refusing it. Formerly, an unwed father had no rights to his illegitimate child, and could be required to support it only upon court order. Further, the child had no inheritance rights unless the father acknowledged him or her and provided an inheritance by will.

The case of *Stanley v. Illinois* (405 U.S. 645, (1972) established the constitutional rights of fathers, whether wed or not, to equal protection of the laws. Fathers now not only have custodial rights and responsibilities, but are entitled to due process of law before they can be deprived of their rights as parents. Thus, before a child can be released for adoption by its mother, the father's parentage must be established and terminated, either by consent or by court decree. Although, as a practical matter, a birth mother will have first custodial rights to her illegitimate child, the father may seek custody on the grounds of the child's best interest. If the mother wishes to release the child for adoption, once the father's parentage has been established—unless he has been declared unfit and his parental rights have been terminated—he will have the right to prevent the adoption and claim custody of the child. In such a case, the mother's parental rights may be terminated by consent or decree.

Q. 12:34 What if an unwed mother does not wish to have the father's parentage declared?

As long as the mother is self-supporting and seeks no public aid for the support of the child, she need not file a parentage action if she does not wish to. The father, if he knows about the child, may do so, but some statutes require that the action by the father be filed within a certain period of time (for example, two years) after the child's birth, or after he becomes aware of the birth. Thereafter, the father may be foreclosed from filing, although in some jurisdictions a parentage action may be able to be filed on behalf of and in the interests of the child—even over the mother's objection—during the child's minority. If the mother applies for public aid for the child, the states (under federal law) must require a parentage action and an order of child support against the father. There is an exception if the mother can establish a very strong personal safety reason for not bringing a parentage action.

Q. 12:35 Can paternity be scientifically established?

Throughout history, only the maternity of a child could be established. During the twentieth century, with the discovery of genetic laws and blood typing, it became possible to establish with certainty that a man was *not* the father, but it was not possible to establish that he *was*—only that he *could have been*. Because the law was loath to illegitimize children, a married woman's husband was irrebuttably presumed by law to be the father unless this was absolutely impossible. Recently, more modern technology—involving human lymphocytic antigen (HLA) typing and chromosomal analysis techniques—has made it possible to establish parentage beyond a reasonable doubt. Statutes may require submission of the putative parent and child to such testing.

Q. 12:36 If a man has been adjudicated the parent of a child, what are his rights and responsibilities?

The father will have all parental rights and responsibilities. He will be entitled to an adjudication of custody, if he wishes it, as well as visitation rights. As a noncustodial unwed parent, he has all the rights that a divorced noncustodial parent would have. He also has all of the responsibilities of support. Whether he wishes it or not, the adjudicated father will be responsible to the child until the child reaches majority. This is a mixed bag for everyone. The relationship between the parents will therefore also continue, neither being free of the other at least until the child grows up. The problems for the child are also evident.

Q. 12:37 What if both parents decide, after such an adjudication, that it is in their best interests that the father be freed of rights as well as responsibilities?

If the parties agree, the father may consent to termination of his parental rights and adoption of the child by the mother alone. Sometimes, depending upon the jurisdiction, the child must be released by both parents to an agency that will then consent to the readoption by the mother alone. In other jurisdictions, it might be preferable or necessary to have the child released by both for adoption to a nominee couple, for example, the mother's parents, who will then rerelease the child to her for adoption. This is complicated and technical and must be done with excellent legal advice.

Child Abuse and Domestic Violence

Q. 12:38 What is child abuse?

Child abuse refers to any form of cruelty to a child's physical, moral, or mental well-being—including any form of sexual behavior or sexual contact with a child—whether or not force or threat is used. In some states, any incestuous behavior, including sibling or cousin incest, is defined as abuse, irrespective of the ages of the participants. Some states include child abuse as a form of neglect. Child abuse is within the jurisdiction of the juvenile court from the perspective of protection of the child. It is also a crime. A child abuser may thus be within the jurisdiction of the juvenile court and also tried in the criminal court.

Q. 12:39 What are child abuse and neglect reporting laws?

In every state, there are statutes requiring certain professionals to report suspected child abuse. The exact details of the statutes will vary from state to state. For example, in some states child abuse is subject to mandatory reporting only if the abuser is a relative or other caretaker, but not if the abuse was committed by a neighbor or other person. In other states, any abuse must be reported. Even if a particular situation or person is not subject to mandated reporting, anyone *may* report suspected child abuse. Every EAP professional must know the child abuse and neglect reporting laws of his or her state *in detail.* (See also Ch. 4, "Confidentiality Requirements," Q. 4:45.)

Most jurisdictions have a child abuse reporting hotline, whose telephone number is available from the Information operator. Child abuse can also be reported to the police. EAP professionals are almost invariably covered under reporting acts as mandated reporters.

Q. 12:40 What should an EAP professional do when child abuse or neglect is suspected?

Do not hesitate, but report it as soon as possible to the proper authorities. Because failure to report can have license or professional liability repercussions, the name or other identification of the person to whom the report was made, along with the date, time, and content of the report, should be recorded. The telephoned report should be followed up by a written report.

Q. 12:41 What are the clinical ramifications if a professional reports child abuse or neglect by a client?

Most authorities suggest that the reporting requirements should be frankly discussed with the client, and that the client be honestly advised that the reporting will occur. Obviously, the client should not be told that a report will be made if there is a valid reason to suspect that the client will harm the child, the other parent, or the EAP professional as a result. In such a case, the situation may be serious enough to warrant other protective measures as well.

The client's feelings about the abuse or neglect and the reporting should be sensitively and empathetically explored, and an attempt must be made to establish or maintain a therapeutic alliance between the client and the reporter. If that is not possible, the client should be offered crisis intervention by referral. If possible, reassurance that the reporting professional will not desert him or her, but will remain available as a resource, will be of great help.

The client should be immediately referred to a lawyer. Because child abuse or neglect is a crime, the client needs legal advice before giving any statements or making any confessions. An admission or confession of child abuse or neglect may be essential from the perspective of the juvenile court, but contraindicated in the event of possible criminal prosecution. Only a knowledgeable, experienced lawyer can properly advise under the circumstances.

Q. 12:42 What are the liability ramifications if a professional reports child abuse or neglect by a client?

Helping professionals are often loath to report child abuse or neglect, not because they do not want children to be protected, but because they feel that abusers or neglecters need care and treatment—not punishment—and because child protection services are often notoriously ineffective. Also, helping professionals are reluctant to get involved with the legal system. Most child abuse and neglect reporting acts provide immunity from civil or criminal liability to persons making good-faith reports of suspected child abuse or neglect. The immunity statutes usually provide for a presumption of the reporting professional's goodwill. Reporting is not likely to result in legal liability to the professional; failure to report, however, has a very high likelihood of liability. (See also Ch. 4, "Confidentiality Requirements," Qs. 4:45–4:48.)

Q. 12:43 What should the EAP professional do if a child protection agency does not respond appropriately?

If the situation is serious, the police should also be called. If the agency refuses to accept the report or otherwise does not respond appropriately or quickly enough, the professional should demand to speak to a supervisor, and go on up the line until someone in authority responds satisfactorily. If nothing seems to work, consider an approach to a local state legislator or to the media. The life and safety of a child are worth the effort.

Q. 12:44 What is domestic violence, and what can an EAP do about it?

Domestic violence refers to any violent or abusive behavior within a household. It includes spouse abuse, elder abuse, and child abuse. Many states have adopted "domestic violence acts," which provide for immediate and meaningful relief to the oppressed family members. Among the remedies that may be available, depending upon the state statutes, is an injunction (a court order prohibiting the abusive behavior). Although spouse or child abuse has historically not been taken very seriously, the violation of a court injunction is a direct insult to the court, and jail may be the result. Other remedies may include exclusive possession of the marital residence (an order allowing the battered spouse and children to remain in the home and requiring the batterer to leave and stay away).

Q. 12:45 What is the "battered wife syndrome"?

The battered wife syndrome is well known among mental health professionals. A battered spouse is often a passive, dependent person who suffers from depression, shame, and such low self-esteem that she (usually she, but sometimes he) is unable to mobilize the courage and strength to take legal steps on her own behalf. The nonbattering parent of a battered child is also often so dependent and passive that she (or he) is unable to mobilize help for the child. The EAP professional can assist with moral support, education, advocacy with the authorities, reporting, counseling, therapy, or referrals. The professional can also be the "friend in court" who accompanies the aggrieved spouse to hearings and appointments and helps free the client from the bond of battery.

Juvenile Court Proceedings

Q. 12:46 What is a juvenile court?

A juvenile court is a court that has special jurisdiction of a parental nature over minors who are alleged to be delinquent, dependent, or neglected. Some jurisdictions call this court a family court, in which event the court may also have jurisdiction over other family-related matters, such as support, parentage, and so forth.

Q. 12:47 What is juvenile delinquency?

Juvenile delinquency is essentially criminal or ungovernable behavior by a minor. A delinquent child is one who violates a state, federal, or local law or ordinance. (See 18 U.S.C. §5001, et seq.) A child who runs away from home or other lawfully authorized place, is habitually truant, habitually disobeys school rules, is ungovernable by his or her parents, or engages in lewd or indecent behavior may be designated a delinquent, or a status offender. A status offense is an act that would not be illegal if committed by an adult, but that is illegal if committed by a minor (for example, sexual activity; leaving home). Delinquency and status offenses are within the jurisdiction of the juvenile court.

Q. 12:48 What is dependency?

All children are dependent upon adults—presumably their parents—for their support, nurturance, and guidance. A child is dependent in the context of a discussion of juvenile court jurisdiction when he or she is without a parent or other adult on whom to depend. This may be a temporary situation (for example, when the parent or parents are hospitalized following an accident), or permanent (for example, when a single parent is physically or mentally disabled, a drug addict, or severely alcoholic).

Q. 12:49 What is child neglect?

A child is neglected when his or her parent or custodian fails or refuses to provide necessary physical, affectional, medical, educational, or other care; or the child is in such a condition of deprivation or suffering, or under such improper care or control, that his or her health or morals are endangered. Neglect includes cruelty or abuse of a child, although some juvenile court acts separate the categories. As a practical matter, it does not matter what the action is called; neglect and abuse both require the child protection powers of the court. The neglect or abuse may be the result of depravity or cruelty (and thus, deliberate), or it may be the result of parental incapacity. In either event, the parent is unfit to care for the child, and intervention is required.

Q. 12:50 Are there preliminary measures taken before a juvenile court intervenes on behalf of the child?

Yes. In the juvenile court, there is usually a prescreening procedure, in which a probation officer makes a determination about whether or not the case is appropriate for diversion from the court. If the matter is not too serious and the probation officer believes it can be handled by referral to therapy or some other nonjudicial intervention, the case will be diverted. Often, the family situation is what will make the difference for a child. If the situation is not chronic, and the family can assure the probation officer that there is adequate parental care and supervision and that the child and the community will be safe with the child and family seeking professional assistance, the probation officer will be inclined to concur.

Q. 12:51 Once the juvenile court intervenes, how are proceedings handled?

If diversion is not indicated, a petition is brought, alleging that the child is delinquent, dependent, or neglected (or abused). In some jurisdictions, a *guardian ad litem* or attorney is appointed to represent the best interest of the child. The child and his or her parents or custodian are named as parties to the proceeding, so the court has jurisdiction over all of them. If the child or parents cannot afford counsel, the court must appoint a public defender or other legal representative without charge in a delinquency proceeding. In other juvenile court proceedings, the local juvenile court act may also require that all parties be represented.

There are two phases to every juvenile proceeding: adjudicatory and dispositional. In the adjudicatory phase, the court hears testimony and makes a finding as to whether the child is, as alleged, delinquent, dependent, or abused. If the child is adjudicated one of these three, he or she becomes a ward of the court.

Q. 12:52 What actions may the court take, once it has decided that the child is delinquent, dependent, or abused?

In this phase of the proceeding, the court will consider social service and clinical reports and make a determination in accordance with what appears to be in the best interests of the child. The child may be placed in his or her own family under certain conditions, in the custody of a child protection agency, in a supervised foster home, or in an institution. If the child is adjudicated delinquent, probation or institutionalization may be ordered. If the child is adjudicated dependent or neglected and placed away from his or her family, reunification of the family is the goal to be sought, and the child protection agency is responsible for providing such services to the family as may be needed to achieve that goal. Treatment services may also be ordered.

If after a reasonable period (for example, 12 months) of placement, the parent has not made sufficient effort or actual progress at rehabilitation to provide permanency and a safe, wholesome environment for the child, a petition for termination of parental rights may be filed; if it is successful, the child can be freed for adoption.

Q. 12:53 What can parents do with an ungovernable child?

Sometimes, a child is so uncontrollable that parents are unable to tolerate his or her acting out behavior. Usually, it is only after protracted misbehavior (which may involve violence) that parents finally seek court help. In cases in which a child is simply ungovernable, but has not yet committed acts that would label him or her a delinquent, parents may have recourse under the state juvenile court act to a proceeding by which the court can adjudicate the child a ward and commit the child for treatment, care, or correction. This proceeding may be known as Minor in Need of Supervision (MINS), Child in Need of Supervision (CHINS), Family in Need of Assistance (FINA), Minor Requiring Authoritative Intervention (MRAI), or something similar. Status offenders may be dealt with under this proceeding. If an adjudicated status offender then disobeys the court's ruling again, he or she may be adjudicated a delinquent or incorrigible, and punished as a delinquent.

Q. 12:54 What is the standard of proof in a juvenile court proceeding?

To some extent, this will be governed by state statute, although certain constitutional principles will apply. In a delinquency proceeding, the child must be proved a delinquent by, at the very least, clear and convincing evidence. Many authorities insist upon "beyond a reasonable doubt," because the child is at risk for loss of freedom.

Dependency, neglect, and abuse may be proved by a preponderance of the evidence. To terminate parental rights, the parent must be adjudicated unfit by at least clear and convincing evidence.

Q. 12:55 If a teenager is accused of a serious crime, will he or she be tried as a juvenile or an adult?

This depends, again, upon state statute. After a certain age (for example, 13 years, or 15 years) juvenile court jurisdiction may be waived in a serious case, and the child may be tried as an adult. Because a sentence under the juvenile court act can last only until the child reaches 21, the prosecutor and judge may both agree that a crime is so serious that a sentence of a few years would be inadequate, both as punishment and as protection for the community. Recently, the U.S. Supreme Court has held that a state may execute a person who was convicted of having committed a capital crime while a juvenile.

On the other hand, a child who is adjudicated delinquent may be kept in a correctional institution until reaching a certain age, usually 21. For example, an adjudication of a 15-year-old child could result in a 6-year sentence as a juvenile. For the same crime, an adult might be given probation or required to serve a maximum of 18 months in prison. In such a case, the juvenile's attorney may seek a waiver to adult court because the sentence would be lighter.

Q. 12:56 How can an EAP professional assist a client whose child is involved in a juvenile proceeding?

In the screening or dispositional phase of the proceeding, an EAP professional can be of considerable help. At these times, the court process is less formal, and the screener or judge will consider any and all information from all relevant sources that may mitigate the situation.

A letter or affidavit from an EAP professional about the EAP's intervention in the situation, the family's involvement in appropriate services, and so forth, will be extremely helpful. A court may be favorably impressed when the parent's employment provides an additional support in straightening out a troubled child.

Criminal Law

Q. 12:57 What is a crime?

A crime is an offense against a penal law. A penal law is one defining criminal offenses and specifying the penalties for their violation. There are state and local, as well as federal, crimes. A misdemeanor is a minor crime, punishable by a relatively small fine or jail sentence of less than a year. A felony is a major crime, punishable by a larger fine and, usually, a prison sentence of more than a year or, under some circumstances, death. (See 18 U.S.C. §1.) State laws vary as to which criminal acts are felonies and what sentences will be imposed.

Q. 12:58 What is a grand jury?

A grand jury is a group of citizens summoned by the sheriff or marshal of the criminal court to receive complaints and accusations and hear the state's evidence concerning the allegations. The grand jury determines whether probable cause exists to believe that a crime was committed and that the accused person committed it. If the grand jury believes that a crime was committed, it issues a true bill—an indictment of the accused. If it believes no crime was committed, it issues a no bill. It is called a "grand jury" because it consists of a greater number of people than the ordinary "petit jury," which hears civil and criminal trials.

Q. 12:59 What is an indictment?

An indictment is a document issued by a grand jury accusing a person of having committed a crime. Usually, the state prosecutor presents the facts to the grand jury, often by testimony of witnesses subpoenaed for the purpose, and requests the issuance of the indictment.

Q. 12:60 After indictment, what happens?

Once the grand jury has issued the indictment, the accused is arrested and arraigned. Arraignment is a procedure in which the accused person is brought before a court to hear the charges against him or her read aloud. He or she is then asked to plead "guilty" or "not guilty." (Some states also permit a plea of nolo contendere, or "no contest.")

Q. 12:61 What is bail or bond?

After the arraignment, in the same hearing or another hearing shortly thereafter, the issue of bail will be decided. Unless the court determines to release the accused pending trial, he or she must remain under arrest. Bail is procuring one's release from custody pending criminal trial. Depending upon the laws and custom of the jurisdiction, an accused can be bailed out of custody on surety bond or on his or her own recognizance.

The court may require that a surety bond be posted to secure the presence of the accused at trial. If the accused has sufficient assets, he or she may post a cash bond, negotiable instruments, or the deed to real estate. Relatives or friends may also be willing to help. If the bond required by the court is more than the accused can raise, a bond may be purchased from a surety company; if the accused does not appear when required, the bond is forfeited. If the court is satisfied that the accused is reliable, he or she may be released on his or her own recognizance—that is a promise to appear, without the requirement of a surety bond.

Q. 12:62 What determines how high a bond will be set?

When the court is concerned about the reliability of the accused, it may set the bond very high to discourage the possibility of bail. The more serious the alleged crime, the greater would be the disincentive to the accused to stay and stand trial. In some jurisdictions, bail is not available when one is accused of a capital crime.

Q. 12:63 If a person is tried for a crime, what is the burden of proof?

Under the U.S. Constitution, a person is presumed innocent until proven guilty. The state has the burden of overcoming the presumption of innocence and proving the defendant guilty beyond a reasonable doubt. This means that the trier of fact, whether a judge or jury, must be fully satisfied and utterly convinced to a moral certainty by the evidence presented that the defendant is guilty of the crime alleged.

Q. 12:64 What is "taking the Fifth"?

The Fifth Amendment to the Constitution provides that no one can be forced to give evidence against himself or herself in a criminal case. A person who is examined before a grand jury or some other tribunal pursuant to a subpoena, and who may be subject to prosecution as a result of anything he or she may say, may refuse to testify on the grounds of possible self-incrimination. This is known as "taking the Fifth." The law does not allow any presumption of guilt to be drawn from a refusal to testify, but such a presumption often occurs in the minds of observers.

Q. 12:65 What is an insanity plea?

An accused person who admits having committed the alleged act, but claims to have been suffering at the time from a mental condition that would render him or her incapable of forming a criminal intent, may plead "not guilty by reason of insanity." The burden of proof is on the accused to establish insanity at the time the crime was committed.

Q. 12:66 What if the accused is mentally ill or otherwise mentally incapacitated at the time of the trial?

An accused person who is suffering from a mental disturbance at the time of trial, or is mentally retarded, may be unfit to stand trial. A person is unfit, or lacks competency, to stand trial if he or she cannot understand the nature and object of the proceedings, cannot consult with counsel, and cannot assist in the preparation of the defense. It is a violation of due process to try someone for a crime if he or she is incompetent to stand trial.

Q. 12:67 May an accused who is unfit to stand trial be required to undergo treatment to restore him or her to fitness?

Yes. The individual may be compelled to undergo treatment and take medication. In one dramatic case, the state was required to provide long-term special treatment and education to a deaf-mute defendant who was probably also retarded, to prepare him to be fit to stand trial of the brutal murder of a prostitute. As of this writing, he remains in custody after many years, still receiving "treatment and training." (*People v. Lang*, 498 N.E.2d 1105 (1986))

Q. 12:68 In a criminal trial, may the defendant refuse to testify?

Yes, under the Fifth Amendment. The prosecution may not call the defendant as a witness against himself or herself. The defendant's attorney must decide as a matter of strategy whether to call the defendant in his or her own defense.

Q. 12:69 When is a court likely to give probation, rather than a prison sentence, after a person is found guilty of a crime?

In some states, there are categories of serious crimes in which a court has no discretion to sentence a convicted criminal to probation, but must impose a prison sentence. Further, there are minimum sentences for specific crimes. A judge who has discretion may decide on probation, in theory, if this is the person's first offense; there are mitigating circumstances; he or she has a good personal family and job record; and it appears that he or she is not likely to commit another crime, or pose a danger to the community, and can be rehabilitated in the community.

In fact, there is much criticism of sentencing practices, because they vary so widely from judge to judge and jurisdiction to jurisdiction. Community outrage may influence a court's sentencing in a case, to the defendant's benefit or detriment. Numerous sociological and penological studies have suggested that minorities are overrepresented in prison populations and underrepresented among probationers. In large urban centers and states in which prisons are overcrowded, there is frequent outcry because dangerous criminals are not incarcerated.

Q. 12:70 What alternative sentencing techniques are available?

This depends upon the jurisdiction. Some jurisdictions have work release programs, in which a convicted prisoner is permitted to leave prison to go to work, but is in prison at all other times. Other jurisdictions are experimenting with house arrest and electronic surveillance of prisoners. The electronic surveillance is conducted by an ankle bracelet that is applied to the prisoner and cannot be removed or tampered with without alerting a monitor. Sometimes this is combined with work release.

Depending upon the nature of the crime, a judge may sentence the criminal to make restitution to a person wronged by the criminal behavior. Sentences of a certain number of hours of community service are also imposed. Because of the spate of commercially successful books by "famous" convicts, laws have been passed prohibiting convicted felons from profiting from their crimes or convictions under certain circumstances. (There is a constitutional question here: prior restraint of free expression. It seems that the convict cannot be prevented from writing or publishing, but can be prevented from receiving money for it.)

So-called white-collar criminals may be sentenced to "country club" low-security facilities to serve their time in relative comfort. There is criticism of this practice, of course, again on the ground of discrimination, while others support it on the theory of "let the punishment fit the crime."

Q. 12:71 What is parole?

Parole is the conditional release of a prisoner after having actually served part of a sentence. Usually, the prisoner is released under the supervision of a parole officer and is subject to certain very stringent conditions. Generally, the parolee must have a job; must live in approved housing; may be subject to a curfew; must not consort with known convicts or other criminals or violate any laws; and may be forbidden to drink. The parolee will be required to report at specified times to the parole officer. Any parole violation will result in the person being returned to prison.

A parole board reviews prisoners after they have served their minimum sentences and determines whether or not parole is to be granted. A good prison record is mandatory for a grant of parole. Even with an exemplary record, if the prisoner was convicted of a serious or notorious crime, the chances of parole are likely to be small.

Q. 12:72 What are an EAP's rights if a crime is committed or threatened against the EAP or its personnel?

The EAP is in the same position as any other complaining witness. The law enforcement authorities may be contacted, and information can be conveyed to them under an exception to confidentiality laws.

Q. 12:73 What is the EAP's responsibility when a client informs a counselor of a crime committed against the employer?

Authorities disagree on this, but the best rule seems to be that a crime against the employer or program sponsor cannot be tolerated on clinical grounds. It is suggested that in the EAP policies and all publicity and literature referring to confidentiality in EAP participation, criminal acts against the EAP or employer should be stated exceptions to confidentiality. To do otherwise establishes an insupportable situation in which trust cannot truly exist, and creates a complicated transference/countertransference issue far beyond the training and skill of any but the most advanced psychoanalyst. (See also Ch. 4, "Confidentiality Requirements," Qs. 4:36–4:37.)

Q. 12:74 Is there a duty to report prospective criminal acts?

There is a common-law duty upon every citizen to act to prevent the commission of a felony. If a client discloses a plan for the future commission of a crime, in some jurisdictions the EAP counselor may be considered a conspirator or accessory if he or she does not report it. Most authorities take the position that one does not report a past crime, but there is an obligation to report an intended one. It is a difficult situation clinically. The clinical question is, "Why are you telling me this?" (See also Ch. 4, "Confidentiality Requirements," Qs. 4:35 and 4:37–4:41.) The counselor should seek immediate legal consultation for advice on handling a future crime issue.

Chapter 13

Preparing for Trial: The Courts, Evidence, and Expert Testimony

EAP professionals are finding themselves in court more frequently today than ever before, whether as parties or witnesses. In either capacity, they will be called upon to respond to writs of the court and to testify. This chapter presents an overview of the legal system; the trial process; common rules of evidence; and helpful hints about choosing and working with a lawyer, preparing for trial, and testifying.

Q. 13:1 How does the legal system work in the United States?

There are essentially two systems of law in the United States—state and federal.

State Legal Structure: Each state has its own laws and a court system in which any matter other than a federal matter will be heard. Each state has trial courts, in which all cases are heard and evidence is taken, and appellate courts, which decide appeals brought by litigants who were unsuccessful at trial and wish to have their cases reviewed. Most states have a three-tier system, with trial courts, appellate courts, and a supreme court. The supreme court ordinarily hears appeals from the appellate court. Some states have two types of state supreme court appeals: appeals of right, which any litigant who was unsuccessful at the appellate level is entitled to bring, and appeals that may be accepted or refused at the discretion of the supreme court.

Federal Legal Structure: The federal court system is composed of districts across the country, with trial and appellate courts for each. The U.S. Supreme Court hears appeals from the federal courts and will hear certain appeals from state courts.

Q. 13:2 Are there any other systems in the United States that can impose law?

Yes. A system of administrative law is created by administrative agencies of the state and federal governments. These agencies hold hearings both to decide what rules and regulations they should enact and to determine facts and administer compliance with those rules and regulations. Examples of cases that are often decided in administrative hearings are workers' compensation claims, civil service disputes, license discipline or disputes over failure to issue a license (for example, professional licenses, or licenses to operate certain businesses, such as a tavern or restaurant), and disputes over taxes. Often, a person who is dissatisfied with the outcome of an administrative hearing may seek review of that outcome in the courts.

State Courts

Q. 13:3 How are state court judges chosen?

This varies from state to state. In some states, judges are elected; in others, they are appointed.

Q. 13:4 Are all nonfederal cases heard by state court judges?

This depends upon the state. In some states, municipalities, counties, or townships have their own courts to hear minor matters involving small sums of money or criminal misdemeanors (petty crimes).

Federal Courts

Q. 13:5 How does a case come to a federal court, rather than a state court?

The following types of cases will be heard in a federal court: those involving treaties; criminal prosecutions arising out of crimes committed against the federal government or on federal property; civil cases in which the parties are citizens of different states (diversity of citizenship) and the amount in controversy is in excess of $10,000, or in which the United States is a party; civil rights or other cases arising out of federal constitutional or statutory law; and cases between or against states. Almost all other cases are heard in state courts.

Q. 13:6 If parties are citizens of different states, in what federal court will the case be heard?

Usually, the case will be heard in the state in which the defendant lives or does business or in which the act complained of took place. Sometimes, many state sites are involved, or the witnesses or other evidence are more readily available in one state than another. A party may move the court to transfer the case on the theory of *forum non conveniens* (inconvenient forum) to another jurisdiction that is more convenient.

Q. 13:7 Is there an advantage in having one's case heard in federal court?

Some people think so. In theory, the federal courts have the finest, most learned judges in the land. Further, because federal judges are appointed for life, they are theoretically less prone to being influenced by public sentiment or political pressure. Because there are fewer cases brought in federal court, it is likely that a case brought there may be heard sooner than in a state court with a considerable backlog.

Q. 13:8 How are federal judges selected?

Federal judges are nominated by the senators from the district in which they will sit. They are then chosen and appointed by the president, subject to the "advice and consent" of the U.S. Senate. Federal judgeships are frankly political appointments, but federal decisions are so important to the running of the country that it is rare, if ever, that a president will choose an unqualified person. If, however, that appears to be the case, the Senate can reject the president's choice, as occurred dramatically during the last months of the Reagan administration.

Role of the Jury

Q. 13:9 What is the role of a jury?

A jury is a body of citizens who hear the evidence and decide on the facts in a case. When they decide what the facts are, they then render a verdict—a formal decision or finding as to the matters submitted to them in the trial. In a criminal case, the jury will decide if the defendant is guilty or not guilty and, in some states, what the penalty shall be. In a civil case, the jury will decide which of the litigants wins and, usually, the size of the award.

Q. 13:10 How many jurors must there be?

Traditionally, there are 12 jurors, but it is not uncommon for a jury to consist of 6 members. In federal court and some state courts, the parties may agree on a number fewer than 12.

Q. 13:11 Is a litigant always entitled to a jury trial?

Under the Constitution, the right to trial by jury is guaranteed in criminal cases and suits at common law in which the amount in controversy is in excess of $20. In equity cases (cases in which a common-law court has no jurisdiction or way to give relief), a jury is usually not available. A suit for money damages is a lawsuit. A suit for an injunction (to force someone to do or not do something), specific performance (to require a person to perform his or her obligations under a contract in a situation in which the payment of money damages will not suffice), divorce, and certain other types of actions are equitable actions.

Q. 13:12 If there is no jury, who decides the facts?

The judge decides in the absence of a jury.

Q. 13:13 Besides deciding on the facts in a case, what is the role of the judge?

The judge conducts the trial and rules on the admissibility of the evidence—what may be admitted, and what may not. He or she makes the decisions about the applicability of the various rules of law to the particular case being heard. When there is a jury, the judge instructs the jury on the law. If the judge feels that the jury's verdict is "against the manifest weight of the evidence," he or she will overrule the jury by entering a "judgment notwithstanding the verdict."

Trial Proceedings

Q. 13:14 Who are the litigants in a civil case?

The plaintiff is the party who brings the action by complaining against the defendant. In some proceedings, the party bringing the action is called the petitioner; the person who must respond to the petition is called the respondent.

Q. 13:15 What is evidence?

Evidence is any means by which the existence or nonexistence of a fact may be proved. It may consist of oral testimony by witnesses, documents, records, exhibits, concrete objects, and so forth. For example, the murder weapon is concrete evidence.

Q. 13:16 May any statement, document, or item be admitted as evidence in a case?

Only pertinent and proper evidence may be considered in reaching a decision. Evidence is admissible when it is:

- *Relevant.* It must apply to the matter in question and tend to make the existence of a fact that is of consequence in determining the outcome of the case either more or less probable.
- *Material.* It must be pertinent to the case being decided and necessary to the consideration of the controversy.

- *Probative.* It tends to prove, has the effect of proving, or actually proves facts that are required to reach a decision in the case.

Q. 13:17 What are the typical documents in a civil case?

A civil case is commenced by the filing of a complaint or, in some instances, a petition. This initial document sets out the plaintiff's side of the story: the allegations of fact and the prayer for relief (what redress is wanted). If the defendant believes the suit is not sufficient in law—that is, the facts alleged do not state a claim on which the court can give relief—the defendant may move to strike and/or dismiss the complaint on procedural or legal grounds.

If the complaint is not stricken or dismissed, the defendant must file an answer admitting or denying the plaintiff's allegations, and seeking dismissal of the suit and/or other relief. If the defendant believes that he or she also has a grievance against the plaintiff, a counterclaim may be filed, which must then be responded to by the plaintiff.

During the course of the proceeding, the parties file motions or petitions seeking orders or rulings of the court in connection with the proceedings. For example, during the pendency of divorce litigation, the parties may file motions for temporary child custody, visitation, and spousal or child support; to prevent a spouse from concealing assets or wasting the marital estate; and so forth.

Q. 13:18 What are discovery proceedings?

Modern judicial theory seeks to conserve judicial time and provide for an orderly trial. The idea is to allow for full knowledge by all parties of all of the facts in the case and the evidence to be presented. Once this knowledge is available, parties can often reach an out-of-court settlement and save themselves and the community the cost and stress of a trial. The pretrial device used by parties to obtain facts and information from each other about the case is discovery. Discovery is governed by the rules of procedure of the court in which the case is brought.

Discovery may be by depositions upon oral and written questions, written interrogatories (questions), production of documents or things, permission to enter and inspect land or other property, physical and mental examinations, and requests for admissions. A deposition is a proceeding outside of court in which a witness is under oath and is asked questions about the case. The person being deposed is called a deponent. A court reporter makes a verbatim transcript of the deposition, which can then be used at the trial for purposes of impeaching the witness if his or her trial testimony is inconsistent with the deposition testimony.

Q. 13:19 How is a suit commenced?

The plaintiff files a complaint with the clerk of the court in which the case is being brought. The clerk issues a summons, which is a writ of the court summoning the defendant to appear before the court and answer the complaint. The plaintiff submits himself or herself to the jurisdiction of the court by filing the case.

In order for the court to have jurisdiction over the defendant, the summons and a copy of the complaint must be served upon the defendant. Service is made in person; by leaving a copy at the home of the defendant under such circumstances as the law requires under the circumstances; or in some instances, by mail (ordinarily certified or registered). Personal service is the best service and is required in many instances. Personal service is made by the sheriff, marshal, or other officer of the court. Under some circumstances, service of some documents may be made by a person who is not an official, in which event a court order may be required.

Once the defendant has been served (has received a copy of the summons and complaint), he or she has a certain number of days in which to file a document called an appearance, and to plead (file a written answer). If the defendant fails to appear or plead, he or she will be held in default, and the plaintiff will be awarded a judgment. Thus, it is absolutely essential that legal advice be sought immediately upon receipt of a summons or complaint.

Q. 13:20 When does discovery take place?

The code of procedure and court rules determine when discovery proceedings take place, but, by and large, they start very early in the case and continue until the statutory cutoff or cutoff by the judge. If a party does not cooperate with discovery, the court will impose sanctions, such as an award of attorneys' fees to the opposing lawyer or striking the pleadings of the noncooperator. If a nonparty witness refuses to appear or turn over documents, the party who subpoenaed him or her for deposition may apply to the court, which can have the witness arrested and punished for contempt. Discovery rules are complex and vary widely from jurisdiction to jurisdiction.

Q. 13:21 What is a bench trial?

A trial by a judge is called a bench trial.

Q. 13:22 If a jury is available for the type of suit being brought, why might a litigant prefer to have a bench trial?

The issue of whether or not to demand a jury is a strategic one that must be determined by the litigator (trial lawyer). Because it takes time to choose a jury, jury trials are longer than bench trials and therefore more expensive. Also, if a party is unattractive, inarticulate, or unsympathetic, or the subject of the suit is inflammatory, the litigator may feel it best to try the case before a judge, who is less likely to be swayed by irrelevancies. Some lawyers prefer a bench trial in cases involving complex facts; others do not. Either party may demand a jury, and the other party is bound by that choice.

Q. 13:23 How is a jury chosen?

After any preliminary motions to the court, the jury will be chosen from a panel of citizens who have been summoned for the purpose. Each potential juror will be examined by both attorneys and, perhaps, the court, to ascertain his or her suitability to sit in judgment in this case. This is called *voir dire.* A juror may be excused for cause if he or she is likely to be prejudiced for or against a party or has preconceived ideas about any issue in the case. Each party is also given a certain number of peremptory challenges, which allow him or her to refuse a juror without cause. Lawyers sometimes have theories about who makes a sympathetic juror for a certain type of case. However, systematically excluding a particular demographic group (for example, blacks, women, or white-collar professionals) is unconstitutional. Once a jury is selected, it is sworn, and the trial begins.

Q. 13:24 What is the "burden of proof"?

The burden of proof consists of two concepts:

1. The burden of persuasion—the plaintiff must persuade the trier of fact that his or her position in the case is the correct one by affirmatively proving the facts necessary to entitle him or her to win; and
2. The burden of going forward with the evidence—a party must refute or explain some fact that has been alleged or as to which evidence has been introduced.

Q. 13:25 What is the "standard of proof"?

The standard of proof is the burden of proof required to prevail in a given type of case. In a criminal case, the state must prove the defendant guilty beyond a reasonable doubt. In a civil case, the party who proves his or her case by a preponderance of the evidence will prevail. Preponderance of evidence is evidence of greater weight or more convincing than the evidence offered by the opposition. It establishes that a fact is more probable than not.

Between beyond a reasonable doubt and preponderance of evidence is an intermediate level of proof—clear and convincing. This standard, which is used in cases in which the absolute standard required for criminal cases is not deemed necessary, but a mere preponderance is not held to be sufficient, is difficult to define. It approaches beyond a reasonable doubt, but does not reach it. Some cases describe it as "more than a preponderance, but less than is required in a criminal case." Obviously, this will be subjective. The clear-and-convincing requirement may, depending upon the jurisdiction, be used in such cases as termination of parental rights, commitment for involuntary treatment, adjudication of incompetency, and adjudication of delinquency.

Q. 13:26 How does the trial proceed?

The plaintiff has the burden of proof in his or her case, and therefore is given the right to open and close the case. The plaintiff's lawyer usually makes an opening statement, explaining what the case is about and what the lawyer expects to prove. The witnesses are then called in turn for direct examination. After each witness has testified, the opposing counsel may cross-examine, but only on matters brought up in direct examination. Cross-examination is intended to point out the flaws and weaknesses in the witness's testimony and to attack his or her credibility, if possible. After the cross-examination, the lawyer who called the witness in the first place may redirect (question the witness again), but only on matters brought up on cross-examination.

Q. 13:27 What must the plaintiff do to ensure that the trial goes forward?

During the plaintiff's case, he or she must establish a *prima facie* case: sufficient evidence to establish all facts necessary for a verdict in the plaintiff's favor, assuming that the defendant cannot refute them. For example, in a malpractice case, the plaintiff must establish the following elements:

1. The defendant owed a duty to the plaintiff;
2. The defendant negligently breached that duty; and
3. The plaintiff suffered damages as a proximate result of the negligence.

At the close of the plaintiff's case (after presenting all of his or her witnesses), if the plaintiff has failed to establish any one of those elements, the judge directs the jury at that point to find for the defendant. If it is a nonjury case, the judge grants the defendant's motion to dismiss.

If the plaintiff does establish a *prima facie* case, the burden of going forward shifts to the defendant, whose lawyer, after an opening statement, must now present witnesses to refute the plaintiff's case. At the close of the defendant's case, the plaintiff may offer rebuttal evidence to explain or refute the defendant's evidence.

Following all the evidence, the plaintiff's lawyer makes a closing argument, the defense responds, and the plaintiff has the right to the last word.

If there is a jury, the lawyers and judge must agree on what instructions as to the law the judge gives to the jury to guide them in their deliberations and decision. The judge instructs the jury, which then retires to deliberate.

Q. 13:28 How does a jury decide a verdict?

A jury elects a foreperson to chair its deliberations. When the jury has reached a unanimous decision, it returns to the courtroom, and the foreperson delivers the written verdict to the clerk or the judge, who then reads it. The losing lawyer may wish to poll the jury, asking each juror if he or she concurs. If the judge agrees that the verdict is consistent with the manifest weight of the evidence, he or she will enter judgment on the verdict. If, however, the jury's verdict is against the manifest weight of the evidence (this sometimes happens when a jury gets carried away and influenced by histrionics, rather than facts), the judge enters a judgment notwithstanding the verdict.

Q. 13:29 After the trial, does the losing side have any recourse?

After judgment is entered, the losing lawyer may file posttrial motions, such as a motion for a new trial—based on a theory of error or unfairness in the proceeding—a motion for relief from the judgment, or a motion for a stay of execution of the judgment pending appeal. Usually, a new trial is not granted at this stage unless some dramatic new evidence turns up that was not previously available. The losing party may, however, decide to appeal to a higher court.

Q. 13:30 What is the basis for an appeal?

The basis for appeal is that there was prejudicial error in the trial procedure or the verdict was against the manifest weight of the evidence. Error might consist of prejudicial comments by a judge or lawyer, admitting evidence improperly, or a misapprehension or misapplication of law.

Q. 13:31 Is testimony or other new evidence taken by the appellate court?

No. The appeal is decided entirely by reviewing the documents and transcript of the trial and reading the briefs of the lawyers. A brief is a statement by each party of his or her point of view about the facts in the case, the issues presented for the appellate court's review, the applicable law, and a written argument on the law. Often, the appellate court will hear oral arguments by counsel. In a case that has implications for a government entity, or a class or group of persons, organizations, or interest groups, petitions may be filed for permission to submit *amicus curiae* ("friend of the court") briefs. With leave of the court, a nonparty may file a brief giving the court technical information and its opinion on the issues being decided. Usually, *amicus* briefs are allowed only in cases of broad public interest.

Q. 13:32 How is an appellate court opinion rendered, and what is its effect?

The appellate court issues a written opinion that is almost always published in several law reporters (volumes of reported case decisions). The opinion sets forth a rule of law in this case that will become legal precedent for all similar cases in the future. If the appellate court agrees with the trial court, it affirms the trial court's decision, and the parties must obey the judgment (for example, pay damages). If the appellate court disagrees with the trial court, it reverses the judgment of the trial court, in whole or in part, and remands the case back to the trial court for further proceedings consistent with its decision. This might include a new trial, for example, or amendment of the judgment to a lower or higher amount.

Admissibility of Evidence

Q. 13:33 What determines whether evidence is or is not admissible?

Every court, whether federal or state, has a code of procedure and rules of evidence. Also, there have been hundreds of appellate court decisions on admissibility of various types and examples of evidence that establish guidelines for judges.

Q. 13:34 What else makes evidence inadmissible?

The rule against hearsay is a primary rule of evidence that confounds, frustrates, and confuses witnesses. Simply put, a witness's testimony can be based only on his or her own direct knowledge. One cannot testify about something that has been heard, ascertained, or obtained from someone else. Hearsay is a statement by a declarant that is not made while testifying at the trial or hearing, and that is offered in evidence by a witness to prove the truth of the matter asserted. Such testimony would proceed not from the witness's personal knowledge, but from mere repetition of what he or she has been told by another person who was not under oath and therefore cannot be assumed to be telling the truth. The rule against hearsay applies not only to oral testimony, but also to documents and writings.

Q. 13:35 Are clinical or other business records admissible?

In many jurisdictions, business records (those kept in the ordinary course of doing business) are admissible under an exception to the hearsay rule. The rationale is that business records are intended to aid in the proper transaction of business and would be useless for that purpose unless they truthfully and accurately reflected what they recorded. The rules about which business records are admissible, and under what circumstances, vary widely from one jurisdiction to another. In Illinois, for example, business records are admissible as an exception to the rule against hearsay, but hospital records are excluded from the exception for most purposes! The matter is extremely technical, and local counsel is necessary for interpretation.

Q. 13:36 Are there any special techniques for clinical recording in cases with legal implications?

Because of the requirement to establish a foundation (see Q. 13:39) in order to use a record as evidence in a legal case, a clinician should take pains to date and fully sign every entry in the record. If the record contains information likely to have legal significance, the names of persons with knowledge relevant to an entry, and especially those who were present during the events being recorded, should be written down.

In defensive recording to guard against a charge of professional liability, the clinician should at all times think about the record as a major source of both charges against the clinician and a defense to such charges. There is a saying about records, "If it isn't written down, it didn't happen." This can have advantages or disadvantages, depending upon the circumstances. The rule is: The clinical record should truly and accurately reflect what happened and who knows about it.

Q. 13:37 Can a person's own out-of-court statement be introduced as evidence against him or her?

A witness can testify to certain types of out-of-court statements (usually admissions) made by a party to the case. An admission is a voluntary acknowledgment, concession, or confession made by a party about the existence of a fact relevant to the case being tried. One of the most common types of admission is an admission against interest—when one has previously stated something to be true that is inconsistent with what that person is now claiming in the lawsuit. Sometimes, a party is said to have made an admission by silence if he or she has failed to protest or correct a statement made by someone else of facts that one would be expected to deny if they were not true.

Example. A client admits to the EAP counselor that he has abused his very young child. The law requires that the counselor report the abuse. The client seems truly remorseful; the counselor feels that it would be therapeutic for the client to report himself, rather than be reported; and the counselor encourages the client to do so. Because of the grave nature of the abuse, the state's attorney decides to prosecute the client criminally. The child is nonverbal, and there is no witness against the client. Child protection proceedings are in place, but it would be next to impossible to criminally convict the abuser. However, since he called the child protection authorities himself and admitted his guilt, the child protection worker, as well as the counselor, will be required to testify to his admission, and this will be admitted by the court as evidence against him.

Q. 13:38 Under what circumstances may a spoken statement be admitted into evidence other than to prove the truth of what was asserted in the statement?

Hearsay is not an issue unless one is attempting to prove the truth of what was said by testifying to it. Sometimes, the very fact that a statement was made is significant, irrespective of whether or not it proves a fact. This is called a verbal act. The issue is: Was the statement made? A verbal act is not hearsay and may be testified to. Two examples of verbal acts follow.

Example 1. A woman dies after surgery; the death is caused by barbiturate withdrawal. Her husband sues the physicians and hospital for negligence and wrongful death. The defense is that they knew nothing about her barbiturate addiction. The husband insists that he told a resident physician about it before he left after settling his wife into her room after her admission. A witness to the conversation between the husband and the resident is permitted to testify to the content of the conversation to establish that the husband did, indeed, notify the hospital of his wife's addiction.

Example 2. Employee A sues an EAP counselor for defamation because the EAP has informed the employer that he has started using drugs again, and it is not safe for him to be operating very dangerous machinery. Employee A claims that the counselor's statement was false. The EAP counselor is permitted to testify that Employee B told him that she had seen Employee A using cocaine and behaving in an unsafe manner with the machinery and that she was consequently afraid to work with Employee A.

Q. 13:39 What is required for a witness to be allowed to testify to a conversation?

Assuming that any hearsay objection has been dealt with, a conversation—either in person or by telephone—may be testified to after a proper foundation for the conversation has been established. The witness must be asked, and must testify to, the following questions in order to lay a foundation for the testimony:

- Who was present?
- Where did the conversation take place?
- When?
- What did he say to you, and what did you say to him?

If the witness is testifying to a telephone conversation, he or she must be asked and testify to how he or she knew the identity of the person on the other end of the telephone.

Q. 13:40 What if a witness has no independent recollection of certain facts or details that are written down somewhere?

Often, a trial takes place years after the events about which a witness will be asked to testify. Even when there has not been a considerable lapse of time, details—such as dates, quantities, or the order of events—might not be clearly in the memory of the witness. If a witness does not remember, he or she should so state. The examining lawyer than asks if the witness's recollection is exhausted. If so, the lawyer asks if there is anything that might refresh the recollection. Notes, records, photographs, or any similar item may be used to refresh the recollection. Anything so used will be available for inspection by the opposing counsel and may be used by him or her for purposes of later cross-examining the witness.

Q. 13:41 What if it is not possible to testify by memory as to the facts, even after looking at the material to refresh recollection?

Items such as records, diaries, calendars, and notebooks—in which the witness recorded events, facts, and details—may be introduced into evidence as past recollection recorded. Before such items are admitted into evidence, they must be shown to the opposing counsel and a foundation must be laid for their admissibility as evidence.

Example.

Q: Mr. Counselor, how many prospective client employers did you call on in 1982?

A: I can't tell you the exact number.

Q: Can you tell the jury the names of the companies?

A: No, ma'am. I can't possibly remember their names. There were many.

Q: What were the names of the company representatives with whom you met?

A: I can't remember them either.

Q: Did you make any record of the companies?

A: Yes, ma'am, I made a list of the companies and the people I met on my daily appointment and expense log book.

Q: When did you make the lists?

A: Every evening before I went home.

Q: Was the list always accurate and complete?

A: Yes, ma'am.

Q: Mr. Counselor, would the log book refresh your recollection as to those names?

A: Ma'am, I couldn't possibly remember all of them, even if I looked at the book for a long time.

[The lawyer then has the book marked by the court reporter as an exhibit; shows it to the opposing counsel; asks the court's permission to show it to the witness, and shows it to him.]

Q: Mr. Counselor, I show you what has been marked Plaintiff's Exhibit Number 14 for identification and ask you if you recognize it.
A: Yes, ma'am.
Q: What is it, please?
A: That is my log book for 1982.
Q: Please examine the pages in the book.
A: Okay, I've looked at them.
Q: Is the book in the same condition now as when you made it?
A: Yes ma'am. Nothing has been altered.
Lawyer: I move that Plaintiff's Exhibit Number 14 be admitted into evidence and ask permission to publish it to the jury.

Subpoenas

Q. 13:42 How is a person compelled to give testimony if he or she does not want to?

Because a judicial proceeding cannot be conducted without witnesses to give oral testimony or produce objects and documents that are necessary evidence, the court has the power to command a person to appear at a certain time and place and give testimony or produce books, papers, or other things. For the purpose, the court issues a subpoena (to testify), and/or a subpoena duces tecum (to produce objects). A subpoena or subpoena duces tecum may be used to compel attendance or production at a trial, any other hearing before the court, or a deposition. Subpoenas are also used in administrative proceedings or legislative hearings to compel testimony or production of evidence.

Q. 13:43 What happens if a person ignores a subpoena?

A subpoena is a command of the court. If it is disobeyed, the court has the power to hold the disobeyer in contempt and punish him or her by fine or imprisonment. In some instances, the court may order the sheriff or marshal to arrest the person and bring him or her forcibly before the court.

Q. 13:44 How is a subpoena served?

This is determined by statute and court rules. Some jurisdictions require personal service of subpoenas by an officer of the court or any other person designated by statute. Other jurisdictions permit service by mailing—perhaps requiring certified or registered mail. With the advent and proliferation of fax machines, it is to be anticipated that service by that means will soon be approved in some jurisdictions. There may be rules about the amount of notice time that a witness must be given.

Q. 13:45 What should an EAP counselor or other keeper of records do if a subpoena is served?

The very first step is to notify the EAP administration about the subpoena. The next step is to notify the EAP attorney. If a client record is being sought or the case otherwise involves a client, the client should be located and notified about the subpoena. (There are instances in which a client may be unaware that a subpoena for information about him or her has been served.) If the subpoena relates to litigation in which a client is involved, his or her lawyer should also be contacted.

A subpoena must not be ignored, but it is not unusual for a subpoena to be subject to attack. It may be requesting privileged information, which is protected from discovery even under subpoena. It may be seeking material that is irrelevant or immaterial to the case, or that contains private information about others not involved in the case (for example, a group record). A lawyer must ascertain the circumstances of the case and make a determination about how to respond.

Q. 13:46 What is the remedy if a subpoena is inappropriate or seeks privileged material?

Under no circumstances may a subpoena simply be ignored. Sometimes, a phone call from the EAP's lawyer to the lawyer who issued the subpoena may resolve the problem. For example, a deal may be struck whereby certain information may be given and other information withheld; more rarely, the issuing lawyer may be convinced to withdraw the subpoena. Often, what is required is a motion to quash the subpoena. A motion to quash requests that the subpoena be vacated or voided and sets forth the reasons. Sometimes, it is the lawyer for the litigant who must present the motion; in other situations, the lawyer for the person subpoenaed must do so. The lawyers argue the legal points at a hearing, and the judge makes a decision.

Q. 13:47 If the court refuses to quash the subpoena, is there any other relief available?

Sometimes, the court modifies a subpoena—requiring testimony on certain matters and prohibiting it on others, or requiring production of only part of a record. If a motion to quash appears to be failing, or the court cannot decide it without access to the material being sought for production, the court may be asked to conduct an *in camera* (in the judge's chambers) examination of the witness and/or the documents being sought. The judge then looks at the material privately and may decide to issue a protective order that sequesters (separates) the portion of the record that he or she rules out. Sometimes, the judge holds an *in camera* examination of a witness (usually, but not always, in the presence of the lawyers), to determine an issue of privileged communications or relevancy. Ordinarily, in such a case, a court reporter is present to take a verbatim record of the *in camera* examination, but the record is not accessible to the attorneys or others unless the court rules that the witness may testify and about what.

The main point to be remembered, aside from not ignoring a subpoena, is that a subpoena does not automatically mean that a witness must testify or turn over everything demanded. Someone who is not a lawyer should never make a decision on the response to a subpoena. If, for example, an EAP turns over a record that should have been protected, the client will have a suit for breach of confidentiality, breach of contract, and breach of fiduciary duty.

Example. In a child molestation case, the state's attorney subpoenas the records of the EAP aftercare support group of which the defendant is a member. The state's attorney claims that the Juvenile Court Act, under which the case is being tried, provides an exception in child abuse cases to any communications privilege that might otherwise exist. The EAP files a motion to quash, on the basis that the subpoena is overbroad and that, although the defendant's own record may be discoverable in a juvenile court case in which he is a respondent, the private affairs of other members of the group are privileged. The judge holds an *in camera* examination of the records and sequesters all information about anyone other than the defendant and all information about the defendant that is not relevant to the juvenile court proceeding.

Q. 13:48 To what may a nonexpert, or lay, witness testify?

Ordinarily, a witness is allowed to testify only to facts within his or her own knowledge, but not to opinions. Opinions are generally the purview of the court, which must form them about the ultimate issues to be decided in a case. For example, the value of an object or the nature of a medical condition would ordinarily be a matter of expert opinion, and a nonexpert, or lay, witness would not usually be allowed to testify to it. Sometimes, it is difficult to draw the line between opinion and fact. "Most persons would probably find it difficult to describe the odor of a rose, whisky, beer or limburger cheese, but his [*sic*] difficulty could scarcely be regarded as affecting the value of their testimony that they were familiar with and recognized the particular odor." (*People v. Reed*, 164 N.E. 847 (1929))

In addition to facts, a lay witness may be allowed to testify to opinions based on personal knowledge of facts that give a basis for the testimony. If it is necessary to an understanding of a witness's testimony that he or she give an opinion, a foundation must first be laid to establish that (1) the witness has knowledge upon which to make comparisons to form the opinion, (2) the testimony is rationally based on the witness's perception, and (3) the opinion is one that a person could normally form from observable facts. Examples are "the man attempted to strangle him"; "it smelled like rotten fish"; "he was driving at least 60 miles per hour"; "he was drunk." Condition of health, ability to work, suffering, being in possession of one's mental faculties, hearing, eyesight, and unconsciousness may be testified to by a lay witness. A lay witness will be allowed to testify to "nervousness," fear, state of upset, or excitement. He or she may be required to testify to the observations from which the conclusion was drawn.

Expert Testimony

Q. 13:49 When the court or jury cannot reach a conclusion without assistance in understanding the evidence or determining a fact in issue, what procedure is used?

Expert testimony may be presented to assist the court in such situations. Before expert testimony is permitted, the court must determine that a sufficiently reliable field of specialized knowledge on the subject has been developed, and that the witness called is properly qualified by knowledge, skill, experience, training, or education to provide assistance to the trier of fact (whether the judge or a jury).

Q. 13:50 If an expert is called to testify, in what form is the testimony given?

An expert may give an opinion, or an exposition of relevant scientific or other principles from which the judge or jury can infer or draw conclusions. The testimony of an expert who is called upon to provide scientific or technical data or other specialized knowledge is based on specialized knowledge and experience; in contrast, a lay witness may be permitted, in certain circumstances, to testify to an opinion based on rationally based perception.

Q. 13:51 What factors qualify a witness as an expert?

The lawyer who calls a witness as an expert must establish to the court's satisfaction the expert's special scientific, technical, or other specialized knowledge. An expert is qualified by reason of knowledge, skill, experience, training, and education.

Usually, but not always, the expert witness is a professional in the field. Specific degrees, certificates, or memberships in professional organizations are not necessarily required, but they are often presented to the court as evidence of expertise.

Q. 13:52 What is the method by which the court determines whether a witness is qualified to be an expert?

The witness is sworn, and the calling lawyer asks a series of questions designed to convince the court that (1) the witness has the qualifications necessary to cause the court to rely on him or her to present technical or other special facts and/or opinions that the court can use in decision making; and (2) the witness is more credible than, and his or her testimony should receive greater weight than the testimony of, the opposing side's expert. The questions vary, depending upon the type of case and the expertise being sought.

The calling lawyer then tenders the witness as an expert, and the court rules on whether he or she may testify as an expert. This procedure is called qualifying the expert. It is possible that a person with outstanding academic qualifications may not be qualified by the court as an expert in a particular case if specific knowledge about the issues in the case is not demonstrated.

The opposing counsel may object to the witness being qualified as an expert. The court may, but is not obliged to, allow the objecting opponent to conduct a preliminary *voir dire* examination of the proffered witness prior to his or her being allowed to testify. If the court does not permit a *voir dire* examination, the opposing counsel may nonetheless cross-examine the expert on his or her qualifications after the witness has testified. At that point, if the court becomes convinced that the witness should not have been qualified as an expert, the testimony will be stricken from the record. (This, of course, is comparable to "unringing a bell.")

Q. 13:53 What steps must be taken before an expert witness can testify?

The expert witness is responsible for providing a current copy of his or her resumé to the calling lawyer. If there are any weaknesses in the resumé, these should be pointed out very frankly and discussed in full. The attorney can then decide whether to seek another expert, or to develop a strategy for minimizing the weaknesses and "spiking the guns" of the opponent, who must be expected to recognize and use them to disqualify or neutralize the expert's testimony.

The expert must meet with the attorney and go over the testimony in detail. The attorney must set out for the expert the facts and legal issues in the case, so that the expert can properly prepare for the testimony. There may be certain technical books or articles that the expert witness may wish to consult, and he or she should review all the evidence in the case. A cross-examiner may well inquire into the facts, data, and opinions forming the basis of the expert's opinion. If the expert has relied upon a book or learned treatise, it may be used to cross-examine.

The expert may, but need not necessarily, examine or interview the party or parties in a clinical case. If the expert is experienced at testifying in court, the attorney may decide not to rehearse the testimony. If the expert is inexperienced, a rehearsal of examination and cross-examination is essential. In the unlikely event that the attorney resists or ignores this issue, the witness should insist upon it as a condition of testifying.

Q. 13:54 On what may an expert's testimony be based?

An expert's opinion must be based on facts or data, which may be derived from three sources:

1. First-hand observation, with opinions based thereon;
2. Facts or data presented at the trial; and
3. Data presented to the expert outside of court and other than by his or her own perception, so long as these are of a type reasonably relied upon by experts in the field as a basis for forming professional opinions.

(*The Federal Advisory Committee's Note to Federal Rule 703,* 56 F.R.D. 183, 283–284 (1973))

Q. 13:55 What is an example of first-hand observation?

Examination of a person, site, or object by the witness is an example of first-hand observation. A treating clinician who is called as a witness—a treating expert—will testify from his or her observations of the client or patient.

Q. 13:56 What is an example of expert testimony based on facts or data presented to the court?

There are two ways in which an expert may acquire the facts or data that have been presented to the court and use them as a basis for opinion testimony: (1) attending the trial and hearing the testimony establishing the facts and (2) replying to a hypothetical question posed to the expert on the witness stand as the basis for the opinion testimony.

A hypothetical question is based on an assumed state of facts; it must include those basic facts, data, and opinions not in dispute; and the version, favorable to the side asking the question, of disputed facts and data that reasonably appear to have a bearing upon the opinion that the expert will give.

A hypothetical question is ordinarily, and preferably, based upon facts that have already been adduced in evidence. Sometimes, a court will allow the question to be asked based upon facts not yet in evidence but that, according to the representation of the lawyer asking the question, will be produced later. The latter practice is not considered desirable, and many courts will not permit it.

Q. 13:57 How is an expert witness cross-examined?

Cross-examination may entail an effort to minimize the credentials of the expert and have his or her testimony stricken; or to establish that he or she is biased, and thus little or no weight should be given to the testimony. If the expert is actually very well-qualified and very well-prepared for testimony, this often backfires.

If a hypothetical question has been used by the direct examiner, the court may, at its discretion, allow the cross-examiner to pose a contrary version of the disputed facts. The cross-examiner may also test the knowledge and fairness of the expert by asking how changes of condition or alternative facts would change his or her opinion. The witness may also be asked if his or her opinion would be changed by the knowledge that another expert had testified to the contrary. The cross-examiner may ask about the fee being paid to the expert, and whether the expert has previously testified for or received referrals from the calling attorney. The expert may be asked if he or she agrees that a certain other professional is a reliable authority in the field; if so, the expert may be cross-examined on the views of that authority as expressed in treatises or other literature. To qualify as authority, the material must have been intended for professional colleagues, not written with a view toward litigation.

Q. 13:58 How can a "battle of the experts" be avoided in a case?

Often, it cannot be avoided in a case in which expert testimony is required. Many authorities decry the use of adversary experts, saying that the profession of the experts is discredited by these battles. Under some circumstances, statute may permit the appointment by the court of an independent expert, who is presumably neutral. Sometimes, a party who disagrees with the court-appointed expert offers his or her own adversary expert in contradiction. In any case, either party has the right to cross-examine the other's expert or a court expert.

Q. 13:59 How can a witness prepare for court?

The most important stage in a trial is the preparation. No witness should be put on the stand without sufficient advance discussion with the calling lawyer. The lawyer must know exactly what the witness can or cannot testify to, and what the hearsay and other evidentiary problems may be. Further, a person who is inexperienced as a witness should be given an opportunity to practice answering questions, to be able to testify in a credible and useful fashion.

Q. 13:60 What is the major frustration for clinicians who testify in court?

Clinicians are often frustrated because they are not permitted to tell the court what they know. They are stymied by the rules of evidence. Clinicians are accustomed to gathering facts and arriving at conclusions in a very different manner from the way lawyers do. They regularly rely on the records, observations, statements, and opinions of others in arriving at diagnostic conclusions and employing clinical interventions. All of this is, of course, hearsay—information not known by the clinician of his or her own knowledge—and therefore generally not admissible as evidence. A clinician cannot testify to something in a record, or that he or she heard from someone else. Thus, the clinician witness may be able to testify to very little. This, of course, should never happen if the calling lawyer has properly prepared himself or herself, as well as the witness.

There may be some circumstances in which other clinicians who were eyewitnesses must be located and called upon to testify to the events in question. Some states have adopted a federal evidence rule, Rule 705, which permits an expert witness to testify to any information that he or she may have utilized in arriving at his or her opinion, if that information is of a type generally relied upon by clinicians. Since clinicians generally rely upon the records, reports, and observations of other clinicians, as well as the statements of clients or patients and their collaterals, information that would otherwise be excluded because of the hearsay rule may be placed before the court in those jurisdictions that have adopted Rule 705. The attorney should be aware of this possibility, but this often proves not to be the case. The clinician should inquire about this issue during case preparation.

When the case involves the presentation of clinical facts and opinions, it is important to know what questions to ask. The clinician witness can play a vital role in case preparation as a consultant to the lawyer, by providing books and articles on the clinical entity at issue and explaining the clinical facts and the inferences to be drawn therefrom. In federal law and many state laws, learned treatises may be used as evidence, as a basis for cross-examining an opposing expert, or as a basis for judicial notice. When a court takes judicial notice of a fact, no evidence need be produced to prove it.

Q. 13:61 How should a witness dress for court?

"Packaging" is an important aspect of trial practice. The trial is a show, in some sense, and the image projected by a witness will have a significant impact on the manner in which the witness is perceived. A witness should come to court dressed in a conservative business suit or dress, not work clothes, or sport or leisure clothes. Men should have well-cut hair and be properly shaven or have facial hair nicely trimmed. Women should be coiffed and made up tastefully. Expert witnesses should take care not to distract from the content of their presentations by inappropriate appearance. The objective is for the judge and jury to identify with the witness, find him or her credible, and agree with his or her position.

Q. 13:62 What are some hints for testifying?

The first rule of testifying is: *Answer only what is asked; do not volunteer anything.* Remember that the lawyer who has called the witness is supposedly well-prepared and has planned the questioning carefully. (The witness should satisfy himself or herself in this regard before testifying.) A lawyer who is unsatisfied by an answer will ask another question to elicit further information. A cross-examiner is entitled to question only on testimony that was elicited on direct examination, so the more a witness talks, the more ammunition the cross-examiner has for attack. Under cross-examination, if the witness is concerned that a "yes" or "no" answer demanded by the cross-examiner will result in a false impression being left with the judge, the witness may turn to the judge and ask permission to explain the answer. The judge may or may not allow the explanation, but this will alert the direct examiner to follow up on the material in redirect examination or rebuttal testimony.

Witnesses are often distressed because they feel responsible for the outcome of a trial. This is unnecessary and inappropriate. It is the lawyer, not the witness, who is responsible for seeing to it that the evidence is fairly and completely presented to the court. The witness is responsible for educating the lawyer as to the facts and the limits of the testimony that the witness can give. After that, the witness cannot control the conduct of the trial and should try hard to separate himself or herself from it.

Q. 13:63 Is it proper for opposing counsel to seek an interview with a witness?

This depends upon the circumstances. Usually, in a civil proceeding, the opposing counsel will not seek an interview with a witness outside of formal discovery proceedings. In most jurisdictions, this would be considered unethical practice. In a jurisdiction that permits this type of contact, witnesses may be told that they need not be interviewed if they do not want to be, or they may insist upon an attorney being with them. Any instance of intimidation of a witness should be brought to the attention of the attorney, who may bring it to the attention of the court.

Q. 13:64 What is perjury?

Perjury is a deliberate false assertion under oath of fact, opinion, belief, or knowledge material to the issue that is being tried, made by a witness in an official proceeding as part of his or her evidence. The assertion may be made orally or by affidavit. Perjury is a crime, punishable by fine or imprisonment. Suborning perjury—inducing another person to commit perjury—is also a crime.

EAP Lawyers

Q. 13:65 Does an EAP need a lawyer?

Yes. A lawyer should be consulted at every stage of planning and negotiations in establishing an EAP, whether internal or external. No contract should be entered into without a lawyer's interpretation and advice. An external EAP should have its own legal representative and not rely upon the sponsor's lawyer. On an ongoing basis, legal questions—confidentiality, commitment, professional liability, labor and employment law, and the new field of drug testing—arise regularly in clinical work, and EAPs are no exception. EAP clients frequently have legal problems that affect clinical service delivery, and legal advice may be required to properly address these.

Q. 13:66 What should an EAP look for in a lawyer?

An EAP needs a lawyer familiar with clinical concepts, mental health and substance abuse treatment, professional liability issues, labor and employment law, and all areas of federal and local state law that affect EAP practice. If an internal EAP is obliged to rely on corporate counsel, the counsel will find it necessary to become acquainted with some otherwise unfamiliar and unusual areas of the law. Specialized outside consultation is often indicated. When the EAP has a choice of counsel, it will find itself and its clients best served by a lawyer who has an interest in the clinical issues and is willing to research and learn all the law relevant to the particular program.

A good working relationship with a lawyer requires accessibility. Lawyers are notoriously busy and difficult to reach on the phone. The EAP should have an arrangement whereby in an emergency, the lawyer will respond in a timely fashion. Most important, the lawyer must take the EAP and its work seriously.

Appendix A

Policy and Procedure Issues

A-1: Sample Policy: Establishment of an EAP

Scope

The Happy Valley Company, Inc. (Company) will provide an employee assistance program (EAP) to all employees.

Purpose

The Company will provide confidential assistance and/or referral on a voluntary basis to employees when personal problems are contributing to, or may contribute to, deteriorating job performance.

Policy

The Company recognizes that a wide range of problems, not directly associated with one's job function, may have an adverse effect on an employee's job performance. Further, personal problems of a family member can also affect an employee's job performance.

When marital or family discord, financial or emotional crises, alcohol or drug problems, illness, or other difficulties interfere with or threaten job performance or conduct, the Company offers assistance through the EAP. There is no desire to intrude on the employee's private life. These problems are recognized as progressive and potentially destructive, but they are also recognized as treatable disorders. The Company stands ready to assist employees and their families who are willing to help themselves.

Practice

Early recognition of the troubled employee, through application of job performance standards, is a proper function of management.

Employees with identifiable performance problems that are not the result of deficits in knowledge, skills, education, and/or working conditions may have personal problems affecting job performance.

The Company actively supports rehabilitation efforts, when applicable and appropriate, through employee group health benefits, sick leave, and disability policies. An employee may be referred to the EAP by Company supervisory personnel, colleagues, medical personnel, union personnel, or family because of a condition that may affect his or her job performance. The decision to accept assistance is the responsibility of the employee.

Employees are also encouraged to self-refer.

Confidentiality

All records and information about referral, diagnosis, and treatment will be maintained by the EAP and treated as confidential. No information concerning a client's personal problems or participation in the EAP will become a part of the employee's personnel record. Except as set forth herein and in situations of dangerousness, or as may otherwise be required by law, no information, oral or written, will be disclosed without the express written permission of the employee.

In the case of a performance-related or Health Service referral, the only information to be disclosed will be to advise the referring person whether the employee has followed through on the referral.

Employee Discipline and Job Security

Employees participating in the EAP will *not* be given preferential treatment, nor will they be subject to any special regulations by the Company. EAP participation will not immunize an employee against discipline, including discharge, by reason of an infraction of work rules or the rules of conduct. All employees will be evaluated strictly on job performance criteria, irrespective of their participation in the EAP. An EAP client may be disciplined for his or her continued unsatisfactory job performance.

An employee's job security or future career advancement will not be jeopardized as a result of his or her participation in the EAP.

Procedure

The immediate supervisor or manager is responsible for monitoring an employee's job performance. In the case of deteriorating performance, the supervisor or manager, following established procedures, should work with the employee in an effort to reestablish accepted levels of performance. If it appears that the substandard performance is or may be due to problems or impairment, the supervisor should refer the employee to the EAP as part of a performance improvement plan.

In the case of a job-performance-related referral, the supervisor will:

- Document, as part of a performance improvement plan, that the employee was made aware of the EAP as a resource;
- Notify the EAP that a referral has been made; and
- Provide relevant documentation of the performance problem to the EAP.

Health Service personnel may refer an employee to the EAP. They should:

- Document the referral in the employee's medical record; and
- Notify the EAP of the referral.

Employees and their family members experiencing problems that may affect the job performance of that employee are encouraged to voluntarily seek information, referral, and related services on a confidential basis by contacting the EAP.

A-2: Policy and Procedure Checklist

In developing policies and procedures for an EAP, consider the following questions:

Relationship of the EAP to the Sponsor

1. What are the program goals?
2. To whom is the EAP accountable, and how?
3. By what criteria will the EAP be evaluated?
4. How does the EAP relate to various components of the sponsor organization?
   - Management/administration;
   - Personnel department;
   - Medical department;
   - Referral sources: supervisors;
   - Security; and
   - Legal counsel.
5. How is a referral made to the EAP?
6. Who can make a referral?
7. What client information does the EAP share with:
   - The referral source?
   - Other sponsor components?
8. Does the employer have written work rules?
9. Does the employer have a fitness-for-duty policy?
10. How does the EAP interface with the employer disciplinary system?

Program Definition

1. What is the scope of the program?
2. Who is eligible for service?
3. Is the program voluntary or involuntary for employees?
4. What services will be offered?
5. Does service availability or client rights differ, depending upon referral type? If so, how?

6. Where will services be provided?
7. Who provides which service?
8. When does the EAP refer to other providers?
9. What are the circumstances for referring?
10. What are the guidelines for choosing programs and professionals as referees?

The EAP Staff

1. How many EAP professionals are necessary to serve the sponsor's employee group?
2. What are the credentialing criteria for EAP professionals?
3. Will the EAP use volunteers? If so, what will their role be?
4. Who has responsibility for screening EAP hires?
5. How will accountability be assured?
6. How will staff activity be monitored for quality assurance?
7. How does the EAP staff interface with the sponsor's staff?

Administrative Records

1. Which administrative records does the EAP keep?
2. Who is responsible for administrative recordkeeping?
3. What form of clinical record does the EAP use?
4. Who is responsible for setting up the clinical recording system?
5. Who is responsible for monitoring recording?

Clinical Records

1. Which clinical records does the EAP keep?
2. What does the clinical record contain?
3. Who owns the clinical record?
4. If the EAP is terminated or taken over by another provider, what happens to the client records?

Confidentiality

1. Who has access to the clinical record?

2. Who has the right to consent to disclosure of the client's record?
3. What form of consent is required for disclosure?
4. Under what circumstances will records or information be disclosed without client consent?
5. How long are records kept?
6. How will the EAP respond to a court demand for access to records (a subpoena)?
7. How will the EAP respond to a law enforcement demand for access to records (a search warrant)?

Clinical Services

1. Is there a written plan for professional services?
2. What are the program's business hours?
3. What is the after-hours emergency procedure?
4. What methods are used to carry out initial screening?
5. What is the intake procedure?
6. How are the client's significant others involved in screening, intake, referral, and treatment?
7. At what stage, and under what circumstances, are family and/or supervisors involved?
8. How is initial contact made with the client? Significant others?
9. What methods are used to deliver services?
10. What methods are used for treatment planning and review?
11. What is the discharge planning and postdischarge process?
12. How does the EAP provide or arrange for:
    - Medical, psychiatric, and other specialty assessments;
    - Therapeutic services;
    - Emergency services and crisis intervention;
    - Client transportation;
    - Continuity of care;
    - Client education; and
    - Sponsor staff consultation.

13. What is the EAP's role in fitness-for-duty evaluations?
    - Referral process;
    - Evaluation process;
    - Feedback method; and
    - Methods for assuring client rights.
14. What is the EAP's role in drug screening?
    - Drug screening process;
    - Testing methods;
    - Quality assurance;
    - Chain-of-custody procedures; and
    - Methods for assuring client rights.
15. What are the rules for staff relationships with clients?
    - Are dual relationships of any kind permitted?
    - Under what circumstances, if any, is a social relationship permitted with a client or client family member?
    - May a staff member enter into a business relationship with a client or client's family member?

A-3: Sample Form: Supervisory Referral to the EAP

____
Date

Name of Employee: ______________________________

Department: ____________________ Position: ____________________

Level: ____________ Seniority: ____________ Shift: ____________

Referred by: ____

Reason for referral: ____

____

____

Feedback

The above employee:

- ☐ has contacted the EAP and accepted service;
- ☐ has not contacted the EAP;
- ☐ has contacted the EAP, but has not accepted service;
- ☐ has contacted the EAP; after assessment, no service appears to be required at this time.

Thank you for this referral.

____
EAP Counselor

____
Date

A-4: Sample Intake Form: Application for EAP Services

____
Date

Name: ____

Address: ____

Age: __________ Marital Status: ______________________________

Phone: Home: ________________ Work: ______________________

Supervisor: ___________________ Phone: ______________________

Union Rep.: ___________________ Phone: ______________________

Position: _____________________ Referred by: __________________

Employee has given permission to contact:

☐ Supervisor ☐ Union Rep. ☐ Medical ☐ Family ____________

History

Medical: ____

Psychiatric: ____

Substance Abuse: ____

Employment: ____

Performance: ____

Attendance: ____

Presenting Problem: ______________________________________

____

Assessment: ____

____

____

Recommendation: ____

____

Employee's Response: ____

____

Collateral Contacts: ____

____

Disposition: ____

Follow-up:

A-5: Model: Employee (EAP Client) Statement of Understanding

Program

The employee assistance program (EAP) of Happy Valley Company, Inc. (Company) is a confidential, voluntary service made available to all employees and their family members (clients).

Fees

Meetings with the EAP counselor are offered at no direct cost to the employee or family member. If a client needs long-term counseling or some specialized service, the EAP will assist in locating a resource for the client in the community. It is the responsibility of the client to pay for any service(s) provided by outside resources. Insurance coverage under the Group Health Plan provided to employees may defray some or all of the cost of service.

Release of Information

Information concerning the use of the EAP will not be given to anyone outside of the EAP except as required by law or as described below, and will not be made a part of the employee's personnel record:

- *Self-referral.* If an employee or employee's family member initiates the meeting, rather than having been referred by a supervisor as a result of a performance problem, no information concerning an individual's participation in the EAP will be discussed or released without the express written consent of the individual, except as set forth herein.
- *Supervisory referrals.* If an employee is referred by his or her supervisor because of work performance problems, the supervisor will note that the employee has been made aware of the program. The EAP counselor will confidentially advise the referring supervisor only about whether the employee has kept an appointment. The employee will be notified that this is taking place.

  The EAP will not discuss the employee's personal problems with, or release any additional information to, the supervisor or anyone else, except as required or permitted by law, without the express written consent of the employee.

- *Medical referrals.* If an employee is referred by the Health Service due to a medical condition, the referring individual will document the referral in the employee's health record. The EAP counselor will confidentially inform the referring individual about whether the employee has kept the appointment.

  The EAP will not discuss the employee's personal problems with, or release any additional information to, the referring individual, or anyone else, except as required or permitted by law, without the express written consent of the employee.
- *Dangerous situations.* If the referrer or EAP staff believe that the client or another person or property is at risk of harm, or it appears that an illegal act or threat thereof has been committed against the EAP or the Company or their staffs, or on their premises, the EAP staff may disclose information to prevent harm or protect against the criminal acts.

Voluntary Participation

Participation in the EAP is voluntary. Employment or advancement in the Company is not affected by an employee's decision to use (or not to use) the service(s) of the EAP. The Company evaluates an employee on the basis of job performance criteria only, and not on the use of the EAP.

Since the program is voluntary and the services are offered at no direct cost to me or my family, I release and agree to hold harmless Happy Valley Company, Inc., the EAP, and their staffs and agents, from any action or liability arising out of my participation in the EAP.

I have read this Employee Statement of Understanding and understand its contents.

____________________________________ _______________
(Signature of client) (Date)

____________________________________ _______________
(Signature of EAP counselor) (Date)

A-6: Sample Form: Consent for Disclosure of Information to Supervisor or for Referral

____
Date

I, ________________________, authorize the employee assistance program (EAP) to disclose to

☐ my supervisor: ________________________ or his or her successor

☐ members of my family: ____

____

☐ others: ____

____

the following information:

☐ the fact that I have accepted referral to the EAP
☐ the EAP's assessment of my problem, if any
☐ the EAP's recommendations
☐ other information: ____

____

The purpose(s) for which the information may be used are:

____

☐ I understand that I may see and have a copy of any written information to be disclosed.

☐ I understand that I may revoke this consent in writing at any time. If I do so, the revocation will have no effect on disclosures already made.

☐ If I revoke this consent and incomplete information has been provided hereunder, I agree that the EAP may disclose only such additional information as may, in the discretion of my counselor, be necessary to avoid harm or damages that might result from misapprehension of my condition or circumstances.

☐ I agree that ☐ my supervisor ☐ my family will be notified of my termination of service with the EAP, whenever that occurs.

☐ Unless earlier revoked, this consent is valid until ______________.

______________________________ ______________________________

Signature of client Witness

A-7: Sample Policy: Fitness for Duty

Scope

This policy provides for the establishment of criteria of fitness for duty of employees, and for fair and uniform standards for application of the criteria.

Purpose

The purpose of this policy is to assist employees in remedying any medical problems related to the use and abuse of any drug that may adversely affect the satisfactory performance of their job functions. Employment security and advancement opportunities will not be jeopardized by reason of an employee's following this policy and the procedures set forth herein. At the same time, normal administrative and disciplinary procedures relating to unavailability for work or inability to perform satisfactorily will not be avoided, nor special privileges or exemptions granted, as a result of following this policy.

Definition

For purposes of this policy, a drug is: any over-the-counter medication; any prescribed medication; any illegal or unprescribed controlled substance; or any alcoholic beverage.

Policy

The following are conditions of employment and must be adhered to consistently:

1. An employee is obligated to notify his or her immediate superior when reporting for duty or in the course of his or her work shift if use of any drug may adversely affect ability to satisfactorily perform his or her normal job (e.g., drowsiness, dizziness, blurred vision).
2. An employee is obligated to report to the Health Service for a fitness-for-duty evaluation, which may include testing for chemical (e.g., alcohol, other drug) levels in the body at any time when referred by his or her supervisor. This may occur when an employee reports for work, following meal or other breaks, or otherwise during a work

shift. The referral must be made in accordance with the fitness-for-duty procedure. The supervisor must document the reasons for the referral, including observations relative to the employee's ability to safely and properly initiate or continue his or her normal work duties, due to the possible adverse influence of any drug use by the employee, or for any other reason.

3. The purpose of this policy is to protect the health and safety of the employee and the work environment. A suspicion of violation of the Rules of Conduct is not the only (or even the ordinary) reason for a referral under this policy. It is contemplated that a supervisor will refer an employee for a fitness-for-duty evaluation at any time when it appears that there is reasonable doubt about the employee's ability to safely and properly initiate or continue normal work duties because of possible adverse influence of *any* drug usage by the employee, including legal and prescribed drugs, or illness or other impairment.

4. An employee is required to follow the Rules of Conduct, which are, by their nature, conditions of employment. Under the Rules of Conduct relating to this policy, the following behaviors are not permitted:

   - Use, possession, or being under the influence of alcohol or drugs (prescription drugs are excluded) for a period of five (5) hours before the beginning of the work shift or during the work shift (including breaks).
   - Excessive or unexcused absence or tardiness.
   - Violation or neglect of safety regulations.
   - Carelessness or negligence; violation or neglect of safety regulations; or violation of other commonly accepted or published rules of conduct.
   - Reporting for work or working in a condition unfit for duty; failure to follow fitness-for-duty policy and procedures.

5. *Confidentiality.* The medical record of fitness-for-duty evaluation results will be maintained by the Health Service and, in the event of a referral to the EAP, in the EAP office. Under no circumstances will any record or results in the record be released to an employee's supervisor or to any other party without the prior written consent of the employee.

Procedure

The following are the steps and responsibilities for implementation of the fitness-for-duty policy:

1. If deficiencies in employee performance or behavior are observed at any time during working hours, the Supervisor is to document those observations. The documentation must be directly related to the employee's inability to perform his or her work duties in a satisfactory manner and may or may not be due to the possible adverse effects of any drug usage by the employee. Possible observations may include, but are not limited to: drowsiness and/or sleepiness; odor of alcohol on the breath; slurred/incoherent speech; inability to concentrate; lack of attention; unusually aggressive behavior; unexplained work errors; unexplained changes in mood; lack of manual dexterity; lack of coordination in walking; and unexplained work-related accident or injury.
2. If possible, a second supervisory employee may witness and confirm any observed deficiencies in employee performance or behavior.
3. The Supervisor will interview the employee in private to determine the need for a fitness-for-duty evaluation. It is the responsibility of the employee to confirm or deny any current drug (as defined in this policy) use.
4. If the Supervisor determines that a fitness-for-duty evaluation is indicated, he or she will notify the Health Service that the employee has been referred.
5. The Supervisor will escort the employee to the Health Service.
6. The Health Service will perform the fitness-for-duty evaluation. Such elements of a general physical examination and other specific testing procedures deemed medically appropriate will be performed. These may include laboratory testing of blood and urine. It is the responsibility of the employee to cooperate with the requests of the Health Service in the examination and in providing blood or urine samples, if requested. Failure to so cooperate is insubordination and a violation of the Rules of Conduct and gives rise to the presumption that the employee is unfit for duty.
7. The Health Service will determine that the employee is "fit for duty" and able to return to work, or "unfit for duty."
8. If the employee is determined to be unfit for duty, for reasons of physical illness or other impairment unrelated to substance abuse,

and not requiring counseling or other related intervention, the Health Service will notify the employee's supervisor and send the employee home, referring him or her for medical care as indicated.

If the employee is determined to be unfit for duty for any other reason, the Health Service will:

- Offer the employee a referral to the EAP the same day or the next day and make the appointment for him or her; and
- Notify the employee's supervisor that the employee is to be sent home.

The EAP will receive the employee referral from the Health Service and schedule an early appointment. Following an interview and a discussion of the EAP plan, if it appears that the employee is in need of EAP services and the employee consents in writing, the EAP will notify the Supervisor that the employee is seeking EAP assistance.

When an employee is sent home or referred for immediate medical care, the Supervisor will help him or her to get there safely. Under no circumstances is an employee who is sent home as unfit to work to be allowed to drive himself of herself. (A person who is unfit to work is unfit to drive.) If the employee will not be dissuaded from driving, he or she should be advised that the police will be notified, and the police should be called.

The employee's accrued sick time may be used to compensate for any regularly scheduled hours missed. If the employee has no sick time accrued, accrued leave time may be used. If neither is available, the employee's pay will be docked.

If the employee's health condition permits, he or she will return to the Health Service on the next day for reevaluation. Following reevaluation, all procedures in (8) will be followed.

9. If an employee is found to be in possession of any alcoholic beverage or illegal or unprescribed controlled substance while on the company premises (whether or not during the employee's work shift), the Supervisor will:

   - Place the employee on indefinite suspension pending an investigation;
   - Refer the employee for a fitness-for-duty evaluation;
   - Notify Security to initiate an investigation of the incident; and
   - Document the incident.

10. Upon notification, Security will conduct an investigation in its usual manner and will gather any physical evidence, interview the principal parties involved in the incident and any eyewitnesses, and document.

    If illegal controlled substances are found on the premises, the police will be called.

Appendix B

Confidentiality

B-1: Sample Form: Consent to Disclose Information

1. I (name of client) ☐ request ☐ authorize:

2. (name or general designation of program that is to make the disclosure)

   ____

3. To disclose (kind and amount of information to be disclosed)

   ____

4. To (name or title of person or organization to which disclosure is to be made)

   ____

5. For (purpose of the disclosure)

   ____

6. Date (on which this consent is signed)

   ____

7. Signature of client

   ____

8. Signature of parent or guardian (when required)

   ____

9. Signature of person authorized to sign in lieu of the client (when required)

   ____

10. This consent is subject to revocation at any time except to the extent that the program that is to make the disclosure has already taken action in reliance on it. If not previously revoked, this consent will terminate upon (specific date, event, or condition).

____

11. The law provides that information disclosed here may not be redisclosed without an additional consent by the client.

Appendix C

Clinical Issues and Malpractice

C-1: Sample John Doe Petition to Allow Disclosure of Confidential Information

CIRCUIT COURT OF HAPPY COUNTY, ILLINOIS
CHANCERY DIVISION

In re the Matter of HAPPY VALLEY COMMUNITY MENTAL HEALTH CENTER, an Illinois not-for-profit corporation, Petitioner and JOHN DOE, Respondent	NO.

PETITION FOR ORDER PERMITTING DISCLOSURE
OF CONFIDENTIAL INFORMATION

Now comes HAPPY VALLEY COMMUNITY MENTAL HEALTH CENTER, an Illinois not-for-profit corporation, Petitioner, by its attorneys, Mar y Johnson and Associates, and for its Petition, states as follows:

1. Petitioner is a community mental health center that operates as one of its programs an Employee Assistance Program providing, *inter alia,* alcohol and drug abuse diagnosis, referral, and treatment to individuals. As a not-for-profit corporation with tax-exempt status providing said services, Petitioner is governed by 42 C.F.R. Part 2.

2. Pursuant to 42 C.F.R. Part 2, Subpart E, disclosure without client consent of information given by a client in the course of substance abuse treatment is forbidden unless authorized by Order of Court.

3. JOHN DOE (a fictitious name), Respondent, is a client of said program and is undergoing treatment for substance abuse.

4. During the course of counseling, Respondent has revealed to his therapist, JANE SMITH, M.S.W. (SMITH), a certified addictions counselor employed by Petitioner, the following information:

(a) He is involved in a lawsuit with one JAMES BROWN, his former business partner, over certain perceived wrongs perpetrated by said BROWN against him, about which he is enraged and bitter.

(b) The said lawsuit is set for trial on May 1, 1990, two weeks from the date of filing hereof.

(c) If he loses the lawsuit, he intends to kill said BROWN.

5. Notwithstanding the earnest efforts of SMITH over a long period of time to convince him otherwise, DOE persists in his plan to kill BROWN, so that SMITH reasonably believes that, in the event that he loses the lawsuit, DOE will carry out his threats.

6. SMITH further reasonably believes that it is necessary to inform BROWN and the Sheriff of the threats of DOE, so that BROWN can take whatever steps he sees fit to attempt to avert the threatened danger and so that the Sheriff can take appropriate steps for the security of the court and persons therein at the time of the trial.

7. Disclosure is necessary to protect against an existing threat to life or of serious bodily injury, as set forth hereinabove.

8. Other ways of obtaining the information necessary to protect against the threat are not available or would not be effective.

9. The public interest and need for disclosure outweigh the potential injury to DOE, the treatment relationship, and the treatment program.

WHEREFORE, HAPPY VALLEY COMMUNITY MENTAL HEALTH CENTER, Petitioner, prays for as follows:

1. For entry of an Order permitting JANE SMITH to inform JAMES BROWN and the SHERIFF OF HAPPY COUNTY, ILLINOIS, of the threats of JOHN DOE.

2. For such other and further relief as in Equity may be just.

HAPPY VALLEY COMMUNITY MENTAL HEALTH CENTER, Petitioner

by ______________________________

its director.

Appendix D

Legal Issues for EAP Operations

D-1: Model Screening Instrument: EAP Clinician Applicants for Employment

Name: ______________________ Soc. Sec. No.: ______________

Address: ______________________________ Phone: __________

____

____

Licenses: ________________________

Has your license ever been disciplined?
If so, please explain:

Please list previous addresses for the past five years and the dates when you lived at each.

Employment History

List your employers for the past ten years:

Name: ______________________ Phone: ______________

Address: ____

Dates of employment: ____________ Supervisor: ____________

Reason for leaving: ________________________________

Name: ______________________ Phone: ______________

Address: ____

Dates of employment: ____________ Supervisor: ____________

Reason for leaving: ________________________________

Name: ______________________ Phone: ______________

Address: ____

Dates of employment: ____________ Supervisor: ____________

Reason for leaving: ________________________________

Name: ______________________ Phone: ______________

Address: ____

Dates of employment: ____________ Supervisor: ____________

Reason for leaving: ________________________________

If there are any gaps in employment, please explain in detail:

Were you ever disciplined by an employer? _______ If so, please give full details.

Education

List all educational institutions and programs you have attended since high school and dates of attendance:

Name: ____________________ Dates of attendance: _____________

Address: ____

Did you complete the program? ______ If not, why? _____________

____

Degree or certificate: ________

Name: ____________________ Dates of attendance: _____________

Address: ____

Did you complete the program? ______ If not, why? _____________

____

Degree or certificate: ________

Name: ____________________ Dates of attendance: _____________

Address: ____

Did you complete the program? ______ If not, why? _____________

____

Degree or certificate: ________

Name: ____________________ Dates of attendance: _____________

Address: ____

Did you complete the program? ______ If not, why? _____________

____

Degree or certificate: ________

Name: ____________________ Dates of attendance: _____________

Address: ____

Did you complete the program? ______ If not, why? _____________

____

Degree or certificate: ________

Were you ever expelled or suspended from an educational program? _______ If so, please explain in detail.

Have you ever been convicted of a crime? _______ If so, please explain in detail, giving dates and locations.

To what professional associations do you now belong?

Have you ever been charged with an ethics violation? _______ If so, please give full details.

I certify that the above answers are complete and truthful. I understand that untruths on this application will subject me to immediate dismissal. I hereby consent to verification of every fact asserted herein, and request the persons, companies, and institutions named herein to reply to inquiries concerning the same and agree to indemnify and hold them harmless from any loss or injury by reason thereof.

Date	Witness	Applicant

D-2: Model Screening Instrument: Verification of Information Provided by Prospective EAP Clinician

To:

Re: Name: ______________________ Date of birth ___________

Address: ____

____

____

Social Security Number: _________________

The above-named applicant for a position as ____________________ has provided the following information:

We request that you verify the same, if you are able to do so, or advise us as to any discrepancies of which you are aware. Please also provide us with a copy of the applicant's last three evaluations. A consent to disclose, containing an indemnification and hold-harmless clause protecting you against any loss by reason of your compliance with this request, is attached.

Your comments as to the suitability of the applicant for the position contemplated will be of great help to us and will be held confidential.

We appreciate your assistance.

____

Hiring Officer

D-3: Model Indemnification for Reference Providers of Prospective EAP Clinicians

I authorize the person, company, or institution to whom this verification is directed to provide the information requested. I further consent to the release of copies of my personnel record, including but not limited to evaluations and notations of discipline, if any, and I agree to hold harmless and indemnify the person, company, or institution against any liability or loss by reason of compliance with this authorization.

__________	____________________	____________________
Date	Witness	Applicant

Index

[References to Chapter One and the Appendices are to pages; references to the remaining chapters are to specific Questions]

[References to Chapter One and the Appendices are to pages; references to the remaining chapters are to specific Questions]

[References to Chapter One and the Appendices are to pages; references to the remaining chapters are to specific Questions]

[References to Chapter One and the Appendices are to pages; references to the remaining chapters are to specific Questions]

[References to Chapter One and the Appendices are to pages; references to the remaining chapters are to specific Questions]

[References to Chapter One and the Appendices are to pages; references to the remaining chapters are to specific Questions]

[References to Chapter One and the Appendices are to pages; references to the remaining chapters are to specific Questions]

[References to Chapter One and the Appendices are to pages; references to the remaining chapters are to specific Questions]

[References to Chapter One and the Appendices are to pages; references to the remaining chapters are to specific Questions]

[References to Chapter One and the Appendices are to pages; references to the remaining chapters are to specific Questions]

[References to Chapter One and the Appendices are to pages; references to the remaining chapters are to specific Questions]

[References to Chapter One and the Appendices are to pages; references to the remaining chapters are to specific Questions]

[References to Chapter One and the Appendices are to pages; references to the remaining chapters are to specific Questions]

[References to Chapter One and the Appendices are to pages; references to the remaining chapters are to specific Questions]

[References to Chapter One and the Appendices are to pages; references to the remaining chapters are to specific Questions]

[References to Chapter One and the Appendices are to pages; references to the remaining chapters are to specific Questions]

[References to Chapter One and the Appendices are to pages; references to the remaining chapters are to specific Questions]

[References to Chapter One and the Appendices are to pages; references to the remaining chapters are to specific Questions]

-T-

[References to Chapter One and the Appendices are to pages; references to the remaining chapters are to specific Questions]

[References to Chapter One and the Appendices are to pages; references to the remaining chapters are to specific Questions]